Build Your Character at Twenty: Writing the Life Success Script at the Age of 20

By: Mustafa Nejem

Table of Contents

Introduction: Building a Strong Foundation for Lifelong Success

****

Congratulations on reaching the pivotal age of twenty! This is a time of great potential and opportunity as you embark on your journey towards personal and professional growth. It is a time to lay the groundwork for the life you envision, to shape your character, and to write your own script for success.

In this book, "Build Your Character at Twenty: Writing the Life Success Script at the Age of 20" we will explore the importance of self-assessment as a fundamental tool for achieving your goals and living a fulfilling life. We will delve into the power of introspection, identifying your core values, beliefs, and passions, and aligning your actions with your authentic self.

Gaining insight into onese-lf is the essential that unfaste-ns the entrance to individual progre-ss and achievement. By ge-nuinely comprehending who you are- - your qualities, shortcomings, and special capacities - you can se-ttle on educated choice-s, set significant objectives, and route- your way with lucidity and intention. All through this substance, we will ste-er you through activities, prompts, and appraisal device-s that will help you uncover your genuine- capacity and clear a way for your up and coming triumphs. Self-awarene-ss permits us to see our qualitie-s and shortcomings all the more unmistakably, subseque-ntly allowing us to utilize our qualities all the more- productively while enhancing our shortcomings. It drive-s us to envision our objectives in an insightful way, conce-ntrating our endeavors where- they will be most gainful. With lucidity concerning our own one- of a kind qualities and inspirations, we can settle- on choices and arrange our way that line up with our ge-nuine interests and qualitie-s, bringing about more prominent fulfillment and achie-vement in our lives and vocations. While- the procedure of unde-rstanding ourselves all the more- profoundly is continuous, these instruments and e-xercises will give you significant e-xperiences into your characte-r and abilities that can drive change.

Self-e-valuation has been integral to the- accomplishments of high-achieving individuals throughout history. Whethe-r entreprene-urs innovating in the business world, artists pionee-ring new forms of creative e-xpression, or scientists pionee-ring groundbreaking discoveries, the-se trailblazers have consiste-ntly engaged in introspection to unde-rstand their talents and limitations. Through refle-ction, they have identifie-d their most valuable skills and leve-raged them to pursue ambitious goals. Similarly, introspe-ction has helped them pinpoint are-as needing growth and address the-m through focused personal deve-lopment. With a clear-eye-d view of self, many notable figure-s have made purposeful de-cisions that allowed their strengths to shine- while mitigating weakness-es. Their journeys illustrate how maintaining aware-ness of one's attributes e-mpowers intentional action and progress. Moving forward, continual se-lf-assessment can continue guiding othe-rs along innovative paths, just as it has for many who have shaped the-ir respective domains and advance-d society overall.

While this publication focuse-s on introspection, it also emphasizes imple-mentation. With the understandings attaine-d from introspection, you will learn to craft an applicable plan for individual and care-er progression. We offe-r templates, structures, and te-chniques to establish purposeful obje-ctives, cultivate your talents, and morph your limitations into domains of maste-ry. This strategy will function as a navigator, steering you through forthcoming te-sts and ambiguities. The plan highlights action items to work on stre-ngths and circumvent weakness-es. It provides milestones to track progre-ss towards goals. Revisiting this written plan periodically ke-eps you accountable and on course. Ove-rall, the book equips you with tools for self-analysis and a roadmap for se-lf-development.

Remember, self-assessment is not a one-time event but a lifelong practice. As you grow and evolve, your values, passions, and skills may change. This book will equip you with the tools and mindset to adapt your action plan, ensuring that you stay true to your authentic self and continue to pursue success on your own terms.

So, are you pre-pared to embark on this transformative journe-y? Let us work together to construct a robust foundation for continual achie-vement as we author the- life success narrative at this pivotal age-of twenty. Let us wholehe-artedly embrace se-lf-reflection, dete-rmine our priorities, hone our tale-nts, and envision a tomorrow that expresse-s our authentic capabilities. The mome-nt has arrived, and the opportunities are- boundless. Let our voyage comme-nce.

"Remember, twenty is the age of discovery, where the world is your canvas and the possibilities are boundless. It's a time to embrace the unknown, take risks, and shape your own destiny. Your journey at twenty sets the stage for a life filled with adventure, growth, and endless opportunities. Embrace each chapter with open arms, for it is the beginning of a remarkable story that only you can write."

Part 1:
Self-Discovery
at Twenty

Chapter: 1

The Power of Self-Assessment: Knowing Who You Are

***

Understanding the Importance of Self-Assessment

As young people- in their early twentie-s start their voyage towards individual and caree-r progression, self-refle-ction becomes an esse-ntial device for accomplishment. By de-dicating time to comprehending the-mselves, people- can make more intellige-nt choices, establish purposeful targe-ts, and guide their route with lucidity. While- embarking on this journey of self-discove-ry, it is important to thoughtfully analyze strengths as well as are-as of improvement. This helps gain de-eper insights to apply towards continual learning and improve-ment. Self-assessme-nt also aids in recognizing interests and making choice-s aligned with natural talents and abilities.

Gaining aware-ness of one's own qualities, abilities, and limitations is e-ssential for accurately evaluating one-'s own performance. It require-s identifying personal strengths, are-as needing improveme-nt, principles, perspective-s, and interests that drive passion. Pe-ople with a clear sense- of who they are can make de-cisions that genuinely refle-ct their true selve-s better than those without se-lf-knowledge. Knowing your talents along with your limitations assists in focusing e-fforts and energy on tasks playing to your strengths, while- acknowledging where e-xtra work or assistance may be nee-ded. Self-assessme-nt allows one to pursue opportunities aligne-d with innate skills and values.

Effective- people in a variety of occupations attribute- internal examination as a main consider in the-ir achievements. The-y realize that by comprehe-nding themselves, the-y had the option to utilize their qualitie-s, concentrate on their shortcomings, and make- intentional choices that pushed the-m ahead. By taking an unbiased take a gande-r at their qualities and shortcomings, these- fruitful individuals had the option to channel their vitality into the- regions where the-y could sparkle, while working on territorie-s that required further improve-ment. Their self-mindfulne-ss permitted them to ze-ro in on utilizing their abilities to make progre-ss, while additionally dealing with regions that re-quired more work. This adjusted way to de-al with self-evaluation and self-improve-ment empowere-d them to deliberate-ly drive forward and accomplish their objective-s.

For instance, re-nowned businesswoman Sara Blakely, the- creator of Spanx, attributes her achie-vement to her proce-ss of self-evaluation. When cultivating he-r thought for shaping underwear, she pe-rceived her e-nthusiasm for solving issues and her capacity to ponder outside- the case. This comprehe-nsion empowered he-r to take measured dange-rs and at last make a organization estee-med at over $1 billion. While de-veloping her thought, Blakely unde-rstood her strong suits, for example, he-r innovative spirit and problem-solving abilities. She- utilized these qualitie-s to imagine a cutting edge ite-m that filled an unmet nee-d. Her comprehension of he-r own qualities gave her the- boldness to take chances and pursue- her vision, driving to her accomplishment as the- founder of Spanx.

By highlighting these examples and emphasizing the power of self-assessment, "Build Your Character at Twenty" encourages readers to embark on their own journey of self-discovery. It stresses the importance of taking the time to reflect on personal values, beliefs, and passions in order to make informed choices that align with one's authentic self.

Through engaging ane-cdotes and thought-provoking research, re-aders are motivated to e-xplore their inner se-lves more thoroughly. The book offe-rs different activities and que-stions that lead readers through the- journey of self-refle-ction, aiding them in discovering their individual passions and obje-ctives. For instance, reade-rs may examine past expe-riences to understand patte-rns in their interests or value-s over time. As another e-xample, readers can e-nvision their ideal day to glean clue-s about purposes that light them up. While se-lf-study takes patience, making small e-fforts regularly can provide meaningful insights that support living life- more joyfully and purposefully.

Furthermore-, "Build Your Character at Twenty" introduces re-aders to evaluation methods and proce-dures that help in recognizing stre-ngths and places for progress. By capitalizing on strengths and conce-ntrating on shortcomings, people can boost their e-xecution and expand their odds of accomplishme-nt. While assessment tools can offe-r insight, true developme-nt comes from regular self-asse-ssment and effort toward self-be-tterment.

To further assist re-aders in self-evaluating, the- book examines how to appraise one-'s abilities and talents. It inspires individuals to gauge- their expertise- in domains like interacting with others, solving issue-s, guiding teams, and additional regions. This appraisal constructs a base for pe-rsonal and career progress, highlighting the- perpetual require-ment of studying. While the e-valuation offers a starting point for growth, one must acknowledge- their limits to strengthen we-aknesses over time- through practice and experie-nce.

While "Build Your Characte-r at Twenty" encourages re-aders to craft an action plan stemming from self-re-flection, developing a strate-gy for improvement nee-d not be an overwhelming or solitary proce-ss. Taking stock of one's strengths and weakne-sses allows for focused progression toward individually me-aningful objectives. The te-mplates furnished help e-stablish objectives and associated actions in a structure-d way, with an emphasis on reevaluating pe-riodically to incorporate evolving aims and a changing self. Working to e-nhance character nee-d not be a static or one-time unde-rtaking but rather a dynamic process of continuous bette-rment that can be aided ye-t not rigidly defined by the guidance- offered in the book.

Reflecting on Personal Values, Beliefs, and Passions:

Through this passage, we- will undertake an inward journey of se-lf-reflection, escorting re-aders in examining their fundame-ntal principles, convictions, and interests. Compre-hending one's dee-pest standards and coordinating deeds consiste-nt with them is pivotal for accomplishing overall fulfillment and conte-ntment in life. While core- values may seem abstract, ide-ntifying a few that profoundly motivate us can provide clarity and dire-ction. As we consider what truly matters most, small acts aligne-d with our principles compound over time. Though the- process of introspection is gradual, making efforts to live- conscientiously in accordance with our dee-pest truths cultivates meaning.

To thoughtfully commence- this contemplative process, take- a few moments to ponder what ge-nuinely resonates with your core- values. Which principles and ideals do you firmly uphold? What stirs your soul and sparks your inne-r passion? By introspectively examining the-se inquiries, you can attain further insight into your authe-ntic self and the journey you aspire- to embark upon. What truly drives your purpose e-ach day and motivates you to keep le-arning? These refle-ctions can offer perspective- on nurturing your strengths and individuality.

Through various exe-rcises and prompts, we aim to help you discove-r your distinctive passions and motivations. One such activity involves crafting a value-s outline. Begin by recording traits and qualitie-s you admire in other people-. Note what themes strike- a chord with you and symbolize the person you want to be-come. These principle-s could encompass honesty, empathy, inve-ntiveness, or adaptability. Additionally, refle-cting on life experie-nces that have shaped you as an individual can provide- valuable insight into your core values. What stre-ngths have helped you ove-rcome challenges? What role-s have been most fulfilling and why? Answe-ring questions like these- in an exploratory, non-judgmental manner may re-veal patterns about what truly matters most to you.

As you dete-rmine your core values, think critically about e-ach one's role in your life. Spe-nd time examining which principles guide- you most strongly and which ones you find non-negotiable. Orde-r your values from most essential to le-ast impactful based on deep introspe-ction. Consider why certain belie-fs are meaningful pillars that shape who you are-. Ranking your values will shine a reve-aling light on those defining virtues at the- heart of your character. This exe-rcise of thoughtful prioritization will bring understanding to the value-s that truly resonate strongest within you.

Another exercise involves reflecting on your passions and interests. Take a moment to think about activities or topics that bring you joy and excitement. This could be anything from playing an instrument to volunteering for a cause you care about. Make a list of these passions and consider how you can incorporate them into your daily life.

Once you have identified your core values and passions, it is crucial to consider how they align with your actions. Are you currently living in line with these values and pursuing your passions? If not, reflect on what changes you can make to bring greater alignment into your life. This may involve revaluating your career choices, personal relationships, or daily habits.

Remember, self-assessment is an ongoing process. As you grow and evolve, your values and passions may shift. Regularly revisit these reflections and make adjustments accordingly. By understanding and honouring who you truly are, you can navigate life with purpose and authenticity.

Identifying Strengths and Areas for Improvement

Here- we will take a look at differe-nt assessment methods and strate-gies that can help reade-rs recognize their tale-nts and places needing work. Knowing our stre-ngths permits us to make the most of the-m, boosting our execution and expanding our possibilitie-s of achievement. Additionally, unde-rstanding where we re-quire improvement e-mpowers us to intentionally centre on changing those shortcomings into qualities.

Assessment tools come in various forms, ranging from personality assessments to skills assessments. These tools provide valuable insights into our natural talents, preferences, and aptitudes. By taking advantage of these resources, readers can gain a deeper understanding of themselves and uncover hidden strengths they may not have been aware of before.

One popular assessment tool is the StrengthsFinder assessment. This assessment identifies an individual's top five strengths out of a list of 34 possible themes. By recognizing these strengths, readers can focus their energy and efforts on activities that align with their natural abilities. Embracing and further developing these strengths will not only boost confidence but also enhance performance in various aspects of life.

The DISC asse-ssment evaluates an individual's behavioural style based on four key dime-nsions: dominance, influence, ste-adiness, and conscientiousness. This tool provide-s insight into one's preferre-d communication approach and typical work habits. Gaining awareness of your behavioural te-ndencies can help you capitalize- on your strengths when interacting with othe-rs and contributing as part of a team. In addition, understanding behavioural style-s empowers individuals to adjust their communication me-thods to productively engage with colle-agues who think and act differently. The- assessment offers pe-rspective that allows for effe-ctive collaboration with personalities unlike- your own.

Beside-s standardized evaluation methods, se-lf-assessment activities can also be- useful in determining abilitie-s and shortcomings. Taking a moment for introspection enable-s individuals to pinpoint habits or pursuits that bring happiness and meaning. Consider past occurre-nces, accomplishments, and instances whe-n you felt most assured and satisfied. What inhe-rent talents added to the-se positive encounte-rs? By analysing previous triumphs, people can re-cognize common motifs and employ those stre-ngths to other parts of their journeys.

Rephrase It is wise to conside-r both your talents as well as areas that could use- enhancement. While- our strengths allow us to contribute value, we-aknesses, if addresse-d rightly, can evolve into new abilitie-s. Take inventory of where- you currently excel and whe-re growth still lies ahead. The-se insights need not discourage- but rather motivate continued advance-ment. Once dimly lit passages come- into focus, set forth on pathways leading there-. Consult experts through lessons, coache-s, or advisors who share their gathere-d wisdom so you too may steadily progress toward mastery.

It is important to kee-p in mind that identifying your talents and opportunities for e-nhancement is a continuous process. As time- passes and we learn, our tale-nts may transform while new shortcomings may surface. Consiste-ntly re-examining ourselve-s permits us to adjust our action plans fittingly, confirming consistent individual and expe-rt development.

Through utilizing assessme-nt instruments, deeply re-flecting on oneself, and be-ing receptive to fe-edback from others, reade-rs can attain a clearer comprehe-nsion of their talents and limitations. With this insight, they can capitalize- on their talents to thrive in various are-as while deliberate-ly endeavouring to transform limitations into territorie-s of skilfulness.

Evaluating Personal Skills and Competencies:

As you continue your journey of self-assessment, it is important to evaluate your personal skills and competencies. These are the abilities and qualities that you possess which contribute to your overall effectiveness in various areas of life. By identifying and understanding your strengths and weaknesses, you can make informed decisions about your career path, personal growth, and long-term success.

Effective communication is so important in both work and personal life. It's worthwhile to asse-ss your speaking and writing abilities, as well as how we-ll you listen with empathy. Ask yourself: can you ge-t your thoughts, perspectives, and fe-elings across clearly? Do you adjust how you communicate de-pending on who you're talking to and the situation? Pinpointing whe-re you could strengthen your communication will allow you to conne-ct with others even be-tter. You'll collaborate more smoothly on te-ams. Your leadership skills may grow too as communication upgrades. Conside-r reviewing your communication style - do you make- sure everyone- understands you? Do you listen actively to compre-hend different vie-ws? Focusing on communication can enrich relationships and open up possibilitie-s professionally.

Problem-solving skills are- crucial to assess. How do you personally tackle difficultie-s and barriers? Are you able to scrutinize- circumstances methodically, uncover unde-rlying reasons, and craft resourceful answe-rs? Thinking about your problem-solving talents can help you de-vise tactics to get past setbacks and locate- inventive reme-dies to knotty issues. You may consider se-arching out means and activities that let you practice- and improve your problem-solving abilities.

While le-adership skills are worth assessing e-ven without a formal leadership role-, as cultivating such qualities benefits one- throughout life, evaluating one's le-adership potential and areas for growth provide-s direction. Consider your capacity to motivate othe-rs through inspiring vision, efficiently dele-gate responsibilities, and make- decisions with assurance. Also assess if you e-mbody characteristics like integrity, e-mpathy, and an aptitude to energize- individuals. Acknowledging where le-adership developme-nt is still needed dire-cts one towards opportunities to further stre-ngthen these skills for the- future.

As you refle-ct on your individual talents and abilities, kee-p in mind that pursuing lifelong learning and progress substantially contribute-s to constructing a thriving career and personal e-xperience. Conside-ring your present strengths pe-rmits noticing where extra progre-ssion may be valuable. Search for me-ans like classes, programs, or guidance from othe-rs that match your aims and passions. By dedicating energy toward cultivating your skills and knowle-dge, you'll ready yourself for pote-ntial achievements and promotions down the- road. Continuous studying grants opportunities to broaden your range while- long-term developme-nt nurtures success.

Kee-p in mind that self-assessment is an ongoing proce-dure. As you continue to cultivate and progre-ss, you may distinguish new aptitudes and capacities to surve-y. Consistently revisit your self-asse-ssment to refresh your activity plan and guarante-e that you are consistently synchronizing your choice-s and activities with your real self. By e-mbracing self-cognizance and consistently asse-ssing and improving your individual abilities and abilities, you will be we-ll-outfitted to handle the difficultie-s and vulnerabilities of your twentie-s and past. Self-evaluation permits you to conce-ntrate on regions nee-ding improvement and acknowledge- your qualities. Revisiting your evaluation pe-rmits refining your activity plan as new openings de-velop. Continuously developing give-s you instruments to actualize progress and accomplish obje-ctives for a productive and satisfying profession.

Creating an Action Plan Based on Self-Assessment:

Now that you have gone through the process of self-assessment and gained valuable insights into your values, beliefs, passions, strengths, areas for improvement, and personal skills and competencies, it's time to translate that knowledge into a concrete action plan. This action plan will serve as a roadmap for achieving your goals and aligning your actions with your authentic self.

To create your action plan, consider the following steps:
1. Synthesize Your Insights:

Looking back on the re-sults of your self-assessment allows you to se-e recurring theme-s among your core values, intere-sts, natural talents, and opportunities for growth. Take a fe-w minutes to closely examine- your self-assessment for consiste-nt messages. Certain value-s or strengths may surface repe-atedly, giving clues to priorities you want to targe-t in your action plan. Likewise, areas de-manding further progress may form an obvious pattern. With a care-ful review, you can pinpoint the pivotal spots that matte-r most so your action plan capitalizes on your strengths and addresse-s your weaknesses.

2. Set Meaningful Goals:

Based on your self-assessment, set meaningful goals that align with your values and passions. These goals should be specific, measurable, attainable, relevant, and time-bound (SMART). For example, if one of your strengths is communication and you are passionate about public speaking, a SMART goal could be to deliver a presentation at a local event within the next six months.

3. Define Actionable Steps:

Breaking down your goals into smalle-r, action-oriented steps can he-lp make progress fee-l attainable. For each objective-, identify concrete tasks you can accomplish in the- near future to inch closer to the-ultimate aim. Think critically about what abilities, tools, or assistance may facilitate- completing each milestone-. For example, if strengthe-ning your leadership is a priority, enrolling in upcoming workshops on the- subject or spearheading a ne-w project for a cause you care about could he-lp hone the appropriate skills through hands-on e-xperience. De-termining incremental ste-ps and necessary support ahead of time- sets oneself up for succe-ss versus being overwhe-lmed by the size of the- full endeavor.

4. Create a Timeline:

Assigning specific date-s to each actionable step will he-lp you stay accountable to your goals and ensure ste-ady progress. Be realistic whe-n estimating deadlines, conside-ring any external factors that could influence- your timeline. Though strive to me-et your self-imposed due- dates, remain flexible- if unexpected de-lays occur. The ultimate aim is to sustain motivation by consistently moving close-r to completion, even if some- dates need adjusting along the- way. Prioritize continued forward motion over rigidly sticking to a pote-ntially imperfect schedule-.

5. Revisit and Update Regularly:

As you commence- your action plan, periodically re-evaluate- and re-examine your obje-ctives, actionable steps, and advance-ment. Be amenable- to modifying your plan if essential, as individual progress and fre-sh ambitions may surface throughout the process. Re-main engaged with your deve-loping self and implement alte-rations appropriately.

By creating an action plan based on your self-assessment, you are taking proactive steps towards personal growth and fulfillment. Remember that this plan is not set in stone and can be refined as you gain more clarity about your path. With determination, perseverance, and a willingness to adapt, you have the power to shape your future and live a life aligned with your true self.

Chapter 2

Embracing Change: The Only Constant at Twenty

*****

Understanding the Importance of Self-Assessment

As young people- in their early twentie-s embark on their personal and profe-ssional development, taking time- for self-reflection prove-s essential for achieving succe-ss. By dedicating some introspective- moments to better unde-rstand who they are, individuals can make wise-r decisions, establish meaningful goals, and ste-er their path with clarity. While starting out on this voyage- of self-discovery, it is crucial to thoughtfully examine- strengths along with places for growth. This lends de-eper understanding to the-n apply towards ongoing learning and progress. Self-e-valuation also helps uncover passions and make se-lections aligned with innate skills and capabilitie-s. As these 20-somethings start out, gaining insight into the-mselves through refle-ction can aid their journey in a meaningful way.

Gaining awarene-ss of one's own qualities, abilities, and limitations is e-ssential for accurately evaluating one-'s own performance. It require-s identifying personal strengths, are-as needing improveme-nt, principles, perspective-s, and interests that drive passion. Pe-ople with a clear sense- of who they are can make de-cisions that genuinely refle-ct their true selve-s better than those without se-lf-knowledge. Knowing your talents along with your limitations assists in focusing e-fforts and energy on tasks playing to your strengths, while- acknowledging where e-xtra work or assistance may be nee-ded. Self-assessme-nt allows one to pursue opportunities aligne-d with innate skills and values. With a clear unde-rstanding of personal strengths and weakne-sses, one can direct e-nergy towards opportunities that make the- most of their natural abilities and intere-sts, while recognizing where- extra care or help is re-quired. This type of evaluation also pe-rmits pursuing chances coordinated with inhere-nt expertise and principle-s.

Effective- individuals attribute their achieve-ments to internal examination. By unde-rstanding themselves, the-y could utilize their qualities and focus on shortcomings to make- intentional choices that pushed the-m ahead. Taking an unbiased look at their qualitie-s and shortcomings allowed these succe-ssful people to channel the-ir energy into areas whe-re they could shine, while- working on territories that require-d further improvement. The-ir self-awareness pe-rmitted them to zero in on utilizing abilitie-s to make progress, while additionally de-aling with regions that required more- work. This balanced way to deal with self-e-valuation and self-improvement e-mpowered them to de-liberately drive forward and accomplish the-ir objectives. By gaining insight into their stre-ngths and weaknesses, pe-ople can focus their efforts in the- right places to achieve succe-ss. An impartial look inward provides awareness that guide-s improvement.

For instance, re-nowned businesswoman Sara Blakely, the- creator of Spanx, attributes her achie-vement to her proce-ss of self-evaluation. When cultivating he-r thought for shaping underwear, she pe-rceived her e-nthusiasm for solving issues and her capacity to ponder outside- the case. This comprehe-nsion empowered he-r to take measured dange-rs and at last make a organization estee-med at over $1 billion. While de-veloping her thought, Blakely unde-rstood her strong suits, for example, he-r innovative spirit and problem-solving abilities. She- utilized these qualitie-s to imagine a cutting edge ite-m that filled an unmet nee-d. Her comprehension of he-r own qualities gave her the- boldness to take chances and pursue- her vision, driving to her accomplishment as the- founder of Spanx.

By highlighting these examples and emphasizing the power of self-assessment, "Build Your Character at Twenty" encourages readers to embark on their own journey of self-discovery. It stresses the importance of taking the time to reflect on personal values, beliefs, and passions in order to make informed choices that align with one's authentic self.

Through engaging ane-cdotes and thought-provoking research, re-aders are motivated to e-xplore their inner se-lves more thoroughly in the book. It offe-rs different activities and que-stions that gently guide reade-rs through the journey of self-re-flection. This aids them in discovering the-ir individual passions and objectives. For example-, readers may examine- past experience-s to understand patterns in their inte-rests or values over time-. Did certain hobbies or causes consiste-ntly spark your curiosity? Another activity invites reade-rs to envision their ideal day to gle-an clues about purposes that light them up. What type-s of activities would fulfill you? While self-study re-quires patience, taking small ste-ps regularly can provide meaningful insights. Insights that support living life- more joyfully and purposefully. Making a little progre-ss each day on better knowing yourse-lf can lead to big rewards long term.

Furthermore-, readers are introduce-d to helpful evaluation technique-s in "Build Your Character at Twenty" that aid in identifying stre-ngths and opportunities for growth. By leveraging stre-ngths and focusing on areas needing improve-ment, people can e-nhance their performance- and increase chances of succe-ss. Although assessment tools provide pe-rspective, genuine- development ste-ms from consistent self-refle-ction and a commitment to continuous betterme-nt. This process of critical self-analysis followed by de-dicated work on weak areas allows ongoing progre-ss over time.

To further he-lp readers in self-asse-ssment, the book explore-s how to evaluate one's stre-ngths and gifts. It motivates individuals to measure the-ir skills in areas like communicating with others, solving proble-ms, leading teams, and other sphe-res. This evaluation lays a foundation for personal and care-er advancement, unde-rscoring the constant need for le-arning. Though the appraisal provides a starting point, one must re-cognize their boundaries to bolste-r shortcomings step by step through repe-ated exposure and e-ncounters. While the asse-ssment offers a place to be-gin expanding, a person must acknowledge- where they can ye-t progress to methodically reinforce- weaknesses through habit and e-xposure.

While "Build Your Characte--r at Twenty" encourages re--aders to craft an action plan stemming from self-re--flection, developing a strate--gy for improvement does not ne-ed to be an overwhe-lming or solitary process. Taking stock of one's strengths and we-akne-sses allows one to make- focused progress toward personally me-aningful objectives. The te-mplates provided help e-stablish objectives and associated actions in a structure-d way, with emphasis placed on ree-valuating periodically to incorporate evolving aims and a changing se-lf. Working to enhance one's characte-r does not need to be- a static or one-time undertaking but rathe-r a dynamic process of continuous betterme-nt that can be supported yet not rigidly de-fined by the guidance offe-red in the book. While te-mplates aid in establishing objective-s and associated actions, one should ree-valuate periodically and allow goals and plans to change with pe-rsonal growth.

Reflecting on Personal Values, Beliefs, and Passions:

Through this passage, we- will undertake an inward journey of se-lf-reflection, escorting re-aders in examining their fundame-ntal principles, convictions, and interests. Compre-hending one's dee-pest standards and coordinating deeds consiste-nt with them is pivotal for accomplishing overall fulfillment and conte-ntment in life. While core- values may seem abstract, ide-ntifying a few that profoundly motivate us can provide clarity and dire-ction. As we consider what truly matters most, small acts aligne-d with our principles compound over time. Though the- process of introspection is gradual, making efforts to live- conscientiously in accordance with our dee-pest truths cultivates meaning.

To thoughtfully commence- this contemplative process, conside-r taking a few moments to refle-ct on what genuinely aligns with your core value-s and principles. Which ideals do you truly stand behind? What inspire-s your soul and ignites your inner passion? By introspective-ly pondering these que-stions, you can gain additional understanding into your authentic self and the- path you wish to travel. What genuinely motivate-s your purpose each day and encourage-s you to keep expanding your knowle-dge? These re-flections can provide insight on cultivating your strengths and unique-ness. While introspection may illuminate- your driving forces, the journey of se-lf-discovery is ongoing. Perhaps revisiting the-se questions periodically allows for continue-d growth and understanding of yourself.

Through various exe-rcises and prompts, we aim to help uncove-r your true passions and motivations. Crafting a values outline can provide- clarity. Begin by considering traits you admire in othe-rs. Note themes that re-sonate with you and represe-nt the person you wish to become-. Core principles could include hone-sty, empathy, creativity, or adaptability. Additionally, meaningful life- experience-s that influenced your deve-lopment offer valuable se-lf-knowledge. Which strengths prove-d most useful when facing difficulties? What role-s felt most rewarding, and why did they bring you fulfillme-nt? Contemplating questions like the-se openly, without criticism, can reve-al your deepest prioritie-s.

When de-termining your core values, take- time to critically analyze each one-'s significance in your life. Carefully e-xamine which principles have the- greatest influence- over your decisions and which you consider non-ne-gotiable. Organize your values from most important to le-ast impactful based on deep se-lf-reflection. Think about why specific be-liefs are meaningful corne-rstones that define your ide-ntity. Prioritizing your values will shine a reve-aling light on those defining virtues at the- heart of who you are. This exe-rcise of thoughtful arrangement will provide- insight into the values that truly echo loude-st within you.

Taking a moment to introspe-ct on what sparks your joy and enthusiasm can provide insight into passions worth pursuing. Whethe-r playing a musical instrument, volunteering your time- for an important cause, or another intere-st that stimulates you, making an inventory of such activities is worthwhile-. Once compiled, explore- approaches to better inte-grate at least one of your liste-d passions into regular practice. Small steps to nurture- activities that light your soul could enhance daily life- through productive channels for creativity, social impact, or simply re-laxation and rejuvenation. While othe-r demands take priority at times, re-membering where- you find fulfilment helps maintain overall we-ll-being and life satisfaction.

Rephrase when you've- pinpointed your fundamental principles and inte-rests, it is exceptionally critical to think about how the-y interface with your activities. Are- you at present living consistent with the-se qualities and see-king after your interests? On the- off chance that not, think about what improvements you can make- to bring more prominent coordination into your life. This may include- reassessing your profession de-cisions, individual connections, or regular schedule-s. Perhaps a few regions of your life- need some adjustme-nt to better mirror your centre qualities and what genuinely drive-s you. Consider little changes you can actualize- step by step to enhance- congruity between who you are- and how you spend your time.

Kee-p in mind that self-assessment is a continuous proce-ss. As you develop and change through e-xperiences, your prioritie-s and interests may alter ove-r time. Frequently re-turn to these considerations and modify the-m as needed. By re-cognizing and respecting your inhere-nt qualities, you can journey through living with intention and ge-nuineness.

Identifying Strengths and Areas for Improvement

Let's e-xplore some of the various asse-ssment approaches and tactics that can aid reade-rs in identifying their strengths and are-as requiring further deve-lopment. Recognizing our talents allows us to capitalize- on them, thereby e-nhancing our performance and broadening our opportunitie-s for success. Furthermore, compre-hending where we- need refine-ment empowers us to purpose-fully focus on transforming those weakness-s into strengths. Here are- a few assessment me-thods that provide helpful insight: self-e-valuations, which give us a chance for introspection; fe-edback from others, like pe-ers, mentors or supervisors, who offe-r an outside perspective-; and analysing past accomplishments and mistakes, which yields le-ssons for continuous self-improvement. While- assessments reve-al aspects demanding work, reme-mbering to appreciate e-xisting abilities boosts confidence and motivation along the- journey.

Assessme-nt tools, which come in many shapes and sizes, he-lp uncover our innate talents and proclivitie-s. Whether examining pe-rsonality or evaluating abilities, these- resources offer important glimpse-s into our inherent gifts, what comes naturally to us, and what we- have affinities for. By utilizing these- types of instruments, people- can come to recognize the-mselves at a dee-per level and uncove-r reserves of capability the-y may not have previously known they posse-ssed. Tools for assessment range- from those analyzing character to those me-asuring skills. All provide worthwhile insights concerning our natural be-nts, preference-s, and aptitudes. When we make- the effort to explore- these tools, we ope-n doors to better comprehe-nd our true selves while- also finding untapped strengths of which we had be-en unaware until that point.

The Stre-ngthsFinder assessment is a wide-ly used evaluation method. This e-valuation identifies an individual's top five tale-nts from a list of thirty-four possible themes. By re-alizing these strengths, pe-ople can channel their e-nergy and efforts into tasks that match their innate- skills. Appreciating and cultivating these tale-nts further will not just increase se-lf-assurance but also improve performance- in different parts of life. The- StrengthsFinder assessme-nt helps uncover natural abilities and proclivitie-s. With understanding of top talents, a person can optimize- their time by concentrating on activitie-s playings to inherent strengths rathe-r than struggle against weaknesse-s. Focusing on developing and applying strengths e-nhances well-being and productivity.

The DISC asse-ssment evaluates an individual's behavioural style based on four key dime-nsions: dominance, influence, ste-adiness, and conscientiousness. This tool provide-s insight into one's preferre-d communication approach and typical work habits. Gaining awareness of your behavioural te-ndencies can help you capitalize- on your strengths when interacting with othe-rs and contributing as part of a team. Understanding behavioural style-s empowers individuals to adjust their communication me-thods to productively engage with colle-agues who think and act differently than the-y do. The assessment offe-rs perspective that allows pe-ople to collaborate effe-ctively with those who have pe-rsonalities unlike their own. By gaining insight into behavioural styles, one can recognize- how to communicate in a way that works best for differe-nt types of colleagues. This aware-ness helps foster productive- discussions and partnerships, even with those- who approach tasks and conversations very differe-ntly. The DISC tool provides a framework to appre-ciate diverse working style-s.

While standardize-d tests provide objective- metrics, self-examination can also offe-r useful insight. Taking time for introspection allows one- to identify habits or pastimes that cultivate joy and purpose-. Reflecting on past happenings, achie-vements, and moments whe-n you felt most confident and content yie-lds understanding. What innate skills contributed to the-se favorable interactions? Analyzing pre-vious victories enables re-cognition of recurring themes and e-mploying those talents in new are-nas. Consider past occurrences, accomplishme-nts, and instances when you felt most assure-d and satisfied. What inherent tale-nts added to these positive- encounters? By analyzing previous triumphs, pe-ople can recognize common motifs and e-mploy those strengths to other parts of the-ir journeys.

It is prudent to e-valuate both your capabilities as well as domains that could be-nefit from refineme-nt. While our strengths enable- us to provide worth, shortcomings, if addressed suitably, can blossom into nove-l skills. Take stock of where you curre-ntly shine and where advance-ment still remains. These- understandings need not dishe-arten but rather ene-rgize continued evolution. Once- dimly illuminated passages come into vie-w, embark on routes guiding there-. Seek guidance from spe-cialists through tutorials, mentors, or counsellors who impart their accumulate-d knowledge so you too can methodically advance- toward expertise.

It is crucial to reme-mber that recognizing your skills and chances for improve-ment is an ongoing process. As time progre-sses and we gain knowledge-, our abilities may evolve while- new weaknesse-s may surface. Regularly reasse-ssing ourselves allows us to modify our action strategie-s appropriately, ensuring steady pe-rsonal and professional evolution. While tale-nts may transform over time, consistent se-lf-reflection helps us adjust plans to maximize- strengths and address areas for growth, supporting life-long learning and developme-nt.

By thoughtfully employing e-valuation tools, thoroughly contemplating one's own qualities, and be-ing open to input from others, reade-rs can develop a more lucid unde-rstanding of their strengths and weakne-sses. With this introspection, they can le-verage their stre-ngths to prosper in various domains while intentionally striving to modify constraints into re-alms of competence. While- assessment can provide clarity, true- understanding emerge-s through reflection.

Evaluating Personal Skills and Competencies:

As you continue your journe-y of self-assessment and pe-rsonal development, taking the- time to deeply e-valuate your unique talents and capabilitie-s is worthwhile. The skills and qualities you have- cultivated, through both experie-nce and natural inclination, compose your repe-rtoire of abilities that impact how successful you are- in different realms of your life-. By thoughtfully considering your strong suits alongside areas with room for improve-ment, you gain valuable self-aware-ness to guide impactful choices about your profe-ssional direction, ongoing learning, and long-term achie-vement. What gifts do you possess that could se-rve you well if refine-d further? Similarly, where might additional e-ffort yield growth?

Effective- communication is so important in both work and personal life. It allows us to share our thoughts, pe-rspectives, and fee-lings with others while also understanding diffe-rent viewpoints. Taking some time- to reflect on how we communicate- can provide valuable insights. Asking yourself que-stions like whether you can cle-arly convey your ideas and if you adapt your approach based on your audie-nce are great place-s to start. Identifying specific areas that could use- improvement will help stre-ngthen your ability to connect with others. With e-nhanced communication skills, you'll find collaborating with teams become-s smoother. Leadership abilitie-s may grow too as you upgrade your communication style. Be sure- to consider if you ensure compre-hension and listen actively. Focusing e-fforts on refining communication can enrich relationships and ope-n up new professional opportunities.

Problem-solving skills are- crucial to assess. How do you personally tackle difficultie-s and barriers? Are you able to scrutinize- circumstances methodically, uncover unde-rlying reasons, and craft resourceful answe-rs? Thinking deeply about challenge-s you've faced can help you unde-rstand your problem-solving talents and devise- new tactics to get past setbacks. Re-flecting on inventive solutions you've- found to complex issues in the past may give- you ideas for approaching new difficulties. You could conside-r seeking out projects, classe-s or hobbies that allow you to strategize cre-atively and strengthen your ability to analyze- problems from multiple perspe-ctives.

Assessing your le-adership abilities, eve-n without having a formal leadership role, can be- worthwhile since deve-loping these qualities is advantage-ous throughout life. By evaluating your potential as a le-ader and areas for growth, you gain direction. Conside-r your ability to motivate others through an inspiring vision and efficie-ntly delegate re-sponsibilities while making decisions with confide-nce. Also assess whethe-r you embody characteristics like inte-grity, empathy, and a talent for ene-rgizing individuals. Recognizing where le-adership developme-nt is still needed points you towards chance-s to further enhance the-se skills for the future. While- leadership skills are worth e-xamining regardless of title, cultivating such traits be-nefits a person in all aspects of life-. Looking at your capacity to guide others through a compelling vision, skillfully distribute- tasks, and make judgments with assurance provide-s understanding. Additionally, determine- if you display high ideals like integrity, compassion, and a knack for inspiring folks. Acknowle-dging where leade-rship refinement is still re-quired aims one towards possibilities to incre-asingly strengthen these- abilities for tomorrow.

As you refle-ct deeply on your unique tale-nts and capabilities, remembe-r that consistently pursuing learning and advanceme-nt notably contributes to building a thriving career and pe-rsonal journey. Considering your current stre-ngths allows noticing where additional progress could be- beneficial. Look for approaches like- courses, initiatives, or advice from othe-rs that align with your goals and interests. By committing time toward e-nhancing your abilities and understanding, you'll prepare- yourself for potential accomplishments and advance-s further along the path. Continuous studying provides possibilitie-s to widen your scope while long-te-rm growth cultivates success. Gaining dee-per insights into your present stre-ngths through reflection helps pinpoint are-as with room for further refineme-nt. Small steps toward broadening your expe-rtise over the ye-ars through learning opportunities outside your comfort zone- support an ever-evolving skillse-t. Progress happens gradually, so remain ope-n to new experie-nces that help strengthe-n existing talents or uncover fre-sh ones.

Here- is a minimally expanded version of the- input text with an intermediate- depth and purpose to clarify:

Self-asse-ssment is an ongoing process that allows continual growth. As you progress, take- time to reconsider your skills and re-cognize any new abilities. Re-visit your self-evaluation regularly to update- your goals and ensure your choices align with your true- strengths. Embracing self-awarene-ss means regularly evaluating your tale-nts and areas for improvement. This will pre-pare you for life's challenge-s throughout your twenties and beyond. Evaluation he-lps focus on where you can strengthe-n your skills while celebrating your natural gifts. Re-visiting your analysis periodically permits adjusting your plans as opportunities arise-. Constant development provide-s tools to enact change and accomplish objective-s for a fulfilling career. Kee-p cultivating self-knowledge through consiste-nt self-assessment in orde-r to refine your path forward.

Creating an Action Plan Based on Self-Assessment:

Now that you have gone through the process of self-assessment and gained valuable insights into your values, beliefs, passions, strengths, areas for improvement, and personal skills and competencies, it's time to translate that knowledge into a concrete action plan. This action plan will serve as a roadmap for achieving your goals and aligning your actions with your authentic self.

To create your action plan, consider the following steps:

1. Synthesize Your Insights:

Looking back on the re-sults of your self-assessment allows you to se-e recurring theme-s among your core values, intere-sts, natural talents, and opportunities that can be de-veloped further. Take- a few minutes to examine- closely the response-s within your self-assessment e-valuation for consistent messages and patte-rns. Certain values or strengths are- likely to surface repe-atedly, providing indications of priorities you want to target in cre-ating your action plan. Similarly, areas requiring more progre-ss may clearly show a noticeable patte-rn. With a thoughtful review, you have the- ability to pinpoint the pivotal aspects that matter most, e-nabling your action plan to capitalize on your strengths and address any we-aknesses identifie-d.

2. Set Meaningful Goals:

Based on your self-assessment, set meaningful goals that align with your values and passions. These goals should be specific, measurable, attainable, relevant, and time-bound (SMART). For example, if one of your strengths is communication and you are passionate about public speaking, a SMART goal could be to deliver a presentation at a local event within the next six months.

3. Define Actionable Steps:

Here- is a minimally expanded text with inte-rmediate depth and clarity of purpose-:

Breaking down your goals allows you to tackle them in smalle-r, more manageable chunks. Whe-n you divide larger objective-s into specific, action-oriented ste-ps, making progress feels within re-ach. For each goal, identify discrete- tasks you can accomplish in the near future to ste-adily move closer to the ultimate- aim. Critically examine what abilities, tools, or assistance- may help complete e-ach milestone.

For instance, if be-coming a stronger leader is important to you, re-gistering for upcoming workshops on leadership or spe-arheading a new project for a cause- you care about could aid in developing the- relevant skills through hands-on expe-rience. Dete-rmining incremental steps and the- necessary support in advance se-ts oneself up for achieve-ment rather than fee-ling overwhelmed by the- scale of the entire- endeavor. Taking goals piece- by piece makes the-m seem less daunting and more- doable.

4. Create a Timeline:

Breaking your goals down into smalle-r, time-bound steps will help you stay accountable- and ensure steady progre-ss towards your aims. When estimating deadline-s for each action, be realistic in your conside-rations - think about any external factors that may impact your timeline-. While your self-imposed due- dates should be targets to hit, re-main adaptable if unexpecte-d delays arise along the way. The- key goal is sustaining your motivation by continuously advancing nearer to comple-tion, even if dates ne-ed adjusting occasionally. Prioritize kee-ping the momentum going rather than rigidly sticking to a sche-dule that may not fully align with how things unfold.

5. Revisit and Update Regularly:

As you begin putting your action plan into motion, make- sure to periodically reasse-ss and reexamine your obje-ctives, action items, and progress. Be- open to making adjustments to your plan if nee-ded, as your developme-nt and new goals may emerge- throughout the process. Stay engage-d with your ongoing growth and implement changes suitably. Ke-ep evaluating how things are going so you can re-vise your approach if your circumstances or priorities e-volve. Check in with yourself re-gularly to see what's working well and whe-re you may benefit from twe-aking your strategy. Remain rece-ptive to reflections that could he-lp refine your plan into something e-ven more effe-ctive for supporting your interests and moving your e-fforts forward.

Creating an action plan grounde-d in self-reflection allows you to active-ly work on personal developme-nt and finding purpose. Understand this outline is a work in progre-ss, amendable when you gain additional insight into your journe-y. By persevering through challe-nges with adaptability and resolve, you control your ability to de-sign tomorrow and exist congruent with your authentic se-lf. Exploring strengths and weaknesse-s through introspection helps craft achievable- objectives. Regular revaluation helps adjust approach as comprehe-nsion increases, supporting steady growth. Although obstacle-s may appear, maintaining direction empowe-rs consistent progress aligning daily acts with important values.

Chapter 3

Defining Your Core
Values and Beliefs

****

Core values and beliefs

When starting out on your path toward se-lf-improvement and accomplishment in your twe-nties, it is extreme-ly important to pinpoint your fundamental ideals and convictions. These- root aspects act as directives that mold your choice-s, behaviors, and overall fee-ling of intention. By taking the effort to re-cognize and comprehend your basic value-s, you can experience- life in a more genuine- and coordinated way.

The value-s closest to one's heart are- the guiding lights that steer conduct and affe-ct judgments made. They mirror what matte-rs most and serve as an internal compass, assisting navigation through life-'s tests and doubts. With lucid values, choices harmonize-, resulting in deepe-r meaning and contentment.

Without a solid understanding of your core values and beliefs, it is easy to get swept away by external influences or societal expectations. By defining your values, you take control of your own narrative and create a life that is meaningful to you. Your values provide a sense of direction and purpose, giving you a solid foundation on which to build your character and make choices that align with who you truly are.

Gaining insight into your fundamental principle-s also permits you to prioritize what genuine-ly signifies in life. By elucidating your principle-s, you have the ability to cente-r your vitality and consideration on the regions that conve-y you the most delight, fulfillment, and individual de-velopment. This intelligibility e-mpowers you to be more inte-ntional in seeking after ope-nings that synchronize with your principles, while additionally pe-rmitting you to tactfully dismiss pursuits that don't resonate with your authentic se-lf.

During the formative- years of your twenties, e-stablishing your fundamental principles and convictions provides a basis for living consiste-ntly with your authentic self. Gaining insight into your own identity capacitate-s assured decision making, recognizing compatibilitie-s with the individual you endeavor to be-come. Whether se-lecting an occupational route, cultivating relationships, or de-dicating efforts to personal growth, possessing disce-rnment of your priorities guarantee-s that your selections respe-ct your genuine character.

RephraseOver the- next few chapters, we- will explore how to uncover your fundame-ntal principles and perspective-s. With self-examination activities, he-lpful direction, and genuine case-s, you will acquire the device-s and understandings expecte-d to discover what genuinely matte-rs to you. By characterizing your center qualitie-s and convictions, you will put yourself on a way towards individual developme-nt, accomplishment, and an existence- filled with objectives and fulfillme-nt.

Self-reflection exercises:

To truly understand and define your core values and beliefs, it is crucial to engage in self-reflection. By taking the time to explore your passions, priorities, and what you hold dear in different areas of life, you can gain a deeper understanding of who you are and what drives you.

Here- are some practical exe-rcises and prompts to help explore- self-reflection:

Writing in a journal daily about your e-xperiences, thoughts, and fe-elings can provide valuable insight. Prompts like- describing a challenging situation

1. Journaling: Set aside dedicated time each day or week to journal about your thoughts, experiences, and feelings. Use writing as a tool for introspection and self-discovery. Reflect on significant moments in your life and consider how they have shaped your values and beliefs.

2. Envisionment: Se-ek out a tranquil locale where- you can loosen up and envision your ideal e-xistence. Picture yourse-lf living a life loaded with importance and re-ason. What does it

resemble-? How does it feel? Focus on the- qualities and convictions that emerge- from these envisionments.

3. The five- why's technique: An individual ought to pick an aspect of the-ir life that is significant to them, such as relationships or profe-ssional objectives. Inquire as to the- reasoning this aspect is critical and compose down the- response. At that point, kee-p inquiring "why" for every ensuing re-action. By digging more profound, one will uncover the- fundamental qualities and convictions that drive the-ir activities and choices.

4. Resource-s for evaluating what matters: Utilize online- resources or books that offer e-xercises to assess what you find me-aningful. These tools freque-ntly present common ideals and ask you to rate- how significant they are to who you are. Care-fully consider the ideals that fe-el most genuine, indicating whe-re your fundamental principles re-side.

5. Gather guidance- from others: Participate in honest discussions with re-liable confidants, relatives, or advisors who can supply invaluable- understandings into your principles and convictions. Inquire as to how the-y view your priorities or what they conside-r to characterize you. Their vie-wpoints may expose facets of yourse-lf that you may have overlooked.

It's important to make time- for self-examination regularly. Sche-dule occasions where you quie-tly think about yourself and your principles. Stay ready to de-tect new aspects of what you e-ssentially consider significant. By willingly taking part in these- activities, you'll achieve a crispe-r comprehension of your authentic prioritie-s and how to synchronize your choices and conduct reasonably.

Discovering what truly matte-rs most helps ensure your e-fforts align with living meaningfully. This part explores ide-ntifying your deepest principle-s and beliefs, with steps to focus on your top prioritie-s when tough choices occur. We'll conside-r techniques for illuminating what guides you, the-n concentrating on those beacons whe-never decisions de-mand discerning trade-offs.

At the start of my journe-y, I took some time for quiet introspe-ction. I reflected on the- different aspects of my life- that I find meaningful, such as my connections with others, my work, pe-rsonal growth, and involvement in my community. I thought about what really holds importance- for me in each of these- domains. What values guide me? What kind of pe-rson do I aspire to be known as?

As you examine- a series of typical principles that corre-spond with diverse aspects of e-xistence, take note- of which ones genuinely touch your spirit. This se-ries might contain integrity, empathy, inve-ntiveness, progress, and autonomy. While- considering the serie-s, focus on which principles truly connect with you. Encircle or spotlight the- ones that honestly talk to your core be-ing.

Years ago, as I se-t out to define what truly mattere-d most to me, I carefully examine-d an array of values that resonated on a pe-rsonal level. To refine- my perspective, I conte-mplated the significance and influe-nce each belie-f held in shaping who I am. I asked myself probing que-stions like: Which principles guide me- during both easy and difficult times? What ideals continue- driving me forward despite se-tbacks? What causes inspire me to ke-ep growing as a person? By refle-cting on how I interact with the world around me during varie-d life experie-nces, both positive and

Through thoughtful self-re-flection on these que-stions, you can begin ranking what matters most to you dee-p down. Bear in mind that your priorities are inte-nsely individualized - a refle-ction of who you are at your core. Your answers re-veal what you find truly meaningful, irrespe-ctive of external norms. This proce-ss illuminates your guiding principles, helping e-nsure future choices align with your authe-ntic self.

Managing conflicting priorities can prove- difficult. In these scenarios, focusing first on what matte-rs most proves key. Refle-ct on how options may affect your guiding principles long-term. Conside-r results and ramifications carefully. Compromise occasionally he-lps, yet aim choices toward values at your core-. Weighing importance assists discerning be-st paths aligning with what you find most meaningful.

true to what re-ally matters can anchor your choices and give life- purpose. My deepe-st motivations guide me well whe-n times are tough. While what drive-s my spirit may transform as years pass, reflecting on my guiding lights re-mains a steady practice, as does following the-ir lead through whatever come-s. Though paths shift and challenges await, reme-mbering what fills my soul with meaning lights the way ahe-ad with reassuring calm.

Making choices that match what matte-rs most is significant for developing as an individual and living intentionally. In this part, we- will look deeper into practically applying what you stand for whe-n making decisions, giving direction on how to assess options and match the-m with your fundamental values and perspe-ctives.

As we e-ncounter crossroads in life, it is prudent to take- a moment and consider how each path re-lates to what matters most dee-ply. Begin by illuminating your guiding lights - what intrinsic truths light your way and shape your steps. With inne-r wisdom shining clear, decision-making nee-d not divide or disorient, but rather conne-ct you to your authentic self and steady course-. Compass in hand, choices need ste-er you not astray from virtue's north.

To align decisions with your core values, consider the following steps:

1. Identify your alte-rnatives: To begin, precise-ly outline the diverse- opportunities accessible to you. Re-gardless of whether choosing a profe-ssion way, making monetary ventures, or choosing whom to spe-nd time with, comprehending the- conceivable decisions is basic.

Considering your principle-s led me to carefully re-think each potential path. I took time to re-visit my deepest motivations and be-liefs. For each option, I contemplate-d how well it mirrored the ide-als most important to me. Asking myself whethe-r the choice upheld or challe-nged my core values he-lped ensure my de-cision represente-d who I am. Evaluating each alternative through the- lens of my principles allowed an inte-ntional selection in line with what I hold most de-ar.

3. Envision potential outcome-s: It is wise to envision the short-te-rm and long-term effects of e-ach option. Reflect on how each path may affe-ct your overall wellness, conne-ctions, and aims ahead. By picturing potential results, you can make- choices more purposefully aligne-d with your guiding principles.

On occasion, one may e-ncounter a complex scenario whe-re multiple paths appear e-qually appropriate. When faced with such a pre-dicament, guidance from respe-cted individuals can offer invaluable wisdom. Consultation with me-ntors or confidants who share your principles or expe-rtise in the rele-vant domain allows alternative viewpoints to inform difficult choice-s. Their insights may provide clarity amid options which see-m indistinguishable, aiding decision-making on thorny matters.

Staying true to what matte-rs most often provides considerable- advantages, but it is prudent to recognize- potential obstacles as well. De-ciding in line with your guiding principles may nece-ssitate sacrificing other options or tackling complex calls. Eve-n so, the benefits of choice-s reflecting who you are at your core- greatly surmount such difficulties.

When making choice-s with careful consideration of what really matte-rs most to you deep down, you nurture a fe-eling of honesty, motivation, and satisfaction. You construct a path that mirrors your authentic se-lf and genuine philosophies. Ke-ep in mind that your principles are spe-cial to you, and accepting them will guide you on a more- significant and driven route.

In this next part, I will e-xamine how embracing our own deve-lopment and genuinene-ss can help us live according to our fundamental principle-s and convictions.

Growing into the pe-rson you want to become and staying true to who you are- lies at the heart of characte-r development in your twe-nties. It is vital that you walk through life in a way that refle-cts your deepest value-s and allows your best self to eme-rge. Continuous personal progress e-nsures you evolve as an individual anchore-d in your authentic principles.

Every chance- to learn holds potential for personal growth. Pursue- pastimes and prospects that match what matters most to you, allowing e-xpansion in new directions. Take up a nove-l interest, sign up for some studie-s, or dare steps beyond familiar comforts - all offe-r ways to progress on your journey. Whethe-r exploring a fresh fascination, furthering your fie-lds of knowledge, or testing tale-nts in areas untried, such trials transport one to highe-r ground.

Connecting with othe-rs with kindred spirits who cheer on your e-volution can notably strengthen the journe-y. Find advisors, trainers, or companions who match your principles and objective-s. Participate in important discussions and joint efforts that motivate and prope-l you to evolve. By linking up with individuals who lift your spirit and test you, you cultivate- a setting encouraging personal e-volution and genuineness.

It is esse-ntial to look inward as well as outward, seeking chance-s and associations. Make time for introspection, conside-ring your ethics, philosophies, and aspirations. Regularly che-ck how your behaviors match your central virtues, adapting whe-n required. This self-re-flection assists you to stay real to yourself e-ven when faced with obstacle-s or social demands.

Every individual unde-rgoes an ongoing process of personal de-velopment throughout their life-. While travelling along this journey, se-tbacks are sure to arise now and the-n. View difficulties as chances to le-arn and improve, rather than defe-ats that determine your worth. Build re-silience and see- mistakes as useful guides that shape- who you become over time-. Understand that though obstacles may hinder progre-ss now, their lessons will serve- you well if you allow each expe-rience to further your growth.

Deve-loping yourself and living according to your true nature se-ts you up for a fulfilling and sustainable future. Strengthe-ning who you are at twenty revolve-s around continual personal developme-nt that matches your deepe-st principles and convictions, permitting you to pursue a life-infused with intention and true to your authe-ntic spirit.

Chapter 4

Cultivating Self-Reliance: Trusting Your Inner Voice

***

Understanding the Importance of Self-Reliance:

Self-reliance plays a crucial role in personal growth and decision-making during our twenties. It is the ability to depend on ourselves, our instincts, and our own judgment rather than constantly seeking validation or relying heavily on others. By cultivating self-reliance, we can develop independence, confidence, and resilience necessary for navigating the challenges and uncertainties of this formative phase.

Relying on our own capabilities and inner voice allows us to make decisions that align with our values, goals, and aspirations. It empowers us to trust our instincts and embrace our unique perspectives, rather than succumbing to external pressures or societal expectations. Through self-reliance, we can take ownership of our choices and pave our own path towards success and fulfillment.

However, it's important to recognize the potential pitfalls of depending too heavily on others for validation and decision-making. Seeking constant approval from others can lead to a lack of self-confidence and self-doubt. Additionally, relying solely on external sources for guidance may result in decisions that do not truly reflect our authentic selves.

In order to cultivate self-reliance, we must understand the importance of trusting our own inner voice. In the following sections, we will explore strategies for identifying and nurturing this inner voice, overcoming self-doubt, making informed decisions, and embracing growth and adaptability. By developing self-reliance in these areas, we can build a strong foundation for personal growth, professional achievement, and financial prosperity in our twenties and beyond.

Identifying and Nurturing Your Inner Voice:

In this section, we delve into the importance of recognizing and nurturing your inner voice as a valuable source of guidance and wisdom. Your inner voice serves as an internal compass, offering insights and perspectives that are unique to you. By tuning into your intuition and distinguishing it from external influences, you can make decisions that align with your authentic self.

To begin, take the time to reflect on moments when you have felt a strong sense of intuition or a gut feeling. These instances often occur when you are faced with important choices or when something doesn't feel quite right. Pay attention to these moments and start trusting your instincts more consistently.

Distinguishing your inner voice from external influences is another crucial aspect of nurturing it. In today's interconnected world, we are bombarded with opinions, expectations, and societal norms that can cloud our judgment. Take a step back and ask yourself whose voice you are truly listening to when making decisions. Is it your own authentic voice or the voices of others? By becoming aware of external influences, you can actively filter out the noise and connect with your own inner wisdom.

Trusting your instincts and embracing your unique perspectives is essential for personal growth and success. Remember that your inner voice is shaped by your experiences, values, and beliefs. It reflects your deepest desires and aspirations. Embrace the fact that your perspective is valuable and valid.

To strengthen your connection with your inner voice, consider incorporating practices such as meditation, journaling, or mindfulness exercises into your daily routine. These activities can help quiet the external noise and allow your inner voice to shine through. Practice self-reflection regularly and listen attentively to what your intuition is telling you.

By identifying and nurturing your inner voice, you will find greater clarity in decision-making and gain confidence in navigating life's uncertainties. Embrace the power within you and trust that your inner voice holds the keys to unlocking your true potential.

Overcoming Self-Doubt and Building Confidence:

During the formative twenties, it is common for individuals to experience insecurities and self-doubt. These feelings can hinder personal growth and prevent individuals from making decisions aligned with their authentic selves. In this section, we will explore techniques to overcome self-doubt and build self-confidence, empowering readers to trust their inner voice and make informed choices.

One effective strategy for overcoming self-doubt is to reframe negative self-talk. Negative thoughts and beliefs about oneself often contribute to feelings of inadequacy and self-doubt. By consciously challenging and reframing these negative thoughts, individuals can cultivate a more positive and empowering mindset. For example, instead of thinking, "I'm not smart enough to pursue my dream career," one can reframe it as, "I have the intelligence and capability to learn and excel in my chosen field." This shift in perspective can help individuals recognize their strengths and potential, boosting their confidence in the process.

Practicing self-compassion is another powerful tool for overcoming self-doubt. It involves treating oneself with kindness, understanding, and forgiveness, especially during times of failure or setbacks. Rather than being overly critical or judgmental, individuals can learn to offer themselves support and encouragement. Engaging in self-compassionate behaviors such as journaling about achievements and positive qualities, practicing mindfulness, or seeking support from trusted friends or professionals can foster a sense of self-worth and resilience.

To further build self-confidence, engaging in exercises and activities that focus on personal growth and cultivating a positive self-image can be beneficial. Participating in activities that align with one's interests and passions allows individuals to showcase their talents and abilities, reinforcing their belief in themselves. Additionally, setting achievable goals and celebrating small victories along the way helps individuals recognize their progress and capabilities.

Self-confidence also stems from taking care of oneself physically and mentally. Prioritizing self-care activities like exercise, healthy eating, and getting enough rest can promote overall well-being and increased confidence. Engaging in activities that bring joy and relaxation, such as hobbies or spending time outdoors, can also contribute to a positive self-image.

By implementing these techniques and actively working towards building self-confidence, readers can cultivate trust in their inner voice and make decisions that align with their authentic selves. Overcoming self-doubt is a continuous process, but with practice and perseverance, individuals can develop the confidence needed to navigate the uncertainties of their twenties and beyond.

Making informed decisions is a crucial aspect of cultivating self-reliance and trusting your inner voice. In this section, we will explore the process of decision-making and how self-reliance plays a vital role in making choices that align with your personal values. We will also introduce practical tools and techniques for evaluating options, considering pros and cons, and setting priorities.

When it comes to decision-making, it is essential to take the time to thoroughly assess your options. This involves gathering relevant information, considering potential outcomes, and reflecting on how each choice aligns with your long-term goals and values. By being diligent in your research and analysis, you can make informed decisions that are more likely to lead to positive outcomes.

One useful tool for evaluating options is creating a pros and cons list. Take a piece of paper or open a document on your computer, and divide it into two columns. In one column, write down all the pros or advantages of each option you are considering. In the other column, write down all the cons or disadvantages. This exercise allows you to see the potential benefits and drawbacks of each option more clearly, enabling you to make a more informed choice.

Another helpful technique is considering the potential impact of each option on different aspects of your life. Think about how each choice may affect your career, relationships, health, and overall well-being. By assessing the potential consequences across various areas of your life, you can gain a better understanding of which option aligns most closely with your priorities and values.

While it is essential to gather information and consider various perspectives when making decisions, it is equally important to trust your instincts and listen to your inner voice. Sometimes, our intuition can provide valuable insights that logic alone cannot capture. If an option feels right deep within you, even if it may not make complete sense on the surface, consider giving it serious consideration.

Taking responsibility for your decisions is another crucial aspect of self-reliance. Understand that decisions may not always lead to the desired outcome, and that's perfectly okay. We learn and grow from both successes and failures. When a decision doesn't turn out as expected, take the opportunity to reflect on what went wrong, what you can learn from it, and how you can make better choices in the future.

Ultimately, cultivating self-reliance means developing the confidence to trust your inner voice while also being diligent in gathering information and considering various perspectives. By making informed decisions aligned with your values and taking responsibility for the outcomes, you can navigate the uncertainties of your twenties with greater clarity and purpose.

Embracing growth and adaptability is a fundamental aspect of cultivating self-reliance. By recognizing the inevitability of change and developing the ability to adapt, young adults can navigate the uncertainties and challenges that arise during their twenties with confidence and resilience.

To embrace growth and adaptability, it is important for readers to acknowledge that change is a natural part of life. Rather than fearing or resisting change, they should view it as an opportunity for personal growth and development. This mindset shift allows individuals to approach new experiences and challenges from a place of curiosity and openness, enabling them to learn and evolve.

Strategies for developing resilience in the face of challenges and setbacks can also empower individuals in embracing growth and adaptability. It is crucial to remind readers that setbacks are not failures but opportunities for learning and growth. By reframing setbacks as stepping stones towards success, individuals can bounce back stronger and more determined than before.

Here are some strategies that readers can implement to cultivate resilience:

1. Cultivate a growth mindset: A growth mindset is the belief that abilities and intelligence can be developed through dedication and hard work. By adopting a growth mindset, readers can view challenges as opportunities for learning rather than insurmountable obstacles.
2. Practice self-compassion: When facing setbacks or difficulties, it is essential for individuals to be kind to themselves. Practicing self-compassion involves acknowledging one's struggles without judgment and offering oneself understanding and support.
3. Seek support: Building a support network of friends, mentors, or family members can provide valuable guidance, encouragement, and perspective during times of change and uncertainty. Surrounding oneself with positive influences can help foster resilience and promote personal growth.
4. Embrace discomfort: Growth often occurs outside of one's comfort zone. Encourage readers to try new things, take risks, and challenge themselves. By embracing discomfort, individuals can expand their horizons and discover new strengths and capabilities.
5. Reflect and learn from experiences: Encourage readers to reflect on their experiences, both successes, and failures, to identify lessons learned and areas for improvement. By continuously learning from their experiences, individuals can adapt and grow, developing the resilience necessary to thrive in a rapidly changing world.

By following these strategies and embracing growth and adaptability, readers can develop the self-reliance needed to navigate the uncertainties of their twenties successfully. Embracing change and seeking opportunities for personal growth will allow them to craft their own narratives of achievement and fulfillment.

Chapter **5**

The Art of Setting
Personal Goals

****

An Introduction to Goal Setting

Setting personal goals at a young age is crucial for long-term success and personal growth. By having clear goals in mind, individuals are more likely to stay motivated, maintain focus, and achieve their desired outcomes. Goal setting provides a sense of direction and purpose, guiding individuals towards their aspirations.

Identifying Your Values and Priorities:

Values play a significant role in goal setting as they reflect what truly matters to individuals. By identifying core values, young adults can align their goals with their beliefs and priorities, fostering a deeper sense of motivation and fulfillment. Self-reflection exercises can help individuals gain clarity on their values and guide them towards setting meaningful goals that resonate with their authentic selves.

SMART Goal Setting Method:

The SMART goal-setting framework is a powerful tool that ensures goals are Specific, Measurable, Achievable, Relevant, and Time-bound. This method helps individuals create well-defined objectives and increases the likelihood of success. By breaking down long-term goals into smaller, actionable steps, individuals can track progress and celebrate achievements along the way.

Overcoming Obstacles and Staying Motivated:

Obstacles are inevitable on the path to achieving goals. However, by understanding common challenges and learning effective strategies to overcome them, individuals can stay motivated and resilient. Techniques such as visualization, positive affirmations, and seeking support from mentors or peers can help individuals overcome self-doubt, fear of failure, and external obstacles.

Reviewing and Adjusting Goals:

Periodically reviewing and adjusting goals is essential for maintaining relevance and staying on track. Progress assessment allows individuals to recognize accomplishments, identify areas for improvement, and make necessary revisions to their goals. This flexibility ensures that individuals can adapt to changing circumstances or discover new passions throughout their journey.

By following this comprehensive five-point plan on the art of setting personal goals, young adults can cultivate a mindset geared towards achievement and personal growth. Understanding the importance of goal setting, aligning goals with values and priorities, utilizing the SMART goal-setting method, overcoming obstacles, and regularly reviewing and adjusting goals will empower individuals to fulfill their potential and craft a successful future.

(Note: The content provided in this chapter will not be repetitive with information discussed in other parts of the book.),Understanding the Importance of Goal Setting:

Setting personal goals at a young age is not only beneficial, but also essential for personal growth and success. By having clear goals in mind, individuals in their twenties can chart a course towards their desired future. Goal setting provides a sense of direction and purpose, serving as a roadmap for navigating through life's challenges and uncertainties.

One of the key benefits of setting personal goals is the motivation it creates. Having specific goals to work towards gives individuals a sense of purpose and fuels their desire to achieve. Goals provide a target to focus on, enabling individuals to channel their energy and efforts effectively. They serve as a constant reminder of what one is striving for, keeping them motivated even during times of adversity.

Furthermore, setting personal goals helps individuals develop a sense of discipline and commitment. It requires dedication and perseverance to consistently work towards achieving one's objectives. This discipline not only aids in accomplishing goals but also cultivates valuable character traits such as resilience, determination, and self-motivation.

Goal setting also enhances clarity and decision-making abilities. When individuals have clearly defined goals, they are better able to make choices that align with their aspirations and values. Goals act as a filter through which decisions can be evaluated, ensuring that choices made are in line with one's overarching objectives. This clarity enables individuals to stay focused and avoid distractions that may hinder progress.

Lastly, goal setting has a direct correlation with achievement. Research has consistently shown that individuals who set goals are more likely to succeed compared to those who do not. By setting measurable targets and establishing action plans, individuals can track their progress and take steps towards reaching their desired outcomes. Goals provide individuals with a sense of accomplishment when achieved, boosting confidence and paving the way for further success.

In summary, setting personal goals at the age of 20 is instrumental in personal growth and success. It brings numerous benefits such as increased motivation, focus, discipline, clarity, and achievement. By recognizing the importance of goal setting and embracing this practice, individuals can lay a solid foundation for a future filled with purpose, fulfillment, and overall life success.

Identifying Your Values and Priorities

In order to set meaningful personal goals, it is crucial to understand the role of values in goal setting. Our values serve as guiding principles that shape our decisions, actions, and overall sense of fulfillment. By aligning our goals with our core values, we increase motivation and create a stronger sense of purpose in our lives.

To begin the process of identifying your values, take some time for self-reflection. Ask yourself what aspects of life are most important to you and what beliefs and principles you hold dear. Consider what brings you joy and fulfillment, as well as what you consider to be essential for a meaningful and successful life.

During this self-reflection process, it may be helpful to ask yourself specific questions to prompt deeper thought. For example:

1. What kind of person do I want to be?
2. What activities or experiences bring me the most fulfillment?
3. What principles or values do I want to live by?
4. What qualities do I admire in others and strive to embody myself?

As you contemplate these questions, write down your thoughts and observations. This can help you gain clarity about who you are and what truly matters to you.

Once you have identified your core values, it is important to align your goals with these values. When your goals are rooted in your values, they become more meaningful and inspiring. They provide direction and motivation that goes beyond superficial desires or societal expectations.

For example, if one of your core values is environmental sustainability, you may set goals related to reducing your carbon footprint, advocating for sustainable practices in your community, or pursuing a career in environmental conservation. These goals will not only be personally fulfilling but also contribute to a greater cause that aligns with your values.

On the other hand, if you set goals that conflict with your values or prioritize external validation over personal fulfillment, you may find yourself feeling unsatisfied even if you achieve those goals. This is why it is essential to regularly evaluate your goals and ensure that they align with your values and priorities.

By identifying your values and aligning your goals accordingly, you create a strong foundation for success and fulfillment. Your goals will have a deeper purpose and meaning, motivating you to work towards them with passion and perseverance. Remember, your values are unique to you, so embrace them fully as you embark on the journey of setting personal goals that truly resonate with who you are.

SMART Goal Setting Method

Setting goals is a crucial aspect of personal growth and success. In order to effectively set goals that lead to achievement, it is important to utilize a framework that ensures clarity, focus, and accountability. That's where the SMART goal-setting method comes in.

The SMART acronym stands for Specific, Measurable, Achievable, Relevant, and Time-bound. Each component plays a vital role in creating goals that are well-defined, attainable, and aligned with your overall aspirations. Let's explore each aspect of the SMART goal-setting method in detail.

1. Specific: When setting goals, it's essential to be specific about what you want to achieve. Vague or ambiguous goals make it difficult to create a clear plan of action. Instead of stating a general objective like "I want to get fit," be more specific by saying "I want to lose 10 pounds in the next three months by exercising for 30 minutes five times a week and following a balanced diet." This specificity gives you a clear target to work towards.

2. Measurable: Goals need to be measurable so that progress can be tracked and evaluated. Measurable goals allow you to determine whether you are moving in the right direction or need to make adjustments. For example, instead of saying "I want to improve my public speaking skills," make it measurable by saying "I want to deliver a confident and engaging presentation at the end of the month by practicing speaking in front of a mirror for 30 minutes every day."

3. Achievable: It's important to set goals that are challenging but realistic. Goals that are too easy may not provide enough motivation, while goals that are too far-fetched can lead to frustration and disappointment. Consider your current resources, skills, and limitations when determining the achievability of your goals. Set targets that push you outside of your comfort zone but are still within reach with effort and dedication.

4. Relevant: Goals should be relevant to your overall aspirations and values. They should align with your long-term vision and contribute to your personal growth and happiness. Ensure that your goals are meaningful and connected to the bigger picture of who you want to become. For instance, if your long-term vision is to make a positive impact on the environment, a relevant goal may be to reduce your carbon footprint by using public transportation or practicing mindful consumption.

5. Time-bound: Goals need to have a specific timeframe for completion. Setting deadlines creates a sense of urgency and helps avoid procrastination. A time-bound goal provides a target date that motivates action and allows for effective planning. For example, instead of saying "I want to learn a new language," make it time-bound by saying "I want to become conversational in Spanish within six months by dedicating 30 minutes every day to language learning."

Implementing the SMART criteria in goal setting ensures that you have a concrete roadmap for success. By making your goals specific, measurable, achievable, relevant, and time-bound, you enhance your ability to stay focused, track progress, and maintain momentum. Remember, breaking down long-term goals into smaller, manageable steps is a key strategy for turning aspirations into reality.

As you embark on your journey of setting personal goals using the SMART goal-setting method, take some time to reflect on what you truly want to achieve and how each SMART component applies to your aspirations. By doing so, you will set yourself up for greater clarity, motivation, and success in reaching your goals.

Overcoming obstacles and staying motivated are crucial aspects of the goal-setting journey. In this section, we will discuss common obstacles that individuals may encounter and provide effective techniques for overcoming them. Additionally, we will explore methods to stay motivated throughout the goal-setting process.

1. Identifying and Overcoming Self-Doubt:

Self-doubt is a common hurdle that can hinder progress towards achieving personal goals. It often stems from fear of failure or a lack of confidence in one's abilities. To overcome self-doubt, it is essential to:

✓ Practice self-compassion: Embrace self-acceptance and acknowledge that making mistakes is a part of the learning process.

✓ Challenge negative thoughts: Replace self-limiting beliefs with positive affirmations and empowering thoughts.

✓ Surround yourself with positivity: Seek support from friends, family, or mentors who uplift and encourage you.

2. Confronting the Fear of Failure:

Fear of failure can hold individuals back from taking risks and pursuing their goals. However, it is important to recognize that failure is not synonymous with defeat but rather an opportunity for growth. To conquer the fear of failure:

- ✓ Shift your mindset: Embrace failures as stepping stones to success and view them as valuable learning experiences.
- ✓ Break down goals into smaller tasks: By breaking goals into manageable steps, you can track progress and celebrate achievements along the way.
- ✓ Take calculated risks: Start small and gradually push yourself outside your comfort zone. Each small success will boost your confidence and diminish the fear of failure.

3. Overcoming External Challenges:

External challenges, such as lack of resources, unsupportive environments, or unforeseen circumstances, can present significant obstacles to goal achievement. To navigate through these challenges:

- ✓ Seek alternative solutions: Brainstorm creative ways to work around limitations or find alternative resources.
- ✓ Build a support network: Surround yourself with individuals who share similar ambitions and can offer guidance and encouragement in times of difficulty.
- ✓ Stay adaptable: Embrace flexibility and adjust your approach when faced with unexpected challenges. This resilience will help you navigate obstacles and stay on track.

4. Maintaining Motivation:

Sustaining motivation throughout the goal-setting journey is essential for long-term success. To stay motivated:

- ✓ Visualize success: Envision your desired outcome and regularly remind yourself why your goals are important to you.
- ✓ Set milestones and rewards: Break larger goals into smaller milestones and reward yourself upon reaching each one. This will reinforce positive behavior and create a sense of accomplishment.
- ✓ Find accountability partners: Share your goals with others who can help hold you accountable and provide support when motivation wanes.
- ✓ Practice self-care: Prioritize self-care activities that rejuvenate you, such as exercise, meditation, or spending time in nature. Taking care of your well-being will boost your energy levels and maintain motivation.

By implementing these techniques and strategies for overcoming obstacles and staying motivated, individuals can overcome self-doubt, address the fear of failure, conquer external challenges, and sustain their drive towards achieving their personal goals.

Reviewing and Adjusting Goals

As readers embark on their journey of setting personal goals, it is imperative to emphasize the significance of periodically reviewing and adjusting those goals. While it is essential to have a clear plan in place, life is unpredictable, and circumstances change. Therefore, being flexible in goal setting is crucial for long-term success and personal growth.

Regularly reviewing goals allows individuals to assess their progress and determine if any adjustments need to be made. This step provides an opportunity for self-reflection, allowing readers to evaluate whether they are still on track or if their goals need to be modified to align with their evolving aspirations.

When reviewing goals, it is important to consider both short-term and long-term objectives. Short-term goals may require more frequent reviews, while long-term goals may be assessed less frequently. However, regardless of the time frame, it is essential to dedicate time to reflect on one's progress.

During the review process, readers should carefully evaluate their achievements and challenges. Celebrating successes is crucial as it reinforces motivation and boosts self-confidence. Recognizing accomplishments, no matter how small, helps build momentum for further progress.

In addition to celebrating successes, individuals must also identify any obstacles that may have hindered their progress. Self-doubt, fear of failure, or external challenges can sometimes derail one's path towards achieving their goals. By acknowledging these obstacles during the review process, readers can develop strategies to overcome them and navigate around potential roadblocks.

Besides reviewing goals objectively, it is equally important to remain open to adjusting them when necessary. As individuals evolve and grow, their passions and priorities may change. It is essential to embrace these shifts rather than rigidly adhering to outdated goals.

Flexibility in goal setting allows for exploration and discovery of new interests and passions. Readers should not view adjustments as failures but rather as opportunities for growth and self-discovery. By adapting goals to reflect newfound passions or changing circumstances, individuals can ensure that their goals remain relevant and aligned with their current aspirations.

Ultimately, the review and adjustment process is an ongoing one. As readers progress through different stages of life, they should continue to reflect on their goals regularly. This practice will allow them to stay focused, motivated, and in tune with their authentic selves.

In summary, periodically reviewing and adjusting goals is an integral part of the goal-setting journey. It allows individuals to assess their progress objectively, celebrate successes, overcome obstacles, and adapt to changing circumstances or newfound passions. By integrating this practice into their lives, readers can ensure that their goals remain aligned with their evolving aspirations, paving the way for long-term success and personal fulfillment.

Part 2:
Personal Development and Growth

Chapter 1

Turning Weaknesses into Strengths: A Guide for Your Twenties

****

Strengths and Weaknesses Discussed:

Grasping the ide-a of our talents and limitations is fundamental for individual progress and care-er achieveme-nt. In this section, I will investigate the- definition of talents and constraints in various settings and diffe-rentiate betwe-en inborn talents and gained tale-nts.

While conside-ring our positive attributes, most commonly we re-late them to innate tale-nts or skills that feel instinctive. The-se strengths can encompass traits like- creativity, analytical reasoning, compassion, leade-rship, or issue resolution abilities. Howe-ver, it is crucial to acknowledge that stre-ngths also evolve through education, re-petition, and exposure. Our inhe-rent gifts interact with dedicate-d efforts to cultivate expe-rtise, wisdom, and efficacy.

While ce-rtain skills may not come as naturally to us, weakness-s present opportunities to cultivate-new strengths. It is how we approach the-se areas for deve-lopment that matters most. With a focus on growth over judgme-nt, we can identify where- expanded practice, study or e-xperience could broade-n our abilities over time. Continue-d effort to strengthen what doe-s not yet come easily e-ncourages progression - what starts as a challenge- need not remain so inde-finitely. Therein lie-s the possibility for profound change.

Gaining insight into our personal tale-nts and limitations provides helpful perspe-ctive not only in career se-ttings but also in relationships. For instance, in our close bonds with othe-rs, recognizing our own strong suits alongside areas ne-eding work allows for more successful inte-raction, resolution of disagreeme-nts, and placing ourselves in another's shoe-s.

We all have- areas that could use strengthe-ning. By acknowledging our shortcomings, we open doors to de-velop those weak points into stre-ngths. This perspective e-mpowers us to face difficulties he-ad on and treat setbacks as chances to gain unde-rstanding. Where others se-e problems, we find pote-ntial - opportunities to broaden our skills and dee-pen our knowledge through e-xperience. While- change requires e-ffort, this growth mindset lifts our sights above temporary trouble-s and towards continual progress.

In this chapter, I will e-xplore how to turn weakness-s into strengths through adopting a growth mindset, pursuing learning opportunitie-s, utilizing feedback, and deve-loping perseverance-. Readers will uncover me-thods for transforming their weakness-s. Additionally, I will discuss the value of using strengths to re-ach personal and professional aims, while e-mphasizing balanced developme-nt involving self-care, mental he-alth, and caring relationships.

Gaining insight into one's talents and limitations, as we-ll as comprehending how each can de-velop, allows individuals to establish a base for both pe-rsonal and occupational achievement in the-ir twenties and for years afte-rwards. By comprehending strengths and shortcomings, and the- capacity for either to progress with time- and experience-, one acknowledges possibilitie-s for changing limits into talents through dedication and effort, se-tting the stage for satisfaction in both caree-r and private life.</

Gaining insight into onese-lf is important for capitalizing on talents while young. Taking stock of strengths, we-aknesses, chances, and difficultie-s through self-examination gives a rounde-d view for enhancing skills and progressing. This inward look he-lps recognize what you exce-l at and where there-is room for fostering abilities, what prospects are- available and what could hinder deve-lopment, supplying a basis for optimizing potential and evolving as a pe-rson in your twenties.

Undertaking a se-lf-assessment require-s both introspection and obtaining perspective-s from others. Start by taking the time to care-fully consider your qualities, strengths, and traits. Re-flect on what endeavours or re-sponsibilities you flourish in, where challe-nges lie, and any particular skills or aptitudes you hold. Gauge- your assets objectively ye-t compassionately to gain insight for developme-nt and team utilization.

I found it bene-ficial to request viewpoints from truste-d companions, loved ones, advisors, or partners. Ge-tting input from others offered important unde-rstandings and helped me se-e issues I may have ove-rlooked. I remained re-ceptive to thoughtful criticism and focused on othe-rs' remarks and proposals with an open attitude. Alte-rnative perspective-s allowed me to consider ne-w angles I had not before thought of.

While re-flecting on my talents and shortcomings, I endeavoured to highlight my talents and mitigate we-aknesses. Common threads in my stre-ngths caught my eye, prompting examination of how applying such skills e-lsewhere could prove- fruitful. For instance, adept problem-solving se-rves me well at work, in re-lationships, and for individual aims. With care and effort, weakne-sses may strengthen, and stre-ngths find new soil in which to flower. Ever mindful of progre-ss made and yet to make, I face-each challenge with confide-nce born of constant betterme-nt.

We all have- room for improvement. When asse-ssing your limitations, see them as chance-s to expand instead of faults. Pinpoint exact actions or tactics that can assist you in e-nhancing those regions. You may search out e-ducational openings, sign up for related classe-s or workshops, or locate an advisor who can offer direction and backing.

It is crucial during a SWOT analysis to pinpoint potential chance-s to capitalize on your capabilities and lesse-n the dangers prese-nted by your shortcomings. Notice how your distinguishing capabilities can ge-nerate possibilities for de-velopment in your occupation or individual life. Like-wise, think about the dangers or complications that may obstruct your advance-ment and scheme approache-s to reduce their influe-nce.

Taking the time- in your twenties to thoughtfully consider your inte-rnal strengths and weaknesse-s as well as external opportunitie-s and threats can help guide your pe-rsonal and career journey. Engaging in se-lf-reflection through a SWOT analysis offers valuable- insight into who you are today and who you aspire to become-. With a clear view of your talents and are-as for growth, you can make strategic choices and targe-ted efforts to bolster we-aker areas. Facing challenge-s with purpose and direction allows continuous evolution towards your de-sired destination. Embrace se-lf-awareness and using what you learn about yourse-lf to navigate life's terrain toward achie-ving your dreams.

Strategies for transforming weaknesses into strengths:

In this part, we will look at various tactics and me-thods that can be used to address and be-tter understand weakne-sses. By taking on a growth attitude and facing challenge-s, people can continuously gain new abilitie-s and change weaknesse-s into strengths. A few helpful strate-gies to think about include:

1. Enhancing weake-r areas necessitate-s pursuing applicable knowledge and guidance-. One approach involves engaging le-arning experience-s like courses or workshops dedicate-d to cultivating certain talents. Alternative-ly, gleaning priceless pe-rspectives and recomme-ndations from a mentor who has relevant e-xperience can be- illuminating. Their valuable insights may shed light on skills de-manding improvement. Actively se-arching for growth chances equips one with tools to stre-ngthen less deve-loped abilities.

2. Taking advantage of fe-edback cycles is important for continuous growth. Solicit opinions from trusted source-s like superiors, coworkers, and me-ntors. Their perspective-s offer valuable insights into where- enhancements could be- made. Make an effort to le-arn from constructive criticism. It highlights opportunities to refine- skills and advance competencie-s over time. Maintain an open mindse-t when receiving fe-edback. Analyze suggestions to gain aware-ness of strengths as well as aspe-cts requiring additional focus. Apply this knowledge to chart a course- of self-improvement.

3. Highlight persiste-nce and toughness: Turning shortcomings into abilities ne-cessitates sticking with it and toughness facing impe-diments or hardships. It's critical to method difficulties with an optimistic outlook, se-eing them as chances for progre-ss instead of obstructions. By keeping re-solved and devoted to advance-ment, people can ge-t past obstructions and change shortcomings into abilities.

4. Rephrase Focusing on weakne-sses can feel quite- daunting if you try to tackle everything at once-. A wise approach is breaking down big aims into smaller, achie-vable steps. Pick one re-gion to concentrate your efforts, and se-t targets you can reach along the road. Achie-ving each target dese-rves recognition, as it confirms progress and inspire-s you to continue. Once complete- with that region, move to the ne-xt until all areas are addresse-d. Breaking goals into bite sized pie-ces makes the route- less overwhelming while- still getting you to your destination.

5. Leve-rage your talents while improving limitations: To de-velop well-roundelay, it is prude-nt to build on existing aptitudes at the same- time as focusing on restrictions. Discover your spe-cial skills and capabilities and find approaches to employ the-m alongside facets requiring work. The- fusion of aptitudes and deliberate- endeavours to bette-r shortcomings can result in extraordinary progress and accomplishme-nt.

While progre-ss takes determination, e-ach small step forward makes the path cle-arer. Weaknesse-s, once understood, nee-d not define us - with care and practice-, our efforts may guide them into gifts. Though change- happens gradually, a steady approach can transform what once challe-nged into the skills that later sustain. As we- learn, so too shall we lead ourse-lves to newer succe-sses, equipped not only for what's ahe-ad but for all that follows in the years to come.

Leveraging strengths to achieve personal and professional goals:

Drawing upon innate tale-nts to accomplish aims and objectives is a pivotal part of individual and occupational evolution. By pinpointing and wie-lding our inherent advantages, we- can bring out the best in ourselve-s and take meaningful steps towards achie-vement.

Discovering our de-fining talents is crucial for uncovering opportunities whe-re they can shine. For e-xample, in deciding on a caree-r, comprehending our strengths he-lps uncover positions or fields that play to our inhere-nt skills. By cantering on domains where- we flourish, we can find dee-per satisfaction and accomplish more substantial success in our se-lected occupation.

We e-ach possess certain qualities that make- us uniquely able to contribute to re-lationships. Noticing our particular talents permits us to impart advantageous attribute-s to how we associate with others. It may be- compassion, communicating effectively, or le-ading well, capitalizing on our strengths can enrich our bonds with che-rished ones, co-workers, and companions. Employing our stre-ngths in these linkages, we- have the power to cultivate- firmer ties, spur teamwork, and craft upbe-at settings where all prospe-r.

While our innate- talents certainly aid advanceme-nt, purposeful progression relie-s equally on ambition appropriately employing one-'s skills. Harnessing inherent stre-ngths to set aspirational yet attainable obje-ctives capitalizes on our capabilities, e-levating likelihood of fulfilment and succe-ss. Deliberately honing proficie-ncies through continuous studying and practicing nourishes inhere-nt gifts, cultivating growth and enhancing performance attainme-nt. Skilled application of inborn talents, matched with re-solute dedication to self-improve-ment, paves a pathway leading e-ver upward both personally and professionally.

At times, whe-n we bring together diffe-ring capabilities, it can produce mighty collaborations providing unusual bene-fits surpassing others. For illustration, an individual with remarkable proble-m-solving talents and potent communication gifts may succee-d in leadership roles whe-re they skillfully convey intricate- ideas to their personne-l and execute innovative- answers. By identifying where- our capabilities converge and inve-stigating how they better one- another, we can uncover fre-sh chances for developme-nt and accomplishment.

In order to make- the most of our talents, deve-loping a course of action is crucial. This involves dividing objective-s into smaller, achievable phase-s that play to our strong suits. For instance, if staying organized and focusing on specifics is one- of our gifts, we could build a process for handling duties and sorting prioritie-s. By matching our talents to clear steps, we- up our odds of success and confirm our energy addre-sses what we exce-l at.

To summarize, capitalizing on our inhe-rent talents to accomplish individual and caree-r objectives is fundamental to thriving in our twe-nties and later. When we- comprehend the worth of our distinguishing skills, we- have the power to contribute- them to diverse sphe-res of living, such as occupations, bonds, and self-improveme-nt. Discerning compatibilities betwe-en diverse stre-ngths and crafting an executable game- plan makes certain we harne-ss our skills productively and take full bene-fit of our capacity for long-run achievement and conte-ntment.

A comprehe-nsive perspective- on personal developme-nt transcends exclusively improving flaws and cultivating tale-nts. It necessitates acknowle-dging the significance of self-care-, emotional wellness, and nurturing caring re-lationships as well as expanding abilities. Ove-rall well-being stems from atte-ntion to the complete pe-rson, not just specific parts of one's character or care-er.

Taking care of one-'s health served as an important first ste-p in my own development. Se-eing to my physical, mental, and emotional ne-eds proved integral to staying we-ll. Getting sufficient rest, fue-ling my body with nutritious foods, maintaining an exercise re-gimen, and wrangling worries into submission - all formed the- groundwork allowing me to grow. Prioritizing myself create-d a sturdy base from which flourishing could follow. Through practices ensuring my we-ll-being, I cultivated the me-ans for moving forward.

Caring for one's se-lf as well as nurturing meaningful bonds with others both significantly influe-nce personal evolution. Forming significant associations that provide- a feeling of belonging, aid, and compre-hension further deve-lops an individual. Having good people and optimistic supporters around some-one not only advances their e-volution but additionally contributes to emotional health and joy. It is e-ssential to dedicate time- and energy into deve-loping sturdy relationships with relatives, companions, advisors, and coworkers.

Taking a holistic approach to my own deve-lopment emphasized linking physical he-alth, emotional skills, and spiritual wellness. Maintaining my body through e-xercise, good nutrition, and routine doctor visits care-d for my physical health. Growing self-awarene-ss, empathy, and strong communication abilities to handle re-lationships and direct feelings de-veloped my emotional skills. Discove-ring meaning and intention in life and bonding to some-thing more than just myself covere-d my spiritual wellness. By focusing on all these- parts of personal growth, people can accomplish a balance-d and satisfying way of living.

The pursuit of continuous le-arning and nurturing curiosity are mighty drivers for personal e-volution and self-awareness. Cultivating a me-ntality of learning throughout life enable-s people to broaden the-ir understanding, obtain new talents, and conform to changing situations. It involve-s searching out fresh encounte-rs, chasing interests outside of one-'s safe territory, and staying willing to diverse- viewpoints. Welcoming inquisitivene-ss fuels mental progress, inspire-s imagination, and prompts a deeper compre-hension of one's self and the- world around us.

Each individual possesse-s a singular array of qualities, abilities, and viewpoints that can be- employed for the be-nefit of all. Realizing and embracing what se-ts one apart allows one to support their community in purpose-ful manners. This may present itse-lf through donating time, participating ir civic undertakings, or following vocations that align with one's principle-s and enthusiasm. Uplifting others and leaving an e-nduring impression are formidable source-s of personal developme-nt anɹ contentment. Furthermore-, taking hold of one's remarkable characte-ristics and applying them to make valuable additions to socie-ty and the world is integral to individual progress. By acknowle-dging and embracing their singularity, persons can contribute- to their neighborhoods in meaningful ways.

Ultimately, taking a comple-te perspective- on individual progress includes realizing the- significance of caring for oneself, cultivating sound re-lationships, incorporating physical health, emotional knowledge-, and spiritual welfare, embracing continuous studying and inquisitive-ness, and employing one's distinctive- qualities to make optimistic contributions to the community and the- planet. By accepting this encompassing outlook, pe-ople can embark on a voyage of se-lf development and satisfaction during the-ir twenties and further.

Chapter **2**

Learning New Skills: A Roadmap for Lifelong Growth: The Importance of Lifelong Learning

****

Learning New Skills:

Continuous learning is a fundamental aspect of personal and professional development, especially during the critical phase of one's twenties. In "Build Your Character at Twenty: Writing the Life Success Script at the Age of 20," we emphasize the significance of lifelong learning and how acquiring new skills can lead to increased opportunities and personal fulfillment.

Research has shown that lifelong learning not only enhances cognitive abilities but also contributes to overall well-being. Engaging in continuous education and skill acquisition can improve mental agility, boost self-confidence, and broaden perspectives. By embracing a mindset of lifelong learning, individuals in their twenties can cultivate a thirst for knowledge and personal growth that will serve them throughout their lives.

In today's rapidly evolving world, acquiring new skills is crucial for remaining competitive in the job market. Employers increasingly value individuals who demonstrate adaptability, resilience, and a willingness to learn. By continually developing new skills, young adults can stay ahead of the curve, seize emerging opportunities, and position themselves for long-term success.

Beyond professional advantages, lifelong learning enriches our personal lives. Acquiring new skills opens doors to hobbies, interests, and passions that bring joy and satisfaction. It allows individuals to explore different fields, expand their horizons, and discover hidden talents or aspirations they may have never considered before.

Embracing lifelong learning also helps us develop additional layers of empathy and understanding. By immersing ourselves in unfamiliar subjects or pursuits, we gain insight into different cultures, perspectives, and ways of life. This expanded knowledge fosters greater connection and appreciation for the diversity of the world around us.

In summary, lifelong learning is an essential ingredient for personal growth, professional success, and overall well-being. By embracing the importance of continuous education and skill acquisition, individuals in their twenties can create a solid foundation for a fulfilling and prosperous future. Through this chapter and the comprehensive roadmap provided, readers will be equipped with the necessary tools and mindset to embark on a lifelong journey of learning and growth.

Identifying Areas for Skill Development

In this section, we will explore techniques to help readers assess their current skill sets and identify areas where they can benefit from acquiring new skills. It is important to remember that skill development should align with readers' passions, interests, and career goals.

1. Self-Assessment Techniques:

- ✓ Encourage readers to reflect on their past experiences, both academically and professionally, to identify skills they have already acquired.
- ✓ Suggest making a list of strengths and weaknesses, considering both hard and soft skills.
- ✓ Ask readers to consider feedback received from mentors, teachers, or supervisors in order to gain insights into areas for improvement.
- ✓ Share the importance of conducting self-assessments periodically as skills requirements evolve with time.

2. Reflecting on Passions and Interests:

- ✓ Urge readers to think about their passions, hobbies, and personal interests.
- ✓ Discuss how pursuing skills related to these areas can lead to greater personal fulfillment and engagement.

✓ Provide examples of how passions and interests can be leveraged in various career fields.

3. Aligning Skills with Career Goals:
✓ Encourage readers to envision their desired future career paths and research the skills required for success in those fields.
✓ Suggest exploring job descriptions in target industries to identify common skills demanded by employers.
✓ Provide guidance on prioritizing skill development based on the relevance to readers' long-term career aspirations.

4. Utilizing Resources and Tools:
✓ Offer suggestions for resources that can assist in identifying skill gaps, such as online self-assessment tools, career quizzes, or personality assessments.
✓ Mention career development centers at universities or local community centers that offer guidance on skill identification.
✓ Highlight the benefits of networking with professionals from desired industries who can provide insights into skill requirements.

By utilizing these techniques for self-assessment and reflection, readers will be able to identify specific areas where they can benefit from acquiring new skills. This process will ensure that skill development aligns with their passions, interests, and long-term career goals.

Setting Goals for Skill Acquisition

Setting goals is a crucial step in the process of acquiring new skills. Without clear goals, it is easy to get lost or lose motivation along the way. In this section, we will discuss the importance of setting SMART (Specific, Measurable, Achievable, Relevant, and Time-bound) goals for skill development.

1. Specific: When setting goals, it is important to be specific about what skill you want to acquire. Instead of a vague goal like "I want to learn programming," specify the programming language or framework you want to focus on, such as "I want to learn Python programming."
2. Measurable: Goals should be measurable to track your progress effectively. In this context, measurable means breaking down the skill into smaller milestones or sub-skills that you can measure your progress against. For example, if your goal is to learn Python programming, you can set milestones like understanding basic syntax, building simple programs, and eventually developing a web application.
3. Achievable: Setting achievable goals ensures that they are within your reach and not too overwhelming. Consider your current skill level and available resources when setting goals. It's great to aim high, but make sure the goals are realistic and attainable with effort and dedication.
4. Relevant: Goals should be relevant to your overall personal or professional aspirations. Think about how acquiring the skill will contribute to your long-term goals and align with your passions or career path. This relevance will help keep you motivated throughout the learning process.
5. Time-bound: Setting a timeline for achieving each goal provides a sense of urgency and helps you stay focused. Break down your goals into smaller time-bound milestones and allocate specific periods for each milestone. For example, you can set a goal of understanding basic syntax within two weeks and building a simple program within a month.

Now that we understand the components of SMART goals for skill acquisition let's discuss strategies for staying motivated and accountable throughout the learning process.

1. Break goals into actionable steps: Once you have set your SMART goal, break it down into smaller, actionable steps. This will make the overall goal more manageable and less overwhelming. For example, if your goal is to learn Python programming, your actionable steps can include completing an online course, practicing coding exercises daily, and building mini-projects.
2. Create a timeline: Assign specific deadlines or timeframes to each step or milestone. By creating a timeline, you create a sense of urgency and give yourself a clear structure for accomplishing your goals. Make sure to be realistic with the timeframes and adjust them as needed based on your progress.

3. Track your progress: Regularly track your progress towards your goals. Keep a journal or use a goal-tracking app to monitor your achievements, identify areas where you may need to put in more effort, and celebrate milestones along the way. Seeing tangible progress can be motivating and keep you engaged in the learning process.

4. Seek support and accountability: Share your goals with a trusted friend, mentor, or accountability partner who can provide guidance and hold you accountable. Regular check-ins with someone who understands your aspirations can help you stay on track and provide encouragement when facing challenges.

5. Celebrate small victories: Acknowledge and celebrate each small achievement along the way. Rewarding yourself for reaching milestones will not only boost your motivation but also remind you of the progress you have made. Treat yourself with something you enjoy or take a break before moving on to the next step.

Setting SMART goals for skill acquisition and implementing strategies for staying motivated and accountable will enhance your learning experience and increase your chances of success. Remember that acquiring new skills is a journey, and staying committed to the process is just as important as reaching the end goal.

Strategies for Learning New Skills:

One of the keys to personal growth and professional success is continuously learning new skills. In this chapter, we explore various strategies for acquiring these skills, ensuring that readers have a solid roadmap for lifelong growth. Here are some effective methods and resources to consider:

1. Online Courses: The internet offers a wealth of online courses covering an array of topics. Platforms such as Coursera, Udemy, and LinkedIn Learning provide access to high-quality educational content taught by experts in their respective fields. These courses offer the flexibility to learn at your own pace, making them ideal for busy individuals.

2. Workshops and Seminars: Attending workshops and seminars can be a great way to acquire new skills in a focused and immersive environment. Look for local events or conferences related to your areas of interest or career goals. These gatherings often provide opportunities for hands-on learning, networking, and collaboration with like-minded individuals.

3. Mentorship Programs: Seeking guidance from experienced professionals through mentorship programs can accelerate skill acquisition. Mentors offer invaluable insights, advice, and support as you navigate the process of learning new skills. Look for mentorship programs offered by industry associations, community organizations, or through networking connections.

4. Books and Literature: Never underestimate the power of reading books to expand your knowledge base. Seek out books written by experts in the field you want to develop skills in. They often provide in-depth information, case studies, and practical tips that can enhance your understanding and ability to apply what you've learned.

5. Networking and Collaboration: Engaging with others who share similar interests or goals can facilitate skill development through collaboration and shared knowledge. Attend meetups, join relevant professional organizations or communities, and participate in online forums or discussion groups. Building connections with others in your industry or field can expose you to diverse perspectives and new learning opportunities.

6. Establishing a Routine: Consistency is key to effective learning. Create a schedule and allocate dedicated time for skill acquisition. Treat your learning journey as seriously as you would a job or other commitments. By establishing a routine, you ensure that learning becomes a regular part of your life.

7. Practicing Active Listening: When acquiring new skills, it is crucial to actively engage in the learning process. Practice active listening by fully immersing yourself in courses, workshops, or mentoring sessions. Take notes, ask questions, and seek clarification to deepen your understanding of the subject matter.

8. Seeking Feedback: Feedback plays a crucial role in skill development. Be open to constructive criticism from mentors, instructors, or peers. Actively seek feedback on your progress and areas for improvement. This input will help you refine your skills and make necessary adjustments along the way.

Remember, learning new skills is not solely an individual endeavor; it can be enhanced through collaboration and networking. Engage with others who possess similar interests or expertise to foster a supportive community of learners.

By utilizing these strategies and resources, you'll be well-equipped to embark on your lifelong learning journey, acquiring the skills necessary for personal growth and professional success.

Overcoming Challenges and Embracing Continuous Growth

Throughout the process of learning new skills, individuals may encounter various challenges that can hinder their progress. It is crucial to address these obstacles head-on and develop strategies to overcome them. By doing so, readers can maintain momentum and continue their journey of personal growth and skill acquisition.

One common challenge when learning new skills is the fear of failure. Many individuals are apprehensive about trying new things because they worry about making mistakes or not achieving immediate success. However, it is important to embrace failures as opportunities for growth. Each setback presents a chance to learn valuable lessons, refine techniques, and ultimately improve. By shifting our mindset and viewing failures as stepping stones towards success, we can approach the learning process with resilience and determination.

Another obstacle that individuals may face is a lack of self-belief. Doubting one's abilities or feeling inadequate can hinder progress and limit personal growth. To overcome this challenge, it is essential to cultivate a growth mindset. By recognizing that skills can be developed through dedication, practice, and continuous learning, individuals can boost their self-confidence and tackle new challenges with a positive attitude. Celebrating small victories along the way can also reinforce belief in one's abilities and provide motivation to keep pushing forward.

Additionally, time constraints and competing priorities often pose challenges when it comes to learning new skills. Many individuals lead busy lives juggling work, relationships, and personal commitments, leaving little time for skill development. To address this challenge, it is crucial to prioritize learning and allocate dedicated time for skill acquisition. By creating a schedule and adhering to it consistently, individuals can ensure that they make progress towards their goals. Breaking down the learning process into smaller, manageable tasks can also help overcome time constraints by making the overall journey more approachable.

Lastly, complacency or resistance to change can hinder continuous growth and skill development. It is essential to maintain a sense of curiosity and embrace new experiences. By seeking out diverse opportunities and exploring different fields, individuals can expand their knowledge base and acquire a broad range of skills. Actively seeking feedback and incorporating it into the learning process can also foster growth and improvement.

To maintain a lifelong love of learning, it is important to approach challenges with perseverance and adaptability. Recognizing that skill acquisition is an ongoing journey allows individuals to embrace new opportunities for growth and personal development. By addressing common obstacles, fostering resilience, and maintaining a growth mindset, readers can overcome challenges and fully embrace the transformative power of continuous learning.

Chapter 3

The Habit of Reading: Expanding Your Mind Daily: The Importance of Reading

****

The Habit of Reading:

I have found re-ading to be an invaluable activity that meaningfully shape-s personal advancement and rational maturation. It pre-sents manifold advantages, broadening the- intellect, ele-vating analytic reasoning talents, inspiring creativity, and multiplying le-arning covering a diversity of topics. While re-ading, one can journey to new place-s, meet fascinating people- and discover fresh perspe-ctives - all without leaving the comfort of a favourite chair. Making time each day to explore- classic and contemporary works nourishes both mind and spirit, offering re-spite during busy moments. Overall, re-gularly opening books proves a simple ye-t profoundly impactful habit for continuous self-improvement and e-ngaged citizenship.

Rephrase Delving into writte-n works provides the invaluable be-nefit of cultivating one's intelle-ct. In contrast with other media that tend to conve-y surface-level facts at a rapid pace-, reading facilitates profound examination of notions and principle-s. It fosters contemplative introspe-ction and interpretation, empowe-ring readers to craft personal vie-wpoints and stances.

Delving into lite-rature expands critical reasoning abilitie-s. When one dee-ply engrosses in diverse-narratives, rationales, and outlooks, reade-rs encounter multifacete-d perspectives that te-st their preconceptions and incre-ase their comprehe-nsion of intricate matters. This expe-rience cultivates the-capacity to think critically, assess evidence- objectively, and make we-ll-informed choices.

Additionally, reading promote-s inventiveness. Within the- pages of books, readers come- across imaginative worlds, nuanced characters, and thought-provoking situations. The- process of visualizing these storie-s nourishes creativity and imagination, motivating reade-rs to think outside conventional limits and investigate- fresh potentials in their own journe-ys.

Beyond foste-ring intellectual expansion, pe-rusing publications additionally augments proficiency in a wide assortme-nt of subjects. Regardless of whe-ther it be fictional or real, se-lf-improvement, biographies, or ve-rse, each classification has something nove-l to bring to the table. Fictional works acquaint peruses with diverse societie-s and encounters, while ge-nuine distributions give important bits of knowledge- into particular fields of enthusiasm. Self-improve-ment books offer practical direction for individual turn of e-vents, biographies demonstrate- the accomplishments and hardships of remarkable- people, and verse- touches on the profundities of human fe-elings. By investigating differe-nt classifications, peruses acquire a we-ll-adjusted training and a more exte-nsive comprehension of the- world around them.

Making reading part of one-'s daily routine is crucial to gain its advantages fully. Dedicating a small amount of time- daily to reading allows individuals to guarantee continual me-ntal excitement and individual progre-ss. Establishing a pleasant reading space fre-e of interruptions, like switching off digital gadge-ts or locating a tranquil nook in a calm room, can aid engrossment and attention.

Reading wide-ly across genres allows one to gain more- from their reading expe-rience. Exploring unfamiliar genre-s exposes reade-rs to new ideas and viewpoints, incre-asing their knowledge and shaping how the-y perceive the- world. Whether one de-lves into timeless lite-rature, explores imaginative- science fiction worlds, or immerse-s themselves in se-lf-help guides, each type- of reading material provides distinctive- understandings and lessons. A varied se-lection ensures continuous le-arning without limitation.

To summarize, making re-ading a habit is a powerful instrument for personal progre-ssion and intellectual maturation. By broadening the- mind, enhancing critical reasoning abilities, boosting cre-ativity, and multiplying knowledge across many topics, reading pre-sents a chance for transformative le-arning and self-exploration. Including reading into e-veryday schedules and inve-stigating different styles can additionally magnify the-se advantages. So get hold of a book, ope-n your mind, and embark on an enriching journey of inquiry and de-velopment through the magnifice-nt realm of reading.

Establishing a regular re-ading routine can unlock many advantages for personal and me-ntal growth. Here are some- practical strategies for integrating consiste-nt reading into one's daily life. De-veloping the habit of dedicating time- each day to open a book allows reade-rs to reap reading's numerous re-wards. With a set schedule and de-dication, one can experie-nce the intelle-ctual development and pe-rsonal gains that come from frequent e-xposure to written works.

Dedicate-d reading time must be sche-duled to develop re-ading into a habit. Prioritizing reading daily transforms it into a non-negotiable routine-. Readers can accomplish this by rese-rving a specific daily period, perhaps in the- mornings, during lunch breaks, or prior to sleeping. Vie-wing reading as integral to one's day e-nsures consistent participation in this enriching activity.

Focusing on novels that match one-'s particular passions and targets is another significant facet of cultivating a thriving re-ading habit. By opting for books that reflect their e-nthusiasm and territories of hoped-for progre-ss, readers are more- apt to remain engaged and spurre-d. Whether leade-rship guides, true stories, imaginary tale-s, factual works, or some other style, discove-ring books that stimulate their inquisitivene-ss will enrich the reading journe-y and nurture personal evolution.

Establishing a relaxing se-tting for reading without disturbances is fundamental for cultivating profound fixation and focus. Choosing a particular spot for pe-rusing, regardless of whethe-r it's a cozy corner in your home or a prefe-rred bistro, can encourage le-ssening diversions and make an e-ncouraging climate for submersion in the book. It is like-wise critical to eliminate pote-ntial disruptions by turning off electronic gadgets or putting the-m on silent mode.

Beyond se-tting a consistent reading routine, avid re-aders can utilize today's technology to inte-grate reading into their e-veryday lives. Electronic publications and audiobooks offe-r practical solutions for consuming written works while traveling or juggling multiple- tasks simultaneously. With applications that support digital texts or platforms for recorde-d books readily available on most mobile phone-s or tablets, readers are- able maintain their curiosity and learning e-ven when time is limite-d, such as throughout commutes or other time-se-nsitive scenarios.

Establishing a steady re-ading habit allows one to experie-nce the life-changing influe-nce of books. Continuing to engage with works of lite-rature empowers re-aders to augment understanding, conside-r other viewpoints, and sharpen analytical abilitie-s in addition to personal evolution and cere-bral satisfaction. Devoting moments to exploring page-s promotes investing in one's own advance-ment, guiding a path of perpetual e-ducation and self-betterme-nt.

Exploring Different Genres:

While e-xploring new genres e-xpands one's horizons, diversifying reading has value-. Literature encompasse-s many genres, each offe-ring unique merits and appeal. Ve-nturing beyond familiar genres allows re-aders to widen their vie-wpoints, fuel their imagination, and uncover fre-sh passions. The literary world prese-nts a wealth of diversity; sampling its varied offe-rings cultivates open-mindedne-ss and fosters discovery.

Academic works transport re-aders to intriguing imaginary realms, permitting the-m to flee actuality and temporarily imme-rse themselve-s in captivating narratives. Whether gripping suspe-nse thrillers arousing one's he-art or heart-warming romance novels moving one- emotionally, fictional creations offer e-ndless opportunities for ente-rtainment, emotional bonding, and persona cultivation. Notable- tomes in this category include "To Kill a Mockingbird" by Harpe-r Lee, a work illuminating societal injustice-; "1984" by George Orwell, a nove-l warning of totalitarian rule; and "Pride and Prejudice-" by Jane Austen, a story depicting the- follies of prejudgment.

Non-fiction: Non-fiction books provide opportunities for readers to expand their knowledge in specific areas of interest. Whether it's delving into scientific discoveries, understanding historical events, or gaining insights from real-life experiences, non-fiction offers the chance to learn and grow intellectually. Some notable non-fiction books include "Sapiens: A Brief History of Humankind" by Yuval Noah Harari, "Becoming" by Michelle Obama, and "Educated" by Tara Westover.

My Journey toward Se-lf-Improvement: Self-he-lp literature provides use-ful direction and practical recommendations for individual progre-ss and evolution. Whether strate-gies for cultivating assurance and enhancing communication or te-chniques for overcoming barriers and accomplishing obje-ctives, self-help books e-mpower readers to take- the reins of their live-s and reach their fullest capacity. notable- works that guide this journey include Ste-phen R. Covey's "The 7 Habits of Highly Effe-ctive People," in which valuable- habits are examined, Jame-s Clear's "Atomic Habits," exploring how behaviors are- built, and Carol S. Dweck's "Mindset: The Ne-w Psychology of Success," sharing insight into fostering a growth attitude.

The storie-s of influential individuals provide insight into achieving gre-at feats. Biographies detail the-experience-s of remarkable people- who impacted their domains, conveying the-ir triumphs over adversity. These- true accounts inspire reade-rs by depicting extraordinary journeys. Re-aders may find motivation in seeing challe-nges overcome by studying the- victories and valleys navigated by othe-rs. Noteworthy biographical works offer glimpses into the- lives of innovators like Anne Frank, Malcolm X, and Ste-ve Jobs. Frank's "The Diary of a Young Girl" outlines surviving life- in hiding during the Holocaust. Co-authored by Malcolm X and Alex Hale-y, "The Autobiography of Malcolm X" relates Malcolm's transformation from criminal to civil rights activist. "Ste-ve Jobs" by Walter Isaacson prese-nts the Apple co-founder's visionary le-adership through intimate intervie-ws. Such biographies commemorate historic figure-s and can encourage reade-rs to pursue their own ambitions despite- life's complexities.

Poetry: Poetry offers a unique form of expression through the use of rhythm, imagery, and language. It allows readers to dive into the depths of emotions, thoughts, and experiences captured within concise and powerful verses. Poetry can evoke strong emotions, inspire reflection, and provide a lyrical escape from everyday life. Notable poetry collections include "The Sun and Her Flowers" by Rupi Kaur, "Leaves of Grass" by Walt Whitman, and "Milk and Honey" by Rupi Kaur.

By exploring different genres, readers can cultivate a diverse reading experience that enriches their understanding of the world and nurtures their personal growth. Each genre offers its own unique benefits, providing readers with endless opportunities for learning, enjoyment, and self-discovery. So why not embark on a literary adventure and uncover the wonders that await within the pages of various genres?,Active Reading Techniques: This section delves into the various active reading techniques that can greatly enhance the reading experience and maximize the value derived from each book. By implementing these strategies, readers can engage more deeply with the material, develop a stronger understanding of the content, and apply the knowledge gained to their own lives.

When de-lving into written works, making notes proves a prude-nt practice. By recording pivotal points, impactful exce-rpts, or introspective impressions, individuals can bolste-r their grasp of the content and re-tain a means to revisit later. Such annotations se-rve as helpful refe-rences for potential consultation, re-view, or dialogue down the line-.

Marking meaningful se-gments can assist retention. By e-mphasizing notable excerpts through unde-rlining or bolding, important ideas or memorable phrase-s become simpler to re-visit later on. This tactic moreover allows for more- interactive involveme-nt with the content, facilitating a more imme-rsive learning process. Varie-d sentence le-ngths and structures foster increase-d engagement while- preserving factual accuracy.

Recapping significant conce-pts is an additional dynamic examining methodology that advances compre-hension and retention. Subse-quent to finishing a section or a book, peruse-rs can compose a brief outline fe-aturing the essential focuse-s and lessons learned. This move-ment not just assists with solidifying comprehension ye-t in addition helps with consolidating and inwardly processing the data.

Inquiring minds want to know while absorbing writte-n works is a superb technique to foste-r critical reasoning and spark further examination. By pre-senting introspective inquirie-s regarding the material, re-aders can test their own pre-conceptions, assess the write-r's stances, and cultivate a more comple-te grasp of the subject mate-rial.

Sharing insights with kindred re-aders of common works proves another strong active- reading method. Participating in considerate- dialogues with those who explore-d equivalent books permits obtainme-nt of fresh viewpoints, exchange- of understandings, and investigation of alternate- aspects of the substance. The-se discussions encourage inte-llectual progress and give a stage- for important participation with the content.

When imple-menting these e-ngaged reading tactics into one's re-gular reading habits, readers have- the power to change passive- intake of information into an energe-tic process of studying and progress. These- methods permit reade-rs to immerse themse-lves further into written works, e-xtract more significance, and use the- knowledge acquired to improve- their individual and expert e-xistences.

Upon finishing this piece-, readers are urge-d to capitalize on the insights they accumulate-d throughout. Absorbing information alone holds limited worth; the true- benefit eme-rges from harnessing those le-ssons to cultivate personal and caree-r advancement. Whethe-r implementing strategie-s discussed or pondering perspe-ctives presente-d, may we each leve-rage what we've le-arned to enhance our live-s and work.

After finishing a book, care-fully considering the important lessons, ide-as, and views really helps apply what was le-arned. Taking the time to think de-eply about the key conce-pts and perspectives found in re-ading assists with comprehending the insights be-tter. Reflecting on how the-se pieces conne-ct to personal values, aims, and hopes aids in inte-rnalizing the lessons and making them more- relevant for life e-xperiences. Ponde-ring over what really rings true he-lps with absorbing the messages and figuring out how to pote-ntially implement them going forward.

Applying the le-ssons from one's readings can take the- form of putting helpful hints into action. For instance, if a book on successful time- management outlines approache-s that ring true, you may opt to blend some into your sche-dule. This could mean setting unambiguous aims, portioning assignme-nts into feasible phases, and capitalizing on digital aids for arrange-ment.

Furthermore-, reflect on how you can circulate and de-bate your freshly gained knowle-dge with others. Participating in discussions regarding books and conce-pts is a superb means to strengthe-n your comprehension while also contributing to the- progress of those around you. Joining a book club or study group allows you to trade vie-wpoints, test presumptions, and acquire ne-w understandings. Circulating ideas through discussions, blog articles, or social me-dia can also ignite meaningful dialogue and furthe-r enrich your learning adventure-.

While knowle-dge gained from reading prove-s personally enriching, its application professionally warrants conside-ration. Workplace implementation of conce-pts and strategies from literature- meaningfully influences care-ers and colleagues.

For e-xample, leadership principle-s from a book could guide interactions with others diffe-rently shouldered. Insights applie-d within roles enhance skills, foste-r positive work environments, and progre-ss careers. Reading illuminate-s beyond pages when le-ssons inspire work conduct. Personal deve-lopment converging with professional dutie-s maximizes benefit of e-xploration. Knowledge serve-s fully when sharing wisdom gleaned with those- alongside each day.

It is esse-ntial to bear in mind that the objective- of implementing knowledge- gained from study is not to merely imitate- what others have done, but rathe-r to modify and customize these unde-rstandings to suit your distinctive circumstances. The ge-nuine strength originates from discove-ring innovative approaches to utilize the-se notions, expanding upon them, and inte-grating them into your singular personal and expe-rt voyage.

When one- commits to intentionally implementing the- insights obtained from reading material, ne-w opportunities can unfold, perspective-s can broaden, and personal evolution be-comes continuous. By making conscious efforts to integrate- the teachings acquired from lite-rature into regular living, one e-mbarks on a journey where improve-ment and accomplishment become- a steady process.

Chapter 4

Embracing Creativity and Curiosity: The Importance of Creativity

****

The Importance of Creativity:

In this section, we delve into the significance of creativity in personal and professional development, focusing on its ability to enhance innovative thinking, problem-solving skills, and adaptability in a rapidly changing world. By understanding the importance of embracing creativity, individuals in their twenties can unlock their potential for success and fulfillment.

Creativity is a fundamental aspect of human nature that allows us to explore new ideas, perspectives, and possibilities. It enables us to think outside the box, challenge conventional wisdom, and find innovative solutions to complex problems. In today's rapidly evolving society, where change is constant and unpredictable, creativity has become a vital skill for navigating the challenges and uncertainties of the 21st century.

When we embrace creativity, we open ourselves up to a world of possibilities. We become more flexible in our thinking, better able to adapt to unexpected situations, and more open to exploring alternative paths. Creative individuals are often valued in various professional fields because they bring fresh ideas and unique approaches to their work. They have the ability to see connections that others may miss, leading to breakthroughs and advancements.

Moreover, creativity nurtures an entrepreneurial spirit within us. By fostering our creative mindset, we develop the courage and confidence to take risks and pursue our passions. This entrepreneurial mindset is not limited to starting businesses but extends to all areas of life. Whether it's developing new skills, seeking out new opportunities, or pursuing unconventional career paths, embracing creativity empowers individuals to forge their own paths towards success.

Creativity also plays a crucial role in personal growth and self-expression. It allows us to tap into our authentic selves, uncovering our passions, talents, and purpose in life. When we engage in creative activities such as painting, writing, or playing music, we stimulate our imagination and connect with our deepest desires. Through creative expression, we communicate our thoughts, emotions, and experiences in ways that words alone cannot capture.

Incorporating creativity into our lives at an early age sets the stage for a lifetime of growth and fulfillment. As individuals in their twenties, embracing creativity becomes even more crucial, as this is a time of self-discovery, exploration, and building a solid foundation for our future. By recognizing the importance of creativity and actively nurturing it, we can unlock our full potential and create a life of purpose, joy, and success.

Overcoming Creative Blocks:

In order to fully embrace creativity and curiosity, it is essential to address the common obstacles that can hinder our creative potential. One of the most significant barriers we face is self-doubt. We often question our abilities and fear that our ideas may not be good enough. This self-doubt can hold us back from exploring new possibilities and taking risks.

To overcome self-doubt, it is important to shift our mindset and cultivate a belief in our own capabilities. Recognize that everyone experiences moments of uncertainty, and it is through embracing these challenges that we can grow and learn. Remind yourself of past successes and times when you have taken risks and achieved positive outcomes. By acknowledging your accomplishments, you will build confidence in your abilities.

Fear of failure is another common obstacle that can impede our creativity. The fear of making mistakes or not meeting our own expectations can prevent us from taking the necessary risks to explore new ideas. However, failure should not be seen as a negative outcome, but rather as an opportunity for growth and learning.

To overcome the fear of failure, reframe your perspective on mistakes. Embrace them as stepping stones to success rather than signs of incompetence. Understand that failure is a natural part of the creative process and that some of the most innovative ideas arise from trial and error. By embracing failures as opportunities for growth, you will develop resilience and become more open to taking risks.

Perfectionism is yet another obstacle that can inhibit our creativity. The desire to create something flawless can lead to procrastination or a fear of starting altogether. However, perfectionism hinders progress and stifles innovation.

To overcome perfectionism, shift your focus from achieving perfection to embracing progress. Allow yourself to make mistakes and view them as stepping stones towards improvement. Set realistic goals and break down larger tasks into smaller, manageable steps. By taking incremental action, you can make progress without succumbing to the pressure of achieving perfection.

Incorporating these strategies and techniques into your life will help you overcome creative blocks and tap into your full creative potential. Remember that creativity is not a destination, but rather a journey of exploration and growth. By pushing through self-doubt, fear of failure, and perfectionism, you will unlock your innate creativity and embrace a world full of possibilities.

Cultivating Curiosity: This section highlights the importance of curiosity in fueling personal growth and expanding one's knowledge and understanding of the world. It emphasizes the role of asking questions, exploring new interests, and seeking out diverse experiences to foster intellectual curiosity.

Curiosity serves as a catalyst for learning and discovery. By cultivating curiosity, individuals can develop a thirst for knowledge and a desire to explore different perspectives. This curiosity-driven mindset opens the door to new opportunities, experiences, and ideas that can lead to personal and professional growth.

To cultivate curiosity, readers are encouraged to ask questions about the world around them. Whether it's questioning why something works a certain way or delving deeper into a topic of interest, asking questions sparks curiosity and ignites a passion for learning. Curiosity also involves being open-minded and receptive to different viewpoints, challenging assumptions, and seeking out diverse perspectives.

Exploring new interests is another way to cultivate curiosity. Trying new hobbies or engaging in activities that are outside of one's comfort zone encourages a sense of exploration and discovery. It may involve stepping out of familiar routines and embracing new experiences that provide opportunities for personal growth.

Seeking out diverse experiences is crucial in cultivating curiosity. This may involve traveling to new places, meeting people from different backgrounds, or immersing oneself in different cultures. Exposure to diverse perspectives and experiences broadens one's understanding of the world and fosters intellectual curiosity.

Incorporating these practices into daily life can help individuals develop a lifelong habit of curiosity. By nurturing curiosity and embracing new experiences, individuals can continue to learn, grow, and expand their horizons throughout their lives. It is through curiosity that we unlock our potential for personal fulfillment and gain a deeper understanding of ourselves and the world around us.

Nurturing a Creative Mindset:

To truly embrace creativity and curiosity, it is essential to cultivate a mindset that supports and nurtures these qualities. This section will delve into the mindset and attitudes necessary for nurturing creativity, providing readers with valuable insights on how to develop a positive and open-minded approach towards their creative endeavors.

One fundamental aspect of nurturing a creative mindset is embracing failure as a learning opportunity. Often, fear of failure can stifle creativity and prevent individuals from fully exploring their ideas or taking risks. However, by reframing failures as valuable lessons and opportunities for growth, aspiring creators can overcome this fear and embrace experimentation and exploration. It is important to understand that failure is an integral part of the creative process and often leads to breakthroughs and innovative solutions.

Additionally, maintaining an open-minded approach is crucial for nurturing creativity. Being open to new perspectives, ideas, and experiences allows for fresh insights and inspiration. By actively seeking out diverse sources of inspiration, such as different art forms, cultures, or fields of study, individuals can expand their creative horizons. A broad range of influences fosters a rich creative ecosystem and helps to generate unique and original ideas.

Furthermore, developing a positive attitude towards experimentation is key in nurturing creativity. Embracing the unknown and being willing to try new things opens up endless possibilities for growth and innovation. By viewing experimentation as an exciting adventure rather than a potential risk, individuals are more likely to push past their comfort zones and discover new dimensions of their creative abilities.

In summary, nurturing a creative mindset involves embracing failures as learning opportunities, cultivating an open-minded approach, and fostering a positive attitude towards experimentation. By adopting these attitudes and beliefs, individuals can unlock their full creative potential and embark on a journey of continuous growth and self-expression.

Incorporating Creativity Into Daily Life: This section provides practical suggestions for incorporating creativity into everyday routines. It encourages readers to set aside dedicated time for creative pursuits, allowing them to explore different artistic mediums or hobbies. By seeking inspiration from various sources, such as nature, books, or other forms of art, individuals can infuse their daily lives with creativity.

One way to incorporate creativity into daily life is by keeping a journal or sketchbook. This provides a space for recording ideas, thoughts, and observations. By committing to regular journaling or sketching sessions, individuals can tap into their inner creativity and express themselves freely.

Another suggestion is to engage in activities that involve hands-on creativity, such as cooking, gardening, or DIY projects. These activities not only offer opportunities for self-expression but also provide a sense of accomplishment and satisfaction.

Seeking out new experiences and embracing novelty is another way to foster creativity. Trying a new hobby, visiting an art exhibit, attending workshops or classes, or even traveling to new places can provide fresh perspectives and spark creative inspiration.

Integrating creativity into problem-solving is an essential aspect of incorporating it into daily life. Instead of approaching problems with a fixed mindset, individuals can adopt a creative mindset that encourages experimentation and out-of-the-box thinking. By reframing challenges as opportunities for innovation, individuals can find creative solutions that may have otherwise been overlooked.

Lastly, finding a community or joining groups that share the same creative interests can offer support, motivation, and collaboration opportunities. Engaging with like-minded individuals can inspire new ideas and provide valuable feedback.

By incorporating these practical tips into daily routines, individuals can infuse their lives with creativity and explore the endless possibilities it offers.

Chapter 5

The Growth Mindset:
Building Resilience
****

The Growth Mindset

In this chapter, we delve into the concept of a growth mindset and its significance in personal and professional development during one's twenties. Understanding and embracing a growth mindset is crucial during this formative period as it sets the foundation for resilience, adaptability, and continuous learning.

A growth mindset is the belief that our abilities and intelligence can be developed through dedication, effort, and hard work. It is the recognition that talents and abilities are not fixed traits, but rather skills that can be cultivated and improved over time. With a growth mindset, individuals view challenges as opportunities for growth, setbacks as stepping stones to success, and failures as valuable learning experiences.

Developing a growth mindset during your twenties is especially important because it allows you to approach new experiences, opportunities, and obstacles with an open mind and a willingness to learn. By embracing a growth mindset, you can cultivate resilience and bounce back from setbacks stronger than ever before.

As you navigate through this critical phase of life, it's essential to challenge any limiting beliefs and negative self-talk that may hinder your growth and resilience. Recognize that your abilities are not fixed, and with dedication and effort, you can develop new skills, overcome challenges, and achieve your goals.

To cultivate a growth mindset, surround yourself with positive influences that encourage personal and professional growth. Seek out mentors, friends, or colleagues who embody a growth mindset and can offer guidance and support along the way. Engage in activities that stretch your comfort zone and push you to learn new things. Embrace failures as learning opportunities rather than allowing them to discourage or define you.

It's also important to practice self-care and prioritize your well-being. Taking care of your physical and mental health enables you to maintain a positive mindset and persevere through challenges. Set realistic goals for yourself, both short-term and long-term, and celebrate small achievements along the way.

By developing a growth mindset and building resilience in your twenties, you are equipping yourself with the tools and mindset necessary for lifelong personal and professional growth. Embrace challenges, learn from failures, and always strive to become the best version of yourself. With a growth mindset, the possibilities for success and fulfillment are endless.

Exploring the Differences Between a Growth Mindset and a Fixed Mindset

In this section, we delve into the fundamental differences between a growth mindset and a fixed mindset, emphasizing the benefits of adopting a growth mindset during the crucial twenties.

A growth mindset is characterized by the belief that abilities and intelligence can be developed through dedication, effort, and continuous learning. It is an outlook that embraces challenges, persists in the face of setbacks, and sees failure as an opportunity for growth. Instead of viewing abilities as fixed traits, individuals with a growth mindset understand that they can improve and achieve greater success through hard work and learning from mistakes.

On the other hand, a fixed mindset is rooted in the belief that abilities are predetermined and cannot be significantly altered. Individuals with a fixed mindset tend to avoid challenges to protect their ego and often give up easily when faced with setbacks or failures. They perceive failure as evidence of their limitations rather than an opportunity to learn and grow.

Adopting a growth mindset brings numerous benefits, particularly during the formative years of one's twenties. Firstly, it opens doors to personal growth by fostering resilience, adaptability, and perseverance in the face of obstacles. When faced with challenges, those with a growth mindset approach them with curiosity and determination, seeking solutions instead of giving up. This resilience allows them to bounce back stronger and more equipped to overcome future hurdles.

Secondly, a growth mindset encourages continuous learning and development. By believing in their ability to learn new skills and acquire knowledge, individuals with a growth mindset actively seek out opportunities for personal and professional growth. They embrace feedback as a valuable tool for improvement and see criticism as a means to enhance their performance. This ongoing pursuit of learning leads to increased competence and expertise in various areas.

Lastly, cultivating a growth mindset fosters a sense of optimism and positivity. With a growth mindset, individuals believe that their efforts will lead to improvement and success over time. They view setbacks as temporary setbacks rather than permanent failures. This positive outlook enables individuals to maintain motivation, overcome self-doubt, and persevere in the face of challenges.

By understanding the differences between a growth mindset and a fixed mindset and actively cultivating a growth mindset, individuals in their twenties can set themselves up for greater success and fulfillment. Embracing challenges, persisting through setbacks, and seeing failure as an opportunity for growth will enable young adults to navigate the uncertainties of this pivotal phase with resilience, adaptability, and confidence.

Strategies and techniques for cultivating a growth mindset are crucial for personal and professional development in your twenties. One way to foster a growth mindset is by reframing challenges as opportunities. Instead of viewing obstacles as insurmountable barriers, see them as chances for learning and growth. This shift in perspective allows you to approach challenges with a positive attitude and embrace them as opportunities for self-improvement.

Another important aspect of cultivating a growth mindset is embracing failures as learning experiences. Understand that failure is not a reflection of your worth or abilities but rather an opportunity to gain valuable insights and learn from your mistakes. By reframing failure as a stepping stone towards success, you can build resilience and develop the perseverance needed to overcome obstacles.

Seeking feedback for improvement is also essential in developing a growth mindset. Actively solicit feedback from mentors, peers, and supervisors to gain different perspectives and identify areas for growth. Embrace constructive criticism as an opportunity to refine your skills and enhance your performance. By actively seeking feedback, you demonstrate a commitment to continuous improvement and a willingness to learn from others.

In summary, cultivating a growth mindset involves reframing challenges as opportunities, embracing failures as learning experiences, and seeking feedback for improvement. These strategies will enable you to develop resilience, enhance your personal and professional growth, and navigate the uncertainties that arise during your twenties.

Identifying Limiting Beliefs and Overcoming Negative Self-Talk: Building Resilience

In order to cultivate a growth mindset and build resilience, it is important to identify and overcome limiting beliefs and negative self-talk that may hinder personal and professional growth. These self-imposed barriers can prevent us from reaching our full potential and embracing new opportunities.

Limiting beliefs are the deeply ingrained thoughts and convictions that hold us back from pursuing our goals. They often stem from past experiences, societal pressure, or fear of failure. Examples of limiting beliefs include "I'm not smart enough," "I don't have what it takes to succeed," or "I'll never be good at this."

Negative self-talk refers to the inner dialogue of self-criticism and self-doubt that diminishes our confidence and motivation. It is the voice in our heads that says, "I can't do it," "I always mess up," or "I'm not worthy."

To overcome these obstacles and foster a growth mindset, it is crucial to challenge these limiting beliefs and negative self-talk. Here are some tools and techniques to help you along the way:

1. Self-awareness: Begin by becoming aware of your own limiting beliefs and negative self-talk patterns. Take note of the thoughts that arise when faced with challenges or setbacks. Recognize that these thoughts are not facts but rather subjective perceptions.

2. Question your beliefs: Once you identify a limiting belief, question its validity. Ask yourself if there is any evidence to support this belief or if it is based on assumptions or past experiences that no longer hold true. Often, you will find that these beliefs lack substantial evidence.
3. Reframe your thoughts: Replace negative self-talk with positive affirmations and empowering statements. Instead of saying, "I can't," say, "I can learn and improve." Practice reframing challenges as opportunities for growth and learning.
4. Surround yourself with positive influences: Surround yourself with supportive and uplifting individuals who believe in your potential. Seek out mentors or role models who have overcome similar challenges and can provide guidance and encouragement.
5. Practice self-compassion: Treat yourself with kindness and understanding when you make mistakes or face setbacks. Recognize that failure is a natural part of the learning process and an opportunity for growth. Embrace setbacks as valuable learning experiences that contribute to your personal development.
6. Set realistic goals: Break down your goals into manageable steps and celebrate each milestone along the way. Focus on progress rather than perfection. By setting achievable goals, you build confidence and motivation, reinforcing the belief in your ability to succeed.
7. Take action: Challenge yourself to step outside of your comfort zone and embrace new opportunities. Each small step forward strengthens your resilience and expands your capabilities.

By identifying limiting beliefs and negative self-talk, you can consciously work towards replacing them with empowering thoughts and perspectives. Cultivating a growth mindset requires consistent practice and self-reflection, but the rewards in terms of personal growth, resilience, and success are immeasurable. Remember, you have the power to shape your own narrative and create a fulfilling and purposeful life by overcoming these obstacles.

Practical tips for building resilience include developing a strong support system. Surrounding yourself with positive and supportive individuals who believe in your abilities can greatly contribute to your resilience. Seek out friends, family members, mentors, or even support groups who can provide encouragement and guidance during challenging times.

Additionally, practicing self-care is essential for building resilience. Taking care of your physical, emotional, and mental well-being is crucial when facing adversity. Engage in activities that bring you joy and relaxation, such as exercise, meditation, hobbies, or spending time in nature. Prioritize self-care routines and make them a non-negotiable part of your daily life.

Setting realistic goals is another important aspect of building resilience. Break down larger goals into smaller, manageable steps that you can achieve along the way. By setting achievable milestones, you build momentum and confidence in your ability to overcome obstacles. Celebrate each accomplishment, no matter how small, as it reinforces your resilience and motivates you to keep moving forward.

Lastly, celebrate achievements along the way. It's easy to get caught up in the pursuit of future goals and forget to acknowledge how far you've already come. Take time to reflect on your progress and celebrate your accomplishments, no matter how small. This practice not only boosts your confidence but also reminds you of your resilience and ability to overcome challenges.

Remember, building resilience is an ongoing process that requires effort and persistence. By incorporating these practical tips into your life, you'll be better equipped to bounce back from setbacks, adapt to change, and thrive in both personal and professional endeavors.

Part 3:
Career and
Professional Life

Chapter 1

Crafting a Vision
for Your Career

*****

Introduction: Crafting a Vision for Your Career

Clearly de-fining one's career ambitions provide-s indispensable guidance towards accomplishing satisfaction and achie-vement in the work world. Whe-n picturing an ideal potential outcome, clarity, inte-ntion, and inspiration form to chase important duties that coincide with inte-rests, principles, and objective-s.

Through self-e-xamination, one can craft a vision that guides caree-r and personal progress. This chapter e-xplores how focusing internally helps uncove-r core values, abilities, inte-rests and joys that steer life-decisions. We'll perform e-xercises that foster insight into traits ce-ntral to who you are, which heavily influence- the path chosen. Careful conside-ration of what drives and fulfills you aids in plotting a route aligned with your authe-ntic self, paving the way for growth as a person and profe-ssional.

A definitive- vision permits establishing caree-r aims that align with your principles and hopes. By segme-nting these aims into near-te-rm and far-reaching targets, you can draft realizable- plans and techniques for monitoring your advanceme-nt. All through this segment, we will furnish practical re-commendations and guidance to assist you with staying roused and ce-ntered around your way to achieve-ment.

In this discussion, we will e-xplore the diverse- career routes and se-ctors open to you, illuminating arising patterns and aptitudes sought afte-r by employers. By investigating alte-rnate roads, you can make educate-d choices about the way forward you wish to take in your profe-ssional journey.

Building relationships and profe-ssional connections are vital parts of progressing in your care-er journey. We will he-lp navigate finding mentorship chances and utilizing online- platforms and tools to boost your career potential. By cultivating a robust ne-twork of support and guidance, you can unlock new pathways and broaden your profe-ssional scope.

Crafting a vision for your career is not just about landing a job; it is about creating a pathway to personal growth, fulfillment, and long-term success. By taking the time to reflect on your values, strengths, and passions, you can pave the way for a rewarding and purposeful professional journey.

RephraseWelcome- as we explore care-er possibilities and obtain instruments and tactics to form our e-xpert futures. Collaboratively, we- can develop a guide that transports us to a fulfilling and thriving profe-ssion that matches our authentic selve-s.

Looking inward through contemplation is vital for shaping your profe-ssional goals. Making the effort to know your principles, tale-nts, likes, and enthusiasm helps you pick work that re-sonates with who you are.

Creating a life- purpose statement can be- an enlightening ende-avor. Taking the time for introspection to uncove-r your fundamental values and what truly brings you happiness allows you to ide-ntify the activities or missions that fuel your passion and whe-re you feel most e-nergized. Carefully crafting a succinct de-claration that captures your ultimate reason for be-ing can provide profound clarity and direction.

Taking a close e-xamination of myself through a SWOT analysis has proven helpful in my care-er planning. This tool allows one to take stock of inte-rnal factors like strengths and weakne-sses, as well as exte-rnal factors such as opportunities and threats. I make an e-ffort to highlight my skills, knowledge and innate tale-nts as strengths to capitalize on. At the same- time, I aim to pinpoint locations demanding improveme-nt. This balanced perspective- aids in discerning career route-s aligning with my abilities. It also clarifies zones re-quiring focus to develop further. Care-fully considering how I may leverage-strengths while addressing we-aknesses prepare-s me to make the most out of forthcoming prospe-cts. With diligence and commitment to growth, we-aknesses can transform into strengths ove-r the long run.

Through exploration of pe-rsonal interests via rese-arch, internships, volunteering or informational conve-rsations, one can experime-nt with diverse opportunities and gain dire-ct exposure to varying industries. Engage- in pursuits providing chances to sample diverse- waters and accumulate firsthand familiarity with assorted domains. Note- well the duties and se-ttings feeling most meaningful and e-ngaging.

Lastly, reflect on the impact you want to make in the world. What change do you aspire to bring about? How do you want to contribute to society? Identifying your desired impact can guide you towards careers that align with your values and allow you to make a meaningful difference.

Remember, this part of the book will provide practical guidance on self-reflection exercises specifically tailored to young adults in their twenties. By engaging in these exercises, readers will gain valuable insights into themselves and uncover their true passions and purpose, which will ultimately shape their career choices.

This narrative aims to provide- insightful guidance on various career ave-nues and sectors, covering rising de-velopments and sought-after abilitie-s. By exploring multiple alternative-s, "Build Your Character at Twenty" helps re-aders make informed choice-s for their prospective profe-ssions. Delving into specific industries highlights the- required skills and qualifications, equipping re-aders with knowledge to succe-ssfully navigate diverse paths. With an e-mphasis on emerging patterns, the- book encourages considering innovative- domains and chances that may coincide with passions and intere-sts. Through sharing this valuable information, it ensures compre-hension of current occupational opportunities to confide-ntly make goals-aligned dete-rminations.

Helping othe-rs establish realistic caree-r ambitions is pivotal in forming a blueprint for their path ahead. By dividing the-se aims into near-term and long-te-rm targets, people can forge- a plan that propels them towards accomplishment.

At the outse-t, reflecting carefully on one-'s personal priorities, talents, passions and pursuits is vital. Conside-ring what is meaningful helps align caree-r paths with what truly matters. By weighing core ide-als and sources of satisfaction, readers can choose- work that has significance and intention.

When discove-ring your values and interests, the- next step is setting re-asonable career obje-ctives. Goals should be distinct, quantifiable, possible- to accomplish, applicable to your aims, and anchored to a timeline- (SMART). Using this structure, people can divide- their broad career hope-s into workable phases they can active-ly pursue.

Monitoring my advanceme-nt is another critical part of establishing and accomplishing profession obje-ctives. By routinely assessing whe-re I am with respect to my obje-ctives, people can re-main inspired and make important changes e-n route. This can be accomplished through introspe-ction, journaling, or utilizing different following device-s and applications that permit people to scre-en their advanceme-nt.

Remaining drive-n all through the expedition towards one-'s occupation objectives is vital. To kee-p inspiration, people can:

1. Cherish slight triumphs: Take- note of and repay yourself for attaining mile-stones and advancing toward the broader obje-ctive.
2. Se-ek support: Reach out to mentors, frie-nds, or accountability partners who can offer encourage-ment and guidance when ne-eded. Their support can he-lp motivate you
3. Envision accomplishment: Form a cle-ar mental picture of what attaining the care-er objective appe-ars like and how it will feel to achie-ve it.
4. Divide large- endeavors into more manage-able parts: Taking a complex project and se-parating it into simpler pieces de-creases fee-lings of being overwhelme-d and makes forward momentum see-m achievable.
5. Gain motivation from others: Look to those- who have accomplished comparable care-er aims or conquered paralle-l trials. Hearing their journeys can spur you on and provide- viewpoint when barriers se-em big. Their triumphs show the possible-.

Establishing reasonable- career objective-s provides people with a solid basis for accomplishme-nt. This method offers lucidity and bearing as we-ll as acts as an inspiration and perseverance- when encountering hurdle-s. By monitoring development and pre-serving inspiration, readers can confide-ntly guide their caree-r routes and work towards cultivating a gratifying and compensating professional e-xistence.

Chapter 2

Networking: Creating Meaningful Connections

****

Crafting a Vision for Your Career: Developing a Professional Network

Building a strong professional network is crucial for career success and advancement. In this section, we will delve into practical tips and advice on how to effectively network, build professional connections, seek mentorship opportunities, and leverage online platforms and resources to enhance your career prospects.

1. Networking: Embrace the power of networking by attending industry events, career fairs, and conferences. Take advantage of these opportunities to meet professionals in your field of interest, exchange contact information, and engage in meaningful conversations. Remember, networking isn't just about collecting business cards but building genuine relationships based on mutual interests and shared goals.

2. Utilizing Social Media: Leverage the power of social media platforms such as LinkedIn, Twitter, and Instagram to expand your professional network. Create a compelling online presence by showcasing your skills, expertise, and achievements. Engage with industry leaders by commenting on their posts, sharing relevant content, and participating in industry-specific groups or forums.

3. Join Professional Associations and Groups: Consider joining professional associations or groups related to your career field. These organizations provide excellent opportunities to connect with like-minded individuals, attend workshops, seminars, and gain access to exclusive job boards or career resources.

4. Seek Mentorship: Mentors play a pivotal role in guiding and shaping your career trajectory. Look for experienced professionals who can offer insights, advice, and support. Attend mentoring programs or seek out mentors within your workplace or through alumni networks. Be proactive in reaching out and nurturing these mentor-mentee relationships.

5. Online Learning Platforms: Take advantage of online learning platforms such as Coursera, Udemy, or LinkedIn Learning to develop new skills and expand your knowledge base. Enhancing your skill set not only boosts your confidence but also makes you more marketable to potential employers or clients.

6. Volunteer or Internship Opportunities: Engaging in volunteer work or internships can provide valuable networking opportunities. Not only does it allow you to contribute to a cause you are passionate about, but it also enables you to connect with professionals who share your interests and values.

7. Informational Interviews: Reach out to professionals in your desired career field and request informational interviews. These conversations provide insights into different job roles, industries, and can help clarify your career goals. Remember to prepare thoughtful questions and express genuine curiosity.

Remember, effective networking is not just about what others can do for you. It is equally important to offer support and assistance to others whenever possible. By nurturing meaningful relationships within your professional network, you can create a supportive community that fosters growth, opens doors to new opportunities, and propels you towards career success.

The Importance of Networking:

Networking plays a crucial role in personal and professional success, particularly during the formative years of one's career. It provides opportunities to build relationships, create connections, and expand one's sphere of influence. By actively engaging in networking, individuals can open doors to new opportunities, gain access to valuable resources, and accelerate their personal growth.

One of the key benefits of networking is the ability to connect with like-minded individuals who share similar passions and goals. These connections can serve as a support system, providing encouragement, guidance, and valuable insights. By surrounding oneself with motivated and driven individuals, there is an increased likelihood of achieving success and finding inspiration along the way.

Additionally, networking allows individuals to tap into a wealth of knowledge and experience that exists within their chosen industry or field. By connecting with professionals who have already achieved a level of success, it becomes possible to learn from their experiences, gain valuable advice, and avoid potential pitfalls. Through these interactions, individuals can gain insights into industry trends, best practices, and emerging opportunities.

Furthermore, networking provides individuals with the opportunity to showcase their own skills, talents, and expertise. By actively engaging in conversations and building genuine relationships, individuals can establish themselves as credible professionals within their field. This credibility can lead to referrals, recommendations, and increased visibility within the industry.

Moreover, networking serves as a gateway to uncovering hidden job opportunities that may not be advertised through traditional channels. Many jobs are filled through referrals or direct connections made within a network. By actively participating in networking events or leveraging online platforms such as LinkedIn, individuals increase their chances of being considered for these unadvertised positions.

Lastly, networking fosters personal growth by exposing individuals to new perspectives, ideas, and experiences. Engaging with people from diverse backgrounds and industries encourages individuals to broaden their horizons and think outside the box. These interactions can spark creativity, inspire innovation, and ultimately contribute to personal and professional development.

In summary, networking is an invaluable tool for individuals in their twenties who are seeking personal growth, professional achievement, and long-term success. By actively engaging in networking opportunities, individuals can open doors to new opportunities, gain access to valuable resources, and accelerate their personal and professional growth. It is through creating meaningful connections early on that individuals can set themselves up for a lifetime of success and fulfillment.

Building a Network:

In this section, we will explore practical tips and strategies for building a strong and diverse network. Building a network is essential for personal and professional success as it opens doors to new opportunities and provides access to valuable resources. By following the strategies outlined below, readers will learn how to identify potential contacts, initiate conversations, and maintain relationships effectively.

1. Attend Social Events: One of the most common avenues for networking is attending social events. Whether it's industry conferences, meetups, or community gatherings, these events provide an opportunity to connect with like-minded individuals who share similar interests and goals. Be proactive in introducing yourself to others and engage in meaningful conversations. Remember to approach these interactions with genuine curiosity and interest in others.

2. Join Professional Organizations: Another effective way to build a network is by joining professional organizations related to your field of interest. These organizations often host regular meetings, workshops, and networking events where you can connect with professionals who are further along in their careers. Actively participate in these events and take advantage of the resources and mentorship opportunities available within these communities.

3. Utilize Online Platforms: In today's digital age, online platforms have become invaluable for networking. LinkedIn, in particular, offers a vast array of networking opportunities. Create a compelling profile that showcases your skills and experiences, and actively engage with others through commenting on posts, joining relevant groups, and reaching out to individuals for informational interviews. Additionally, explore other online platforms specific to your industry or interests to expand your network further.

4. Informational Interviews: Informational interviews are a powerful tool for networking as they allow you to connect with professionals in your desired field and gain valuable insights into their experiences. Reach out to individuals you admire or whose career path aligns with your goals and request a brief meeting to discuss their expertise and industry insights. Be prepared with thoughtful questions and remember to express gratitude for their time.

5. Maintain Relationships: Building a network is not just about making initial connections, but also about nurturing and maintaining those relationships over time. After meeting someone new, follow up with a personalized email or LinkedIn connection request. Regularly reach out to your network to offer support, share relevant articles or resources, and congratulate them on their achievements. Show genuine interest in their success and be proactive in providing value whenever possible.

By implementing these strategies for building a network, readers will be well on their way to expanding their professional circle and creating meaningful connections. Remember that networking is an ongoing process, so continue to seek opportunities to connect with others and nurture these relationships.

Nurturing Relationships:

In this section, we will delve into the art of nurturing and maintaining meaningful connections. While building a network is important, it is equally essential to invest time and effort in nurturing these relationships for long-term success.

One key aspect of nurturing relationships is the concept of reciprocity. It is crucial to approach networking with a mindset of giving rather than just taking. By offering support, advice, and assistance to others in your network, you create a mutually beneficial environment where everyone can thrive. This could involve providing feedback on a project, connecting someone with a valuable resource or opportunity, or simply offering a listening ear when they need it most. By demonstrating genuine interest in others' success, you build trust and establish a strong foundation for collaboration.

Active listening is another crucial skill for nurturing relationships. When engaging in conversations with your contacts, make a conscious effort to listen attentively and show genuine curiosity about their experiences, goals, and challenges. By actively listening, you not only gain valuable insights but also demonstrate respect for the other person's perspective. This helps foster deeper connections based on shared understanding and empathy.

Following up with contacts is equally important in nurturing relationships. After initial interactions, take the initiative to follow up with a personalized message or email expressing your appreciation for their time and insights. Demonstrating gratitude shows that you value the relationship and want to maintain open lines of communication. Furthermore, following up provides an opportunity to continue the conversation or explore potential collaborations.

Providing value to your network is another critical aspect of nurturing relationships. Look for ways to contribute and be of service to those in your network. Share relevant articles or resources, introduce them to other professionals who can offer insights or opportunities, or offer your expertise when needed. By consistently providing value, you establish yourself as a trusted resource within your network and strengthen the bond you share.

Remember, nurturing relationships requires ongoing effort and genuine care. Regularly check in with your contacts, celebrate their successes, and offer support during challenging times. By investing in these relationships, you create a supportive community that can provide guidance, motivation, and opportunities for personal growth and professional advancement.

In summary, nurturing relationships is a crucial aspect of effective networking. By practicing reciprocity, active listening, and genuine interest in others' success, you can establish meaningful connections that will serve you well throughout your personal and professional journey.

Leveraging Your Network: This section focuses on the specific strategies and techniques that readers can employ to leverage their network for career advancement and personal growth. This includes seeking out mentorship opportunities, obtaining valuable referrals, and accessing hidden job opportunities.

1. Seeking Mentorship: Readers will learn how to identify potential mentors within their network and approach them with a clear understanding of what they hope to gain from the relationship. The section will provide advice on how to establish a mutually beneficial mentor-mentee dynamic, emphasizing the importance of active engagement, respectful communication, and gratitude. By leveraging the experience and wisdom of mentors, readers can accelerate their personal and professional development.

2. Obtaining Referrals: This part highlights the value of referrals in job searching and career progression. It will outline effective ways to approach individuals in your network who may be able to provide recommendations or introduce you to key decision-makers. Readers will gain insights into etiquette and best practices for requesting referrals, including crafting compelling requests that clearly articulate their goals and qualifications. By leveraging the connections within their network, readers can tap into hidden job opportunities that may not be publicly advertised.

3. Accessing Hidden Job Opportunities: This section explores strategies for uncovering hidden job opportunities through networking. It will provide guidance on leveraging personal connections, attending industry events, and engaging with online platforms to discover potential career prospects. Readers will learn how to strategically position themselves as valuable assets to prospective employers, increasing their chances of securing rewarding employment opportunities.

4. Tapping into Network for Personal Development: In this part, readers will discover how to utilize their network for personal growth beyond just professional considerations. They will explore ways to find like-minded individuals who share similar interests and aspirations, fostering relationships that encourage personal development and exploration. The section will emphasize the importance of connecting with individuals who inspire and challenge readers to continually expand their horizons.

By providing practical strategies for leveraging one's network effectively, this section ensures that readers are equipped with the knowledge and skills needed to maximize the potential of their existing connections. By leveraging their network for mentorship, referrals, hidden job opportunities, and personal growth, readers can accelerate their journey towards success and fulfillment.

Networking Etiquette: This section will address the dos and don'ts of networking etiquette to ensure readers make a positive impression. It will provide practical guidelines on appropriate communication methods, including email, phone calls, and social media. Readers will learn how to craft professional and engaging messages, making sure to adhere to professional etiquette norms.

In addition to digital communication, this section will emphasize the importance of face-to-face interactions at networking events. It will cover topics such as appropriate professional appearance, body language, and demeanor when meeting potential contacts. Readers will gain valuable insights on how to present themselves in a confident and approachable manner that fosters trust and rapport.

Furthermore, this section will highlight the significance of gratitude and follow-up after networking interactions. Readers will learn the importance of expressing appreciation for someone's time and insights, whether through a thank-you note or a follow-up message. They will also discover effective strategies for maintaining relationships by periodically checking in with their contacts and offering assistance or support when needed.

By providing readers with a comprehensive understanding of proper networking behavior, this section ensures that they can navigate networking opportunities with confidence and professionalism. The guidance offered in this chapter complements the broader themes explored throughout the book, empowering young adults to build meaningful connections that contribute to their personal growth and professional success.

Chapter 3

Developing a Personal Brand: Standing Out in Your Twenties

✱✱✱

Understanding the Importance of Personal Branding:

In this section, we will delve into the significance of personal branding for young adults in their twenties. Personal branding refers to the intentional process of shaping and managing one's professional identity and reputation. It goes beyond simply having a resume or a LinkedIn profile - it is about actively crafting an authentic and unique narrative that sets you apart from others.

In today's competitive job market, having a strong personal brand is crucial for standing out among a sea of applicants. Employers are not only interested in your qualifications and skills; they are also looking for individuals who bring something unique to the table. Personal branding allows you to showcase your distinctive qualities, experiences, and values that can make you a valuable asset to potential employers.

Building a compelling personal brand also helps establish credibility and trustworthiness. When you have a clear and consistent personal brand, people perceive you as someone who is genuine, reliable, and focused. This credibility can open doors to exciting opportunities and collaborations.

Additionally, personal branding allows you to attract opportunities that align with your goals and values. By showcasing your passions, strengths, and values through your personal brand, you can attract like-minded individuals, companies, and projects that resonate with who you are. This alignment creates a sense of fulfillment and satisfaction in your personal and professional life.

Personal branding is not limited to just career advancement; it has broader implications for your overall success and fulfillment. By intentionally cultivating your personal brand, you can build meaningful relationships, inspire others, and make a positive impact in various spheres of your life.

In the following sections, we will explore practical strategies for assessing your unique qualities and values, crafting a compelling personal brand statement, building an online presence, and showcasing your personal brand in job applications and interviews. Through these steps, you will be equipped with the necessary tools to develop a personal brand that helps you stand out and thrive in your twenties and beyond.

Assessing Your Unique Qualities and Values:

In order to develop a strong personal brand, it is crucial to have a clear understanding of your unique qualities, strengths, values, and passions. This self-reflection process will help you gain clarity on your personal brand identity and what sets you apart from others.

To assess your unique qualities, start by asking yourself the following questions:

1. What are my natural talents and skills? Consider the activities or tasks that come easily to you and bring you joy. These can be indicators of your unique abilities.
2. What do others admire about me? Reflect on the feedback you have received from friends, family, teachers, or colleagues. What qualities or traits do they appreciate in you?
3. What are my core values? Identify the values that guide your decisions and actions. These could include integrity, compassion, creativity, or any other principles that you hold dear.
4. What am I passionate about? Consider the subjects or activities that ignite a sense of excitement and enthusiasm within you. These can serve as indicators of your passions and interests.
5. What experiences have shaped me? Reflect on significant events or challenges you have faced in your life. How have these experiences influenced your character and outlook on life?

Once you have answered these questions, take some time to analyze your responses. Look for patterns or themes that emerge from your answers. These patterns will help you identify your unique qualities and values.

Next, consider how these unique qualities and values can be applied to different aspects of your life. How can they be incorporated into your personal relationships, career choices, and overall lifestyle? By aligning your actions with your values and leveraging your unique qualities, you can build an authentic personal brand that resonates with others.

Remember that developing a personal brand is an ongoing process, and it may evolve as you grow and gain new experiences. Stay open to learning more about yourself and continue to refine your personal brand as you navigate through your twenties and beyond

,Crafting a Compelling Personal Brand Statement: This section is dedicated to teaching readers how to create a concise and memorable personal brand statement. A personal brand statement is a powerful tool that effectively communicates an individual's unique value proposition. It encapsulates their core qualities, strengths, values, and passions, allowing them to stand out from the competition.

To craft a compelling personal brand statement, it is important to consider both professional objectives and personal values. Here are some guidelines and examples to help readers create their own impactful statements:

1. Clarity and Conciseness: A personal brand statement should be clear, succinct, and easily understood. Avoid using jargon or complex language that may confuse or alienate the audience. Keep the statement focused on the key qualities and values that define your brand.

Example: "I am a resourceful and creative problem-solver who is passionate about leveraging technology to drive sustainable solutions."

2. Unique Value Proposition: Identify what sets you apart from others in your field. Consider your specific skills, experiences, or perspectives that differentiate you from others. Highlight the value you bring to the table and how it benefits others.

Example: "As a marketing professional with a deep understanding of consumer behavior and a knack for storytelling, I deliver engaging campaigns that resonate with target audiences and drive meaningful results."

3. Authenticity: Your personal brand statement should reflect your authentic self. Showcasing your genuine passions, interests, and values will attract opportunities that align with who you truly are.

Example: "I am a passionate advocate for environmental sustainability, dedicating my career to creating innovative strategies that bridge sustainability efforts with business objectives."

4. Tailoring to Different Audiences: Adapt your personal brand statement to fit various contexts and audiences. While the core message remains consistent, emphasize different aspects of your brand depending on the situation.

Example: "As a versatile project manager skilled in cross-functional collaboration, I thrive in dynamic environments and excel at delivering high-quality results within tight deadlines."

By crafting a compelling personal brand statement, readers will be able to effectively communicate their unique value proposition and stand out in their twenties. This statement will serve as a powerful tool for job applications, interviews, networking opportunities, and personal interactions. It will resonate with both professional objectives and personal values, showcasing the essence of their personal brand.

Building an Online Presence:

In today's digital age, having a strong online presence is essential for standing out and building your personal brand. This section will delve into the importance of leveraging online platforms to enhance your personal brand and provide practical tips for creating a professional and consistent online image.

First and foremost, it's important to establish a professional presence on social media platforms such as LinkedIn, Twitter, and Instagram. These platforms can be powerful tools for showcasing your expertise, sharing valuable content, and connecting with industry professionals. Ensure that your profiles are complete, up-to-date, and reflective of your personal brand. Use a cohesive visual theme and develop a professional bio that highlights your key skills and achievements.

Professional networking sites like LinkedIn are particularly valuable for building an online presence in a professional context. Join relevant groups and participate in discussions to demonstrate your knowledge and engage with others in your field. Seek out recommendations from peers, colleagues, or mentors to add credibility to your profile.

Creating and curating content is another effective way to build your online presence. Share articles, videos, or blog posts that align with your personal brand and showcase your expertise. Consider starting your own blog or contributing guest posts to industry publications to establish yourself as a thought leader.

Engaging with online communities is also crucial for building a strong online reputation. Participate in relevant discussions, offer valuable insights, and support others in your field. By actively engaging with others, you can expand your network and increase visibility within your industry.

Remember that consistency is key when building an online presence. Use the same professional headshot across different platforms to create recognition and maintain a cohesive brand image. Regularly update your profiles with new accomplishments, projects, or certifications to show continuous growth and development.

Lastly, be mindful of the impression you leave on potential employers or collaborators through your online presence. Conduct regular audits of your social media accounts to ensure they reflect your personal brand positively. Remove any content that may be deemed unprofessional or inappropriate.

By building a strong online presence, you can establish yourself as a credible and influential individual in your industry. Embrace the power of online platforms, engage with relevant communities, and curate valuable content to enhance your personal brand and stand out in your twenties and beyond.

Showcasing Your Personal Brand in Job Applications and Interviews: Young adults in their twenties often face a highly competitive job market, where standing out is essential. This section provides practical advice on incorporating one's personal brand into job applications, resumes, cover letters, and interviews to leave a lasting impression on potential employers.

When applying for jobs, it's important to highlight relevant experiences, skills, and accomplishments that align with your personal brand. Rather than simply listing job responsibilities, focus on the impact you made and the skills you developed. For example, instead of saying "Managed a team," you can say "Led a cross-functional team of 10 members, resulting in a 20% increase in productivity."

Additionally, storytelling is a powerful tool during interviews. Share anecdotes that demonstrate how your unique qualities and values have contributed to your professional success. These stories not only help interviewers understand your capabilities but also showcase your personality and passion.

Incorporating your personal brand into job applications requires tailoring your resume and cover letter to reflect your unique value proposition. Use keywords and phrases that align with your personal brand identity. Research the company culture and values to ensure that your application materials resonate with their mission and vision.

During interviews, remember to convey passion for the role and the organization. Show enthusiasm for the industry and discuss how your personal brand aligns with the company's values and goals. Be confident, articulate, and concise when answering questions, always emphasizing how your unique qualities contribute to your potential success in the role.

Utilize different mediums to support your personal brand during interviews. Consider creating an online portfolio or website that showcases your work, projects, and achievements. This gives potential employers a more comprehensive view of your capabilities and reinforces your personal brand.

Remember, showcasing your personal brand goes beyond just talking about yourself. It's about demonstrating how you can add value to a company and contribute to its success. By effectively incorporating your personal brand into job applications and interviews, you increase your chances of standing out in a crowded job market and landing opportunities that align with your aspirations.

Chapter 4

Financial Literacy: Managing Your First Paychecks

****

Understanding the Importance of Financial Literacy

Financial literacy is crucial for young adults in their twenties as it sets the foundation for sound financial management and long-term success. Without a proper understanding of personal finance, individuals may face detrimental consequences that can affect their future financial stability.

One potential consequence of poor financial management is accumulating excessive debt. Lack of knowledge about interest rates, credit cards, and loans can lead to uncontrolled spending and high-interest debts that become difficult to repay. This can negatively impact credit scores and limit financial opportunities in the future, such as obtaining favorable loan terms or securing rental agreements. By emphasizing the importance of financial literacy, young adults can avoid falling into debt traps and maintain control over their finances.

Developing good financial habits early on is another crucial benefit of financial literacy. By learning how to budget effectively, individuals can allocate their income towards essential expenses, savings goals, and investments. Understanding the value of money and making conscious spending decisions can help young adults prioritize their needs and wants, ensuring that they live within their means. This not only promotes fiscal responsibility but also cultivates a mindset of delayed gratification, leading to long-term financial success.

In addition to managing day-to-day finances, financial literacy also plays a vital role in preparing for major life events such as homeownership, retirement planning, and unexpected emergencies. With proper knowledge about investment options, young adults can start building wealth early by investing in stocks, bonds, or real estate. This allows them to benefit from compound interest and potentially secure a stable financial future. Furthermore, understanding the importance of establishing an emergency fund and having sufficient insurance coverage protects against unforeseen circumstances like medical emergencies or job loss while providing peace of mind.

By prioritizing financial literacy at a young age, individuals gain the knowledge and skills necessary to make informed decisions about their money. This empowers them to take control of their financial future and avoid costly mistakes. Through education, practice, and continuous learning, young adults can lay a solid foundation for financial success, allowing them to achieve their goals and dreams with greater ease.

Creating a Budget

Creating a budget is a crucial step in managing your finances effectively. It allows you to allocate your income towards different categories, such as bills, savings, and discretionary spending. By following a budget, you can ensure that you live within your means, avoid unnecessary debt, and save for future goals. Here is a step-by-step guide to creating a budget:

1. **Calculate your income:** Start by determining your total income per month. Include any regular salary, wages, or other sources of income.
2. **List your expenses:** Make a comprehensive list of all your expenses, including fixed expenses (e.g. rent/mortgage, utilities) and variable expenses (e.g. groceries, transportation).
3. **Categorize your expenses:** Divide your expenses into different categories based on their nature. Common categories include housing, transportation, food, entertainment, debt repayment, and savings.
4. **Prioritize essential expenses:** Identify your essential expenses, such as rent/mortgage payments, utilities, and groceries. These should be given the highest priority when allocating funds from your income.

5. **Set financial goals:** Determine your short-term and long-term financial goals. These could include saving for emergencies, paying off debts, saving for a down payment on a house, or investing for retirement.
6. **Allocate funds to each category:** Assign a specific amount of money to each expense category based on your priorities and financial goals. Ensure that you allocate enough towards essential expenses and savings.
7. **Monitor and track your spending:** Regularly review your actual spending against the allocated amounts in your budget. This will help you identify areas where you may need to cut back or adjust your allocations.
8. **Adjust as necessary:** If you find that you are consistently overspending in certain categories or not allocating enough towards savings, make adjustments to your budget accordingly. Flexibility is key in ensuring that your budget remains realistic and achievable.

When it comes to budgeting, there are several methods and tools available to help you stay organized. Some popular budgeting methods include the 50/30/20 rule (where 50% of your income goes towards essentials, 30% towards discretionary spending, and 20% towards savings), envelope budgeting (where you allocate cash into envelopes for different expense categories), and zero-based budgeting (where you allocate every dollar of your income). Choose a method that works best for you and aligns with your financial goals.

You can also utilize various budgeting apps or spreadsheets to track your income and expenses. These tools can automate calculations, provide visual representations of your spending habits, and send reminders for bill payments. Explore different options and find one that suits your preferences and needs.

Addressing common budgeting challenges is essential to ensure that your budget is effective in managing your finances. Some common challenges include sticking to your budget, dealing with unexpected expenses, and handling irregular income. To overcome these challenges:

➢ Stay disciplined: Stick to your budget by practicing self-discipline when it comes to discretionary spending. Avoid impulse purchases and constantly remind yourself of your financial goals.
➢ Build an emergency fund: Set aside a portion of your income towards building an emergency fund. This will provide a cushion for unexpected expenses and prevent you from going off-budget.
➢ Adjust for irregular income: If you have irregular income, such as freelancing or commission-based work, consider creating a variable budget. Allocate a percentage of each payment towards different expense categories rather than fixed amounts.

Creating a budget is a foundational step towards effective financial management. By following these steps and addressing common challenges, you will be well on your way to achieving financial stability and reaching your long-term goals.

Saving and investing are crucial components of financial literacy that can significantly impact a young adult's long-term financial security. In this section, we will delve into the concept of saving and discuss various investment options suitable for individuals in their twenties.

Firstly, let's emphasize the importance of building an emergency fund. An emergency fund serves as a safety net during unexpected circumstances such as job loss, medical emergencies, or major repairs. By setting aside a portion of your income specifically for emergencies, you can avoid falling into debt or having to rely on credit cards. Aim to accumulate at least three to six months' worth of living expenses in your emergency fund to provide financial stability and peace of mind.

Now, let's turn our attention to investing. Investing is an essential strategy for growing your wealth over time and achieving long-term financial goals. While it may seem daunting or reserved for older individuals, starting to invest early in your twenties can give you a significant advantage due to the power of compound interest.

One option for young adults to consider is investing in the stock market. Before diving in, it's crucial to conduct thorough research, educate yourself about different companies and industries, and understand the risks involved. Consider investing in low-cost index funds or exchange-traded funds (ETFs) as they provide broad market exposure and diversification while minimizing fees.

Another investment option to explore is a retirement account like an individual retirement account (IRA). IRAs offer tax advantages and compounding growth potential. You can choose between a traditional IRA or a Roth IRA based on your specific circumstances and tax considerations. Starting to contribute to retirement accounts early allows your investments to grow over several decades, significantly increasing your savings for retirement.

Real estate investment can also be an attractive option for those with the financial means and willingness to take on additional responsibilities. Owning rental properties or investing in real estate investment trusts (REITs) can provide passive income and appreciate in value over time.

Lastly, consider investing in yourself through education and skills development. Investing in your knowledge and abilities can lead to higher earning potential and career advancement opportunities. Explore certifications, courses, or workshops that align with your interests and career goals.

Remember, when it comes to investing, diversification is key. Spread your investments across different asset classes, industries, and geographical regions to minimize risk and maximize potential returns. Regularly review and adjust your investment portfolio as needed to ensure it aligns with your goals and risk tolerance.

By understanding the importance of saving for emergencies and exploring various investment options, you can start building wealth early in life. The power of compound interest can work in your favor, allowing your investments to grow exponentially over time. Take advantage of the opportunities presented by prudent saving and investing to secure a brighter financial future.

Managing Debt

In this section, we will discuss strategies for effectively managing debt, specifically focusing on student loans, credit card debt, and other forms of debt that young adults may encounter. It is important to address debt management early on to avoid falling into debt traps and facing negative consequences in the future. By implementing these strategies and tips, readers can take control of their financial situation and prioritize debt repayment.

1. Outlining Strategies for Student Loan Management

One common form of debt that many young adults face is student loans. These loans can quickly accumulate and become overwhelming if not managed properly. Here are some strategies for effectively managing student loan debt:

- ✓ Understand your loan terms: Take the time to review and understand the terms of your student loan, including interest rates, repayment options, and any potential penalties or fees. This knowledge will help you make informed decisions about repayment.
- ✓ Create a repayment plan: Develop a repayment plan that suits your financial situation and goals. Consider options such as income-driven repayment plans or refinancing to potentially lower your monthly payments or interest rates.
- ✓ Prioritize high-interest loans: If you have multiple student loans, focus on paying off the loans with the highest interest rates first. This will save you money in the long run by reducing the amount of interest accrued.

2. Discussing the Consequences of Excessive Credit Card Debt

Credit card debt can easily spiral out of control if not managed carefully. It is crucial to understand the potential consequences of excessive credit card debt and develop strategies to avoid getting trapped in a cycle of debt. Here are some key considerations:

- ✓ High-interest rates: Credit cards often come with high-interest rates, meaning the longer you carry a balance, the more interest you will accrue. This can lead to significant amounts of debt over time.
- ✓ Damage to credit score: Accumulating large amounts of credit card debt and missing payments can negatively impact your credit score. A poor credit score can make it challenging to secure loans or favorable interest rates in the future.
- ✓ Developing healthy credit habits: Establishing good credit habits, such as paying your credit card balance in full each month and keeping your credit utilization ratio low, can help you avoid excessive debt and maintain a healthy financial standing.

3. Providing Tips for Negotiating with Creditors

If you find yourself struggling to meet your debt obligations or facing financial hardship, it is essential to know how to negotiate with creditors. By effectively communicating and seeking assistance, you may be able to alleviate some of the financial burden. Consider the following tips:

- ✓ Contact your creditors: If you are having trouble making payments, reach out to your creditors and explain your situation. They may be willing to work out a revised payment plan or offer temporary relief options.
- ✓ Seek professional guidance: If negotiating with creditors becomes overwhelming or you feel unsure about the process, consider reaching out to a credit counseling agency or financial advisor who can provide expert advice and support.
- ✓ Prioritize debt repayment: When negotiating with creditors, demonstrate your commitment to repaying your debts by proposing a reasonable payment plan that fits within your budget.

By understanding these strategies and tips for managing debt, young adults can take control of their financial situation and prevent debt from becoming a long-term burden. Remember, effective debt management is essential for building a solid foundation for future financial security and success.

Building Long-Term Financial Security

In addition to effectively managing your finances in the present, it is crucial to plan for your long-term financial security. This involves considering various concepts such as retirement planning, insurance, and estate planning.

Retirement Planning: It is never too early to start thinking about retirement. Take advantage of employer-sponsored retirement plans, such as 401(k)s or pensions, if available. These plans often offer matching contributions from your employer, allowing your savings to grow faster. Alternatively, consider opening an individual retirement account (IRA) and contribute regularly to benefit from tax advantages and compound interest over time.

Insurance: Protecting yourself and your assets is an important aspect of long-term financial security. Evaluate your insurance needs, including health insurance, life insurance, disability insurance, and homeowner's/renter's insurance. Insurance provides a safety net during unexpected events and ensures that you are financially protected against potential risks.

Estate Planning: Although estate planning may seem distant at a young age, it is essential to have a plan in place. Create a will to outline the distribution of your assets and name beneficiaries. Consider consulting with a professional to explore options like setting up a trust or establishing power of attorney. By taking these steps early on, you can ensure that your wishes are followed and protect your loved ones in case of any unfortunate circumstances.

Emergency Fund: An emergency fund is an essential component of long-term financial security. Aim to build an emergency fund that covers at least three to six months' worth of living expenses. This fund acts as a safety net during unforeseen events, such as job loss or major medical expenses. Having an emergency fund helps you avoid accumulating debt during difficult times and provides peace of mind.

By incorporating these practices into your financial strategy, you lay the groundwork for long-term stability and security. Taking steps towards retirement planning, insurance coverage, estate planning, and building an emergency fund sets you on a path towards financial freedom and ensures that you can enjoy the fruits of your labor well into the future.

Chapter **5**

Internships and Experience: Laying the Foundation

***

The Importance of Internships:

Internships play a crucial role in laying the foundation for future success. They provide young adults with valuable hands-on experience, industry insights, and networking opportunities that are essential for personal growth and professional development.

One of the key benefits of internships is the opportunity to gain practical experience in a specific field or industry. Unlike classroom learning, internships allow individuals to apply their knowledge and skills in real-world settings. This hands-on experience not only enhances technical abilities but also fosters problem-solving, critical thinking, and decision-making skills that are highly valued by employers.

Internships also offer a unique chance to gain industry knowledge and understand the intricacies of different roles and responsibilities. By working alongside professionals in their chosen field, individuals can observe firsthand how theoretical concepts translate into practical applications. This exposure helps them develop a deep understanding of the industry's trends, challenges, and best practices, setting them apart from other job applicants.

Furthermore, internships provide unparalleled networking opportunities. By immersing themselves in a professional environment, interns can connect with industry experts, mentors, and potential employers. Building relationships with experienced professionals not only opens doors for future job opportunities but also allows for valuable mentorship and guidance that can shape their career paths.

Internships also serve as a valuable platform for individuals to discover their interests, strengths, and desired career paths. By trying out different roles and industries through internships, young adults can gain clarity about their passions and professional aspirations. This self-discovery process enables them to make informed decisions about their future career choices.

In summary, internships are instrumental in building a solid foundation for future success. By providing hands-on experience, industry knowledge, and networking opportunities, internships contribute to personal growth, skill development, and career exploration. Young adults who actively seek internship opportunities position themselves for long-term success by gaining invaluable experiences that set them apart in an increasingly competitive job market.

Finding and Applying for Internships: This section provides practical guidance on finding and applying for internships. It goes beyond the traditional advice of searching for opportunities online or through personal networks, delving into lesser-known strategies and techniques to stand out from the cometition.

1. Unconventional Sources: While online platforms and networking are valuable resources, this section encourages readers to think outside the box when searching for internships. It suggests exploring industry-specific forums, attending career fairs and industry events, and reaching out directly to companies or organizations of interest. By expanding their search methods, readers can uncover hidden internship opportunities that may not be widely advertised.

2. Crafting an Attention-Grabbing Resume: This section provides tips on creating a resume that catches employers' attention. It emphasizes the importance of tailoring resumes to each internship opportunity by highlighting relevant skills, experiences, and achievements. Furthermore, it offers guidance on structuring resumes effectively, using action verbs, and quantifying accomplishments wherever possible. By showcasing their unique qualifications, readers can increase their chances of getting noticed by employers.

3. Writing a Standout Cover Letter: In addition to a compelling resume, this section explores the art of writing a standout cover letter. It guides readers in crafting a personalized letter that demonstrates their enthusiasm for the internship and showcases their strengths and potential

contributions. It also provides tips on addressing any gaps in experience or qualifications and expressing a willingness to learn and grow. By conveying their passion and dedication through a well-crafted cover letter, readers can make a lasting impression on employers.

4. Interview Success Strategies: This section offers practical advice for interview preparation and success. It covers researching the company or organization, preparing responses to common interview questions, practicing with mock interviews, and honing non-verbal communication skills like body language and eye contact. Additionally, it highlights the importance of asking thoughtful questions during the interview to demonstrate engagement and interest. By mastering these interview strategies, readers can confidently showcase their qualifications and increase their chances of landing an internship.

5. Showcasing Transferable Skills: This section addresses the challenge of showcasing relevant skills and experiences when lacking direct internship experience. It encourages readers to identify transferable skills acquired through part-time jobs, extracurricular activities, volunteer work, or coursework. By highlighting these transferable skills and connecting them to the internship role, readers can demonstrate their potential value to employers even without prior internship experience.

By covering these areas in the "Finding and Applying for Internships" section, this chapter provides comprehensive guidance on navigating the internship search process. It equips readers with unique strategies to find internships beyond traditional methods, craft attention-grabbing resumes and cover letters, excel in interviews, and showcase transferable skills that make them standout candidates for internships.

Maximizing Your Internship Experience: This section emphasizes the importance of setting clear goals and expectations during an internship. It guides readers on how to define their objectives for the internship, whether it's gaining specific skills, expanding their network, or exploring potential career paths. By setting these goals, individuals can maximize the value they derive from their experience and stay focused on what they hope to achieve.

Seeking feedback and mentorship is also crucial during an internship. This section provides advice on actively seeking feedback from supervisors and colleagues to understand areas for improvement and capitalize on strengths. It encourages readers to take advantage of mentorship opportunities within their internship, whether it's through formal programs or informal relationships with experienced professionals. By actively seeking guidance and input, individuals can enhance their learning and development throughout the internship.

Engaging in projects and tasks with enthusiasm and dedication is another key aspect of maximizing an internship experience. This section offers strategies for taking on responsibilities proactively, approaching tasks with a positive mindset, and demonstrating a strong work ethic. It emphasizes the importance of being proactive, asking for additional assignments or projects when appropriate, and seeking opportunities to contribute beyond assigned roles. By doing so, individuals can showcase their abilities and make a lasting impression on employers.

Builing professional relationships and networking effectively are essential components of a successful internship experience. This section provides practical tips on fostering connections with colleagues, supervisors, and other professionals in the industry. It covers strategies such as attending networking events, initiating conversations, actively listening, and maintaining professionalism in all interactions. It emphasizes the importance of building a strong network during an internship that can serve as a valuable resource for future job opportunities.

Creating a positive impression in the workplace is also crucial during an internship. This section highlights the significance of professionalism, reliability, and a positive attitude. It encourages readers to demonstrate excellent communication skills, both verbally and in written form, and to be punctual and dependable. By consistently exhibiting professionalism and a positive approach, individuals can leave a lasting impression on their supervisors and colleagues, potentially leading to future opportunities or endorsements.

By discussing these strategies for maximizing an internship experience, this section ensures that readers have the tools and insights necessary to make the most out of their internships. It empowers them to set clear goals, seek feedback and mentorship, excel in their assigned tasks, build professional relationships, and leave a positive and lasting impression.

Translating Internship Experience into Future Success: This section delves into the ways in which individuals can leverage their internship experiences to enhance their future job prospects and overall career growth. While internships provide valuable hands-on experience and industry knowledge, it is crucial to effectively communicate these experiences to potential employers. This section focuses on strategies for showcasing internship achievements on resumes and LinkedIn profiles.

Firstly, it emphasizes the importance of tailoring resumes and highlighting relevant internship projects, responsibilities, and accomplishments. By clearly articulating the skills gained and outcomes achieved during internships, individuals can demonstrate their value to potential employers. Additionally, this section provides guidance on the appropriate use of keywords and action verbs to optimize resume impact.

Furthermore, this section discusses the significance of obtaining strong letters of recommendation from supervisors or mentors within the internship organization. These letters serve as endorsements of an individual's performance, work ethic, and potential for future success. It offers advice on how to approach requesting letters of recommendation and ensures individuals understand the importance of maintaining a positive impression throughout the internship duration.

In addition to resumes and letters of recommendation, this section emphasizes the utilization of internship connections for future job opportunities. Networking is a crucial aspect of professional development, and internships provide a unique platform for building relationships with industry professionals. By nurturing these connections and staying in touch with former colleagues or supervisors, individuals can tap into hidden job markets and gain insights into potential career paths.

Moreover, this section highlights the importance of continuous learning and professional development beyond the internship period. It encourages individuals to reflect on their internship experiences, identify areas for improvement, and seek opportunities to further enhance their skills or knowledge. Whether through attending workshops, participating in webinars or conferences, or pursuing additional certifications, ongoing learning showcases a commitment to personal growth and professional advancement.

By providing practical strategies for leveraging internship experiences, this section empowers individuals to actively shape their future career trajectories. It ensures that readers are equipped with the tools and knowledge needed to effectively communicate their internship experiences, build a strong professional network, and continue their development beyond the confines of the internship period.

Exploring Alternative Experiences: This section provides readers with a comprehensive exploration of alternative experiences that can complement or substitute traditional internships. It delves into various options such as volunteering, freelancing, participating in research projects, starting a side hustle, or pursuing online courses or certifications.

The section emphasizes that while internships are highly valuable, they may not always be feasible or available for every individual. Therefore, alternative experiences offer an opportunity to gain valuable skills, knowledge, and networking opportunities that contribute to personal and professional growth.

By considering volunteering opportunities, individuals can engage in meaningful projects and contribute to causes they care about. This not only develops their skills but also showcases their dedication and commitment to giving back to the community.

Freelancing allows individuals to gain real-world experience by taking on independent projects in their desired field. This experience not only helps build technical skills but also develops communication, project management, and entrepreneurial abilities.

Participating in research projects, whether through academic institutions or independent initiatives, offers a chance to delve deep into a specific subject matter and develop critical thinking and analytical skills. Research experiences also provide opportunities to collaborate with professionals and make valuable connections within the field.

Starting a side hustle allows individuals to explore their entrepreneurial spirit and gain hands-on experience in running a business. This experience can provide valuable insights into marketing, financial management, customer relations, and problem-solving.

Pursuing online courses or certifications allows individuals to learn new skills or deepen their knowledge in a specific area of interest. Online platforms offer a wealth of resources and qualifications that can be pursued at one's own pace and convenience.

Using these alternative experiences creatively and strategically can help individuals build a strong foundation for future success. They provide opportunities to develop essential skills, expand professional networks, and demonstrate adaptability and initiative.

By including this section in the chapter on "Internships and Experience: Laying the Foundation," readers gain valuable insights into the various paths they can explore to gain experience and enhance their personal and professional growth.

Part 4:
Relationships
and Social Life

Chapter 1

Choosing Your Circle:
Relationships that Elevate
*****

The Importance of Choosing the Right Circle

This chapter e-xplores the importance of cultivating re-lationships with empowering individuals and how that can dee-ply influence our personal and care-er developme-nt. The company we kee-p can either encourage- and assist us or hinder us from achieving our highest abilitie-s.

The re-lationships in our lives have immense- power to impact who we become-. The friends, mentors and partne-rs we surround ourselves with shape- our views and help dete-rmine the paths we walk. By re-flecting on the connections we- currently have, we gain insight into whe-ther these bonds are- aiding our advancement or holding us back. Our circle influe-nces what we belie-ve, how we see- the world and what we dare to dre-am for our future. Taking stock of who stands with us now reveals what influe-nces are truly empowe-ring our journey ahead versus what drags us down the- road. Understanding the roles our re-lationships play can grant us clarity to either strengthe-n alliances propelling positivity or redire-ct energy from ties taxing our progre-ss toward what call us.

This narrative e-xplores how relationships impact individual deve-lopment, both personally and professionally. Supportive- relationships offer indispensable- direction, motivation, and assistance that propel growth. In contrast, harmful or unsupportive- relationships deplete- one's energy, diminish confide-nce, and hinder advanceme-nt toward objectives. By thoughtfully considering those- around us, readers can make sure- they inhabit a setting that cultivates se-lf-improvement and caree-r flourishing.

Through these- pages, we invite you to ponde-r the traits you hope to find in your bonds with others. Re-gard, faith, and backing are core bases for sound frie-ndships and loving couplings. We share suggestions for spotting balance-d relationships, including proofs of truth, true care, and e-quitableness. By knowing about danger signs and alarms of unhe-althy relationships - such as control, mistreatment, or lack of e-steem - reade-rs can make educated choice-s about which ties to cultivate and which to rele-ase.

Ultimately, we- aim to bring awareness to considering the- harmony between inve-sting in bonds with others and pursuing self-improveme-nt. Although robust relationships are esse-ntial for a meaningful life, it is just as crucial to prese-rve uniqueness and e-mphasize individual progress. We propose- approaches for attaining this equilibrium productively – acce-ntuating the necessity of se-lf-care, retaining autonomy, and straightforward dialog with cherishe-d people.

When conside-ring how our relationships affect personal and care-er developme-nt, carefully assessing existing conne-ctions and deliberately opting to associate- with uplifting people establishe-s the basis for a supportive network that drive-s progress towards accomplishing goals. Through recognizing influence- of relationships on self and professional e-volution, evaluating current bonds, and intentionally se-lecting encouraging individuals to surround onese-lf with, one will lay the foundation for a supportive ne-twork that propels movement towards achie-vement.

Identifying Healthy Relationships

In crafting a meaningful and accomplishe-d existence, the- bonds we form serve a pivotal function. Nurturing, uplifting re-lationships offer the backing, caring, and inspiration nece-ssary to blossom in both individual and career pursuits. Yet disce-rning these relationships and compre-hending the traits rende-ring them constructive remains crucial. The- following principles may aid recognition of healthy, positive- relations:

1. Estee-m Each Other: A thriving relationship should be base-d on esteeming one- another. Both sides should appreciate- each other's perspe-ctives, limits, and choices. Estee-m permits straightforward and honest corresponde-nce, cultivating an air of trust and comprehension.
2. Faith and Depe-ndability: Faith is the cornerstone of any powe-rful relationship. It signifies having assurance in anothe-r's personality, behaviors, and aims. A sound relationship should also include- dependability, where- both parties can rely on one anothe-r and feel certain that the-ir needs will be addre-ssed.
3. Supportive Surroundings: He-althy relationships furnish a nurturing environment whe-re individuals can blossom and prosper. This involves e-motional backing, motivation, and applauding each other's triumphs. In a good relationship, both side-s boost and stir one another to attain their comple-te capacity.
4. Reciprocity: Healthy relationships are built on reciprocity, meaning that both parties contribute equally and receive benefits in return. There should be a balance of give-and-take, with both individuals investing time, effort, and resources into the relationship.

While asse-ssing relationships, awareness of dange-r signals and cautionary indications of toxic connections proves prudent. Such signs pote-ntially betray an unbalanced rapport that risks emotional or bodily injury. Fre-quent danger signals encompass:

1. Guidance: If you notice- someone consistently ste-ering or directing your emotions, activitie-s, or choices against your will, it may indicate an unbalanced partne-rship. Guiding behavior strives to diminish your indepe-ndence and constrain your individual unfolding.

Respe-ct is vital for building trust between individuals. Whe-n one party consistently fails to honor another's pe-rspectives or personal space-, it undermines the re-lationship's foundation. Healthy bonds require both partie-s feel heard and value- each other's views, e-ven if they sometime-s differ. Disregarding another's boundarie-s, opinions, or core principles erode-s goodwill and breeds rese-ntment over time. To cultivate- understanding betwee-n any two people, honoring each pe-rson's autonomy and validity is key.

2. Abusive Behavior: Physical, emotional, or verbal abuse should never be tolerated in any relationship. If you experience or witness any form of abuse, it is crucial to seek help and distance yourself from the toxic situation.

While maintaining e-quilibrium is essential for healthy re-lationships, imbalance deserve-s understanding. If one finds themse-lves regularly giving more than gaining, or the- other habitually profits from kindness, this could signal a relationship lacking re-ciprocity. Before judgment, re-flect with compassion: are nee-ds and gifts being shared, or is one e-xploiting the other's gene-rosity? True connection require-s effort from all sides. With openne-ss and care, discuss perceptions re-spectfully; rebalancing may eme-rge through deepe-r listening.

Distinguishing nourishing relationships is a fundame-ntal move towards crafting a supportive system that lifts up your individual improve-ment and general prospe-rity. By comprehending these- rules and perceiving cautioning signs, you can cultivate- relationships that convey optimismo, motivation, and fulfillment to your life-. Recollect, surrounding yourself with the- proper individuals will empower you to turn into the- most ideal form of yourself.

Cultivating Supportive Friendships:

I have always found that cultivating strong bonds with pe-ople who share my priorities and ambitions plays a pivotal role- in my development. Those- in my network who think like me and have- comparable aims have significantly shaped my achie-vements and gene-ral welfare. Whethe-r assisting me to overcome obstacle-s or simply providing perspective, my value-d compatriots meaningfully contribute to my journey.

To cultivate supportive friendships, consider the following strategies:

1. Find Shared Passions: Look for chance-s to bond with others who share your enthusiasms and le-isure activities. Sign up for groups, associations, or online ne-tworks focused on things that fascinate you. Taking part in mutual intere-sts gives a natural base for constructing solid affiliations.

Being your authe-ntic self is crucial for building real friendships. Show your true- personality without hiding behind a facade. Fe-el comfortable showing vulnerability by ope-nly sharing life experie-nces, views, and emotions. Forming conne-ctions in this way helps you find people who appre-ciate you for everything that you are-. Don't be afraid to let others se-e the real you through hone-st self-expression. Authe-nticity is what makes friendships genuine-.

Deve-loping strong relationships is built on clear communication. As friends, we- must make an effort to truly understand e-ach other by actively listening with e-mpathy. Maintain eye contact and show your intere-st by asking thoughtful questions to learn more about the-ir experience-s. Offer supportive response-s when others share so the-y feel heard. By paying atte-ntion to what people say and giving them your undivide-d attention, strong bonds of trust will form betwee-n friends.

4. Provide Encourage-ment and Understanding: A network of caring pe-ople stands by our side in joyous moments as we-ll as difficult days. Be present for othe-rs, cheer their accomplishme-nts, and lend a compassionate ear whe-n times are tough. Demonstrate- understanding by imagining how they might fee-l and giving reassurance with hopeful words.

Trustworthiness and alle-giance are esse-ntial for enduring bonds. Relationships are built on re-liability, discretion with private matters, and ke-eping promises. Earning trust nece-ssitates honesty, consistency, and re-spect. Loyalty is equally important - backing friends during tough time-s, protecting their good name, and upholding the-m without reserve.

When issue-s arise betwee-n friends, addressing them re-spectfully is key. Disagree-ments will happen with any relationship, ye-t how conflicts are dealt with can strengthe-n or damage a bond. If tensions eme-rge, bring concerns to light willingly and truthfully, though avoid accusing or fault-finding. See-k solutions together in a cooperative- spirit, aiming for fairness and benefit for all involve-d. Working through difficulties with care, understanding and compromise- nourishes long-term trust.

7. Chee-r Your Friends On: Continuously encourage and motivate- your friends. Applaud their accomplishments, root for the-m in their goals, and be their bigge-st fan. By truly rejoicing in their successe-s, you cultivate a beneficial and e-ncouraging friendship where you have- one another's backs.

Cultivating supportive frie-ndships takes work and commitment. Make building the-se relationships a priority by spending quality time- with people who motivate, push your limits, and ce-lebrate your wins. With genuine- friends, you'll construct a solid support system propelling you towards se-lf-improvement and accomplishment.

Navigating Romantic Relationships

Connecting with anothe-r in a romantic way profoundly impacts our lives, notably affecting our contentme-nt but also our individual evolution. In this part, let us investigate- the essentials for nurturing sound and re-warding romantic bonds, discussing regular tests, and dete-rmining restrictions to confirm shared regard and assistance-.

1. Cultivating Healthy Relationships

Effective- communication plays a key role in building strong relationships. Foste-ring an environment where- open and honest conversations can fre-ely occur betwee-n partners is essential. By cultivating trust and unde-rstanding through open communication, relationships are give-n the room to thrive.

Both parties: Establish a foundation of common value-s and objectives. Discuss your dreams, principle-s and hopes to guarantee consiste-ncy and harmony.

- ✓ **Trust and Respe-ct:** Reliability, transparency, and respe-ct for boundaries, thoughts, and feelings lay the- foundation for any healthy bond betwee-n individuals. Cultivating trust demands that we kee-p our word and remain open while acce-pting differences of opinion or pre-ference.

2. Balancing Personal Goals and Relationships

RephraseWhile in a romantic re-lationship, it is important to nurture individual growth and allow space for personal pursuits. Encourage- your partner to explore the-ir unique interests and support the-ir goals. Maintaining a sense of individual identity within the- connection can enrich the bond through share-d experience-s and mutual understanding.

When making de-cisions together, find a balance be-tween addressing your own ne-eds while also considering your partne-r's wants. Collaborate to choose options that work well for the- two of you.

3. Managing Conflicts

Rephrase Conflicts are an ine-vitable part of any relationship. It is important to learn strate-gies for resolving disagree-ments effective-ly, such as active listening, finding compromise, and se-eking

75

solutions where all partie-s win. By listening to understand each othe-r's perspectives in a disagre-ement, we can ide-ntify areas for potential compromise. Compromise- often involves give and take- from both sides. The most satisfactory resolutions

Rephrase - Establishing Cle-ar Limits: It is important to set clear boundaries and communicate-your expectations openly in orde-r to promote respect and pre-vent conflicts from escalating. Make sure- to make your boundaries known so

4. Setting Boundaries

Rephrase- Establishing Emotional Support Le-vels: It is important to understand each partne-r's needs for emotional intimacy and privacy. Communicate- openly about how much care, affection and alone- time each person re-quires to feel se-cure and balanced in the re-lationship. Healthy boundaries strengthe-n trust when it comes to personal matte-rs, socializing independently, or sharing the-innermost

Rephrase - Managing Your Time- Wisely: It's important to find the right balance be-tween investing quality mome-nts with each other and indepe-ndently pursuing personal hobbies or time- with

Each person de-serves time alone- to recharge and pursue individual inte-rests. Respect e-ach other's need for pe-rsonal space and alone time to follow se-parate hobbies and passions. Allow space for inde-pendent activities that e-nrich your partner as an individual.

Building a romantic connection ne-cessitates work, insight, and concession from both individuals involve-d. By establishing significance on candid dialogue, de-pendability, mutual principles, and sound limitations, a couple can de-velop a robust base for a fulfilling and mutually supportive bond. It is pivotal to be- straightforward with one another regarding de-sires and aims to guarantee a harmonious and prospe-rous collaboration. What matters most is prioritizing comprehension be-tween partners through ope-n lines of communication.

Balancing Relationships and Personal Growth:

On life's journe-y toward success, keeping individuality and se-lf-growth within relationships is key. Relationships offe-r support, camaraderie, and shared adve-ntures, but balancing time for others and pe-rsonal aims is vital. While relationships nourish us, negle-cting one's own needs and dre-ams risks losing oneself. With care and compromise-, close bonds and personal fulfillment can coe-xist for a rich, balanced life.

One key aspect of balancing relationships and personal growth is prioritizing self-care. It is important to remember that taking care of oneself physically, mentally, and emotionally is necessary for overall well-being. This means setting aside time for activities that bring joy, relaxation, and rejuvenation. By prioritizing self-care, individuals can maintain their own happiness and avoid becoming overly dependent on others for their well-being.

Upholding autonomy inside re-lationships is equally crucial. It is easy for personal aims and visions to take- a rear seat when pe-ople are profoundly investe-d in their connections. Howeve-r, it is vital to recollect that individual progress doe-s not need to be re-linquished for the bene-fit of the relationship. Healthy re-lationships are constructed on shared re-spect, trust, and backing for every othe-r's aspirations. By upholding independence- and pursuing personal goals, people can continue- developing and progressing as individuals while- nurturing their relationships.

Establishing proficient communication is anothe-r pivotal facet of balancing relationships and individual progress. It is impe-rative to articulate one's re-quirements, wants, and limitations evide-ntly with their companion or cherished one-s. By sincerely examining pe-rsonal aims and aspirations, persons can collaborate to fashion a supportive e-nvironment that permits both individual progress and whole-some relationships.

Achieving e-quilibrium between prioritizing re-lationships and pursuing self-directed aims ne-cessitates proficient time- administration abilities. It may require allotting de-dicated time for solo intere-sts and being aware of how time is spe-nt with cherished people-. By establishing a routine that makes provisions for both high-quality time- with cherished people- and concentrated time for pe-rsonal progression, individuals can locate a balanced state- that is useful for both parts of their life.

Ultimately, acce-pting the notion of interconnecte-dness can help achieve- equilibrium in relationships and individual progress. Inte-rconnectedness signifie-s identifying that even though we- are solitary beings with our personal aims and ambitions, we- also depend on others for e-ncouragement, counsel, and care-. By embracing interconnecte-dness, people can cultivate- their bonds while still putting individual progress at the- forefront. It incorporates acknowledging that individual progre-ss can be enriched through the- links and lessons gained from our relationships.

Ultimately, achie-ving equilibrium betwee-n bonds with others and self-improveme-nt is pivotal for enduring achieveme-nt and satisfaction. Focusing on self-care, upholding autonomy, engaging in productive- dialog, judiciously allocating time, and embracing interre-liance allows people to e-xpertly handle the nuance-s of connections while chasing their private- objectives. Recall, one- can cultivate robust and significant relationships while still accomplishing pe-rsonal evolution and accomplishment.

Chapter **2**

Communication Skills
for Lasting Relationships
****

Communication Skills for Lasting Relationships:

Communication plays a crucial role in building and maintaining lasting relationships. It is the foundation upon which trust, understanding, and intimacy are built. By effectively communicating with our partners, friends, and family members, we can foster healthy connections and create a sense of belonging.

Effective communication involves more than just speaking; it requires active listening, nonverbal cues, and empathy. Active listening means fully engaging in the conversation by giving our undivided attention, maintaining eye contact, and asking clarifying questions. Nonverbal cues, such as facial expressions and body language, also play a significant role in communication. Being aware of these cues helps us understand the emotions and intentions behind the words being spoken.

Expressing our thoughts and emotions clearly and respectfully is essential for effective communication. Clearly articulating our needs, desires, and concerns allows others to understand us better. Using "I" statements instead of "you" statements can help avoid blame or defensiveness in conversations. Additionally, practicing active self-reflection can help us become more aware of our own communication patterns and identify areas for improvement.

By focusing on these foundational elements of effective communication, we can strengthen our relationships by fostering open and honest dialogue. This approach creates an environment where both parties feel heard and valued, ultimately leading to deeper connections and greater relationship satisfaction.

Conflict Resolution Techniques:

Conflicts are an inevitable part of any relationship, whether it's a romantic partnership, friendship, or familial bond. However, what sets successful relationships apart is the ability to address conflicts and find resolutions through effective communication. In this section, we will explore common sources of conflict and provide techniques to address them constructively.

1. Recognizing the Naturalness of Conflict:

Conflict should not be viewed as a sign of failure or an indication that the relationship is flawed. Instead, conflicts are opportunities for growth and understanding. By reframing conflicts as opportunities for improvement rather than threats, individuals can approach them with a more positive mindset.

2. Identifying Common Sources of Conflict:

Conflict can arise from various sources, including differences in values, expectations, communication styles, and priorities. It is crucial to acknowledge and understand these differences to develop effective strategies for resolution. Taking the time to identify the root causes of conflict can help prevent recurring issues in the future.

3. Active Listening and Empathy:

Active listening is a fundamental skill in conflict resolution. It involves fully engaging in the conversation by giving undivided attention to the speaker, maintaining eye contact, and showing genuine interest. Additionally, practicing empathy allows individuals to understand and validate the other person's perspective, even if they don't agree with it. This fosters a sense of mutual respect and helps create a safe space for open dialogue.

4. Finding Win-Win Solutions:

In conflict resolution, it is essential to shift from viewing conflicts as win-lose situations to seeking win-win solutions. This involves finding creative alternatives that address the needs and concerns of both parties involved. By brainstorming mutually beneficial solutions and using negotiation techniques, individuals can work towards a resolution that satisfies everyone involved.

5. Compromise and Flexibility:

Compromise plays a vital role in resolving conflicts. It requires individuals to be open-minded and willing to find middle ground that meets the needs of both parties. Recognizing that not every conflict can be resolved with a perfect solution is important, as compromise often involves finding a balance that may not entirely satisfy either party but allows for progress and growth.

By developing these conflict resolution techniques and practicing effective communication skills, individuals can navigate conflicts in their relationships more constructively. Conflict should be seen as an opportunity to strengthen bonds, deepen understanding, and find creative solutions that promote long-lasting and fulfilling relationships.

Building Trust and Deepening Connections:

✓ Trust is the foundation of any strong and lasting relationship. It is built upon open and honest communication, where both parties feel heard, respected, and valued. By being transparent and genuine in our interactions, we can establish trust with others. This means being honest about our thoughts, feelings, and intentions, even if it feels vulnerable or uncomfortable.

✓ Building intimacy and deepening emotional connections requires effort and intentionality. It involves creating a safe space where both individuals can be themselves without fear of judgment or rejection. By actively listening to one another, expressing empathy, and validating each other's experiences, we can foster emotional closeness and strengthen our bond.

✓ Vulnerability and authenticity are essential ingredients in building strong and lasting relationships. When we allow ourselves to be vulnerable with others, we invite them to do the same. This vulnerability creates an opportunity for deeper connection and understanding. Authenticity is about being true to ourselves and staying genuine in our interactions. It means showing up as our authentic selves, without pretending to be someone we're not.

To build trust and deepen connections with others, it is crucial to prioritize open and honest communication, actively listen and understand each other's perspectives, and foster an environment of acceptance and support. By doing so, we can cultivate relationships that are built on trust, intimacy, vulnerability, and authenticity, leading to long-lasting and fulfilling connections.

In different types of relationships, such as romantic relationships, friendships, and familial relationships, unique communication challenges often arise. Understanding how to adapt communication styles to meet the needs of different individuals and relationship dynamics is crucial for fostering positive connections.

In romantic relationships, effective communication plays a pivotal role in building trust, enhancing intimacy, and resolving conflicts. Couples may face challenges in expressing their needs and desires clearly, leading to misunderstandings or unmet expectations. By being open and honest with each other, partners can create an environment of trust and understanding. It's important to actively listen to one another, validate emotions, and show empathy towards each other's perspectives. Moreover, finding healthy ways to communicate during times of stress or conflict is essential. This includes practicing patience, taking breaks when needed, and maintaining a calm and respectful tone.

When it comes to friendships, individuals must adapt their communication styles to accommodate the unique dynamics of each friendship. Some friends may require frequent check-ins and emotional support, while others may prefer more independence. By being attuned to the needs and preferences of friends, individuals can build stronger connections. Effective communication involves actively listening, showing genuine interest in their lives, and providing support when needed. Additionally, resolving conflicts within friendships requires open and honest conversations where both parties feel heard and respected.

Within familial relationships, effective communication is vital for maintaining strong bonds and resolving conflicts that naturally arise. Each member of a family may have their own communication style, making it necessary to adapt and find common ground. Active listening and practicing empathy are key components of effective communication within families. It's important to create a safe space where all family members feel comfortable expressing their thoughts and emotions. During times of stress or conflict, finding strategies for open dialogue can help resolve issues and strengthen family ties.

By exploring the unique communication challenges present in different types of relationships and understanding how to adapt communication styles accordingly, readers can foster healthier connections with those around them. The book offers strategies and guidance on effective communication during times of stress or conflict, empowering readers to build lasting and fulfilling relationships in all areas of their lives.

Developing Healthy Boundaries and Assertiveness:

Understanding the importance of setting boundaries in relationships is crucial for maintaining healthy dynamics. Boundaries define acceptable behavior, protect one's emotional well-being, and promote mutual respect. In this section, we will explore effective strategies for establishing and communicating boundaries in different types of relationships.

Firstly, it is important to understand your own needs, desires, and limits before communicating them to others. Take the time to reflect on what is important to you and how you want to be treated in your relationships. This self-awareness will serve as a solid foundation for setting boundaries confidently.

To effectively communicate your boundaries, it is essential to be clear, direct, and assertive. Clearly express your expectations and limits using "I" statements to avoid sounding accusatory or confrontational. For example, instead of saying, "You always interrupt me," try saying, "I feel disrespected when I am interrupted." This approach focuses on your feelings rather than placing blame on the other person.

When addressing a boundary issue within a relationship, choose an appropriate time and place for the conversation. Find a calm and private setting where both parties can express themselves without distractions. Approach the discussion with empathy and understanding, acknowledging that the other person may not have been aware of the boundary. Listen actively to their perspective, allowing open dialogue and seeking compromise when possible.

Navigating situations where boundaries are crossed can be challenging. It is important to address these instances promptly and assertively. Start by stating your discomfort or concern using respectful language. Express how the crossed boundary has affected you personally and emphasize your desire for a resolution that respects both parties' needs and boundaries.

Remember that asserting boundaries does not mean cutting off all communication or severing the relationship entirely. Instead, it allows for growth and mutual respect within the relationship. Recognize that healthy relationships involve ongoing dialogue about boundaries as individuals evolve and grow.

In conclusion, developing healthy boundaries and assertiveness is vital for maintaining positive relationships. By understanding the importance of boundaries, learning effective communication techniques, and addressing boundary violations promptly and respectfully, individuals can establish and maintain healthy dynamics in all types of relationships.

Chapter **3**

Setting Boundaries:
The Key to Healthy Relationships

****

Understanding the Importance of Boundaries:

In this section, we delve into the significance of boundaries and why they play a pivotal role in maintaining healthy relationships. Boundaries serve as the invisible lines that define our personal limits, values, and needs. By setting and respecting boundaries, we can enhance communication, foster mutual respect, and establish a solid foundation of trust within our relationships.

Boundaries are essential because they help us protect our emotional well-being. They act as a safeguard against being taken advantage of, manipulated, or disrespected by others. When we have clear boundaries in place, we can effectively communicate our needs and expectations, ensuring that our relationships are built on honesty, openness, and reciprocity.

Moreover, boundaries help create a sense of balance and autonomy in our relationships. They allow us to maintain individuality while also fostering intimacy and connection with others. When both parties involved in a relationship understand and respect each other's boundaries, it strengthens the bond between them and promotes a healthy dynamic where both individuals feel heard, valued, and understood.

Recognizing the importance of boundaries is the first step towards establishing healthy relationships. It empowers us to take control of our own happiness and well-being while cultivating trust, mutual understanding, and respect with those around us. Through setting and respecting boundaries, we can create an environment that is conducive to positive growth, effective communication, and long-lasting connections.

Identifying Your Personal Boundaries:

This section delves into the importance of self-awareness and introspection in identifying personal boundaries. It encourages readers to reflect on their needs, values, and limits in various types of relationships, such as romantic, platonic, and professional. By engaging in practical exercises and prompts, readers are prompted to explore their comfort zones and define their boundaries.

Through these exercises, readers are encouraged to consider questions such as:

- ✓ What are my core values and beliefs?
- ✓ What behaviors, actions, or words make me uncomfortable or violate my boundaries?
- ✓ What are my non-negotiables in relationships?
- ✓ How do I want to be treated by others?

By actively engaging with these questions, readers gain a deeper understanding of themselves and the boundaries they need to establish in order to maintain healthy relationships. The exercises in this section provide a framework for readers to become more aware of their own needs and assert them in a clear and confident manner.

It is important to note that personal boundaries are unique to each individual. While some may have strict boundaries around certain behaviors or actions, others may have more flexible boundaries. This section encourages readers to embrace their individuality and define their personal boundaries based on their values and emotional well-being.

Furthermore, examples of different types of personal boundaries are provided to help readers navigate this reflection process effectively. These examples serve as guiding points but also encourage readers to develop their own set of boundaries that align with their values, priorities, and comfort levels.

By engaging in this self-reflection exercise, readers can establish a strong foundation for healthy relationships built on mutual respect, trust, and understanding. Identifying personal boundaries sets the stage for effective communication and ensures that individuals enter into relationships with a clear sense of what is acceptable and what is not.

Communicating Boundaries Effectively: This section focuses on the importance of effective communication when it comes to expressing boundaries. It offers practical strategies that readers can implement in order to communicate their boundaries clearly, assertively, and respectfully.

One key aspect of communicating boundaries effectively is using "I" statements. By starting sentences with "I," individuals can express their needs and preferences without sounding accusatory or confrontational. For example, instead of saying, "You always interrupt me when I'm talking," a more effective approach would be to say, "I feel frustrated when I get interrupted while speaking."

Active listening is another crucial component of effective boundary communication. This involves giving full attention to the other person, maintaining eye contact, and showing genuine interest in what they have to say. By actively listening, individuals demonstrate respect for the other person's perspective and create an open space for dialogue.

Non-verbal cues also play a significant role in boundary communication. Body language, such as maintaining appropriate personal space and using assertive posture, can support the verbal expression of boundaries. Additionally, individuals should pay attention to their tone of voice, making sure it is firm but not aggressive or hostile.

It is important for individuals to consider the feelings and perspectives of others when communicating their boundaries. While asserting boundaries is necessary for self-care and maintaining healthy relationships, being empathetic towards others' reactions can contribute to a more compassionate and understanding conversation. By acknowledging the potential impact on the other person and expressing empathy, individuals can foster a sense of mutual respect and cooperation.

By providing practical strategies for effective boundary communication, this section equips readers with the tools they need to express their boundaries confidently and assertively while considering the thoughts and feelings of others.

Navigating Boundary Violations:

In this section of "Setting Boundaries: The Key to Healthy Relationships," we will explore the challenges that can arise when others disrespect or cross our established boundaries. It is essential to address these boundary violations constructively in order to maintain healthy relationships. By implementing the strategies provided in this chapter, readers will be equipped to handle these conflicts effectively and protect their personal boundaries.

One strategy for addressing boundary violations is to set consequences. Clearly communicating the consequences for crossing boundaries helps reinforce the importance of respecting them. By establishing these consequences in advance, individuals ensure they are prepared to follow through with appropriate actions if their boundaries are violated. This not only protects their own well-being but also sets clear expectations for the other party involved.

Seeking support from trusted individuals is another valuable strategy for navigating boundary violations. It can be helpful to discuss the situation with a friend, family member, or mentor who can provide guidance and perspective. These individuals can offer objective advice and support, helping individuals determine the best course of action to address the violation while maintaining their personal boundaries.

Practicing self-care is crucial when dealing with boundary violations. It is important to prioritize one's own well-being and take steps to restore a sense of balance and peace. Engaging in activities that bring joy, practicing mindfulness or meditation, and seeking professional help if necessary are all ways to nurture oneself during challenging times. Remember, taking care of one's own needs allows for better emotional and mental resilience when facing boundary-related conflicts.

Real-life scenarios and examples are provided throughout this section to help readers understand how to navigate common boundary-related conflicts. By examining these scenarios, readers can gain insights into effective communication techniques and problem-solving strategies specific to boundary violations. These real-life examples serve as practical applications of the concepts discussed in earlier parts of the book.

By addressing these boundary violations constructively, readers can maintain healthier relationships and protect their personal well-being. The strategies outlined in this section provide a foundation for handling conflicts that may arise, allowing individuals to navigate boundary-related challenges with confidence and assertiveness. Remember, setting boundaries is an essential aspect of building strong, respectful relationships, and addressing violations is crucial for maintaining these boundaries effectively.

Maintaining Healthy Boundaries in the Long Term: It is crucial to regularly reassess and adjust boundaries as relationships evolve. Boundaries are not set in stone; they need to be flexible to accommodate changing circumstances and dynamics. By regularly reflecting on our boundaries, we can ensure that they continue to align with our needs, values, and personal growth.

One key aspect of maintaining healthy boundaries is recognizing signs of unhealthy boundaries. Unhealthy boundaries often manifest in codependent or enabling behaviors, where one person becomes overly reliant on another and compromises their own well-being. Being aware of these signs can help us identify when our boundaries may be becoming blurred or unhealthy.

To reinforce and maintain healthy boundaries over time, it is important to practice self-care and prioritize our own well-being. This means setting aside time for ourselves, engaging in activities that bring us joy and fulfillment, and asserting our needs without guilt. When we take care of ourselves, we are better able to establish and maintain boundaries that promote healthier relationships.

Regular communication is also key in maintaining healthy boundaries. As relationships evolve, it is important to have open and honest conversations with the people in our lives about our boundaries. This can involve discussing any changes or adjustments that need to be made and ensuring that both parties feel heard and understood.

Additionally, seeking support from trusted individuals can be helpful in maintaining healthy boundaries. Sometimes, we may need guidance or a sounding board to navigate boundary-related conflicts or challenges. By reaching out to trusted friends, family members, or even professionals, we can gain valuable insights and perspectives that help us reinforce and maintain our boundaries.

In summary, maintaining healthy boundaries in the long term requires regular reassessment and adjustment as relationships evolve. Recognizing signs of unhealthy boundaries, practicing self-care, engaging in open communication, and seeking support when needed are all essential components of maintaining healthy boundaries. By prioritizing our own well-being and being proactive in reinforcing our boundaries, we can foster healthier relationships and minimize conflicts in the long run.

Understanding the Importance of Empathy

Empathy, the ability to understand and share the feelings of another person, is a crucial skill for personal growth and professional success. By genuinely connecting with others and understanding their perspectives, we can build meaningful relationships, foster effective communication, and navigate conflicts with grace and compassion.

Research has shown that empathy plays a vital role in various aspects of our lives. In personal relationships, empathy fosters deeper connection and understanding between individuals. It allows us to truly listen to others, validating their emotions and experiences. By acknowledging and validating someone's feelings, we show them that they are seen and heard, which strengthens trust and emotional bonds.

In the workplace, empathy has been linked to improved teamwork and collaboration. When we recognize and acknowledge the emotions of our colleagues, we create a supportive environment where open communication and cooperation thrive. This leads to increased productivity, creativity, and overall job satisfaction.

Empathy also plays a significant role in conflict resolution. By putting ourselves in another person's shoes, we gain insight into their perspective and motivations. This helps us approach conflicts with empathy and understanding, seeking mutually beneficial solutions rather than escalating tensions. Empathy enables us to listen actively, acknowledge the other person's feelings, and find common ground for resolution.

To illustrate the power of empathy, consider a scenario where a coworker is experiencing difficulty meeting deadlines due to personal reasons. Instead of simply judging their performance or becoming frustrated, practicing empathy allows us to understand the underlying challenges they face. By showing support, offering assistance or flexibility when necessary, we not only alleviate their stress but also strengthen the mutual respect and camaraderie within the team.

In personal relationships, empathy can be transformative. For example, imagine a situation where a friend is going through a tough time and needs a listening ear. By approaching this conversation with empathy, we can provide comfort and solace by truly understanding their feelings. Our empathetic response can make them feel supported, validated, and less alone in their struggles.

In summary, empathy is a powerful tool for fostering connection, enhancing communication, and navigating conflicts effectively. By cultivating empathy in our lives, we enhance our personal growth, strengthen relationships, and create a more compassionate and harmonious world.

Chapter 4

Cultivating Empathy and Compassion

****

Developing Self-Awareness

In this section, we delve into the crucial process of developing self-awareness as a foundation for cultivating empathy and compassion. By exploring our own emotions, biases, and perspectives, we gain valuable insights into how others may feel or think.

Self-reflection is a powerful tool that enables us to better understand ourselves and empathize with others. Taking the time to reflect on our personal experiences allows us to uncover hidden biases and assumptions, ultimately broadening our perspective and enhancing our capacity for empathy.

Practicing self-reflection techniques can enhance our empathy towards ourselves and others. One effective technique is journaling, where we can freely express our thoughts and feelings without judgment. By analyzing our own emotions and thought processes, we develop a deeper understanding of our own inner world, enabling us to empathize with others on a more profound level.

Another technique is mindfulness meditation, which involves being fully present in the moment and observing our thoughts and emotions without judgment. Through regular practice, we become more attuned to our own feelings and can better recognize and empathize with the emotions of others.

It is important to approach self-reflection with an open mind and a willingness to challenge our own beliefs and assumptions. By being aware of our biases and acknowledging them, we can actively work towards overcoming them and cultivating empathy towards people who have different backgrounds or opinions.

By focusing on developing self-awareness, we lay the groundwork for building empathy and compassion in our lives. With increased self-understanding, we are better equipped to connect with others, appreciate their perspectives, and respond with kindness and understanding. Through ongoing self-reflection, we continue to deepen our empathy towards ourselves and those around us, fostering harmonious relationships and a more compassionate society.

Building Empathy Skills

In order to cultivate empathy and strengthen our ability to understand and connect with others, it is essential to develop certain skills. By honing these skills, we can improve our relationships, enhance communication, and foster a greater sense of empathy in our daily interactions.

One of the key skills that contributes to building empathy is active listening. Active listening involves not only hearing the words being spoken, but also making a conscious effort to truly understand the speaker's feelings and needs. To practice active listening, we must set aside distractions, maintain eye contact, and give our full attention to the person speaking. By focusing on their words, tone, and body language, we can gain valuable insights into their emotions and experiences.

Nonverbal communication cues play a significant role in understanding others' feelings as well. Observing body language, facial expressions, and gestures can provide important information about someone's emotional state. For example, crossed arms may indicate defensiveness or discomfort, while open and relaxed posture suggests receptiveness. By paying attention to these subtle cues, we can gain a deeper understanding of how others are feeling and respond accordingly with empathy.

Expressing empathy through both verbal and non-verbal expressions is another vital skill. Verbal expressions of empathy involve using phrases such as "I understand," "That must be challenging," or "I'm here for you." These statements convey our willingness to listen, support, and acknowledge the other person's emotions. Non-verbal expressions of empathy can include gentle touches, nods of understanding, or offering a comforting presence.

By practicing active listening, interpreting nonverbal cues, and expressing empathy in both verbal and non-verbal ways, we can strengthen our ability to connect with others on a deeper level. These skills not only enhance our personal relationships but also contribute to creating a more compassionate and understanding society overall.

Cultivating Compassion

In this section, we will explore the concept of compassion and its significance in building strong relationships and fostering a positive impact on others. Compassion goes beyond empathy, as it involves not only understanding and sharing someone else's emotions but also taking action to alleviate their suffering or support their well-being.

It is important to recognize the importance of caring for others' well-being and extending kindness towards them. Compassion allows us to connect with others on a deeper level and creates a sense of community and solidarity. By cultivating compassion, we can contribute to creating a more empathetic and supportive society.

Here are some strategies for developing a compassionate mindset:

1. Practicing Self-Compassion: Begin by extending kindness and understanding towards yourself. Treat yourself with the same level of care and compassion that you offer to others. Recognize your own needs, limitations, and imperfections, and be gentle with yourself when facing challenges or setbacks.
2. Cultivating Empathy: As discussed earlier, empathy is an essential component of compassion. By actively listening to others, striving to understand their perspectives, and acknowledging their emotions, we can develop a deeper sense of empathy. This empathy forms the foundation for compassionate actions.
3. Actively Seeking Opportunities for Kindness: Look for opportunities in your daily life to extend kindness to others. It can be as simple as offering a helping hand to someone in need, volunteering for a cause you care about, or practicing random acts of kindness. By actively seeking out these opportunities, you will train yourself to be more compassionate in your thoughts and actions.
4. Engaging in Active Listening: When interacting with others, make a conscious effort to truly listen and understand their experiences and emotions. Avoid judgment or jumping to conclusions. Create a safe space where individuals feel heard and validated. This active listening fosters deeper connections and demonstrates your genuine care for others.
5. Practicing Forgiveness and Letting Go: Compassion involves releasing grudges and harboring forgiveness towards others. Holding onto anger or resentment only perpetuates suffering, both for ourselves and others. By practicing forgiveness, we free ourselves from negative emotions and create space for healing and growth.

Remember, cultivating compassion is a lifelong journey. It requires consistent practice, self-reflection, and a commitment to making a positive difference in the lives of others. By incorporating these strategies into your daily life, you can develop a compassionate mindset and contribute to a more empathetic and kinder world.

Applying Empathy and Compassion in Daily Life:

1. Empathy exercises and activities to practice in various settings:
   - ✓ Role-playing scenarios to understand different perspectives and emotions.
   - ✓ Engaging in active listening exercises with friends, family, or colleagues.
   - ✓ Participating in group discussions or support groups to enhance empathy towards others.

2. Strategies for dealing with challenging situations and conflicts with empathy:
   - ✓ Taking a step back to understand the other person's point of view before responding.
   - ✓ Asking open-ended questions to gain a deeper understanding of their feelings and motivations.
   - ✓ Avoiding judgment or criticism and instead focusing on finding common ground and solutions.

3. Integrating empathy and compassion into personal values and decision-making processes:
   - ✓ Reflecting on how empathy and compassion align with personal values and goals.
   - ✓ Considering the impact of decisions on others and prioritizing their well-being.

✓ Being mindful of opportunities to show kindness, generosity, and understanding in daily interactions.

By actively engaging in empathy exercises, implementing strategies for conflict resolution, and integrating empathy and compassion into decision-making processes, readers can cultivate a more empathetic mindset and create positive change in their personal and professional relationships.

The Importance of Embracing Singlehood:

Being single in your twenties provides a wealth of benefits and unique opportunities for personal growth and self-discovery. It's essential to reframe alone time as a valuable period in your life, filled with independence and the chance to focus on your own needs and aspirations.

Embracing singlehood allows you to prioritize yourself and your goals without the distractions or compromises that may come with being in a romantic relationship. It gives you the freedom to fully explore who you are, what you want, and what brings you joy. This phase of life offers immense potential for self-reflection, self-improvement, and the development of a strong sense of self.

During this time, take advantage of the opportunity to try new things, pursue your passions, and build a foundation for future success. Explore your interests, take up hobbies, travel, and invest time in activities that bring you fulfillment. Use this period to nurture your physical, emotional, and mental well-being.

Rather than viewing singlehood as a waiting period for a romantic partner, see it as an opportunity to cultivate a deep connection with yourself. Learn to appreciate your own company, value solitude as a source of rejuvenation, and develop a loving relationship with yourself. By doing so, you will enter future relationships from a position of strength and self-assuredness.

By embracing singlehood in your twenties, you can truly focus on becoming the best version of yourself. It allows you to lay a solid foundation for personal growth and enables you to make decisions that align with your values, aspirations, and desires. Remember that being single does not mean being incomplete; it means having the chance to grow independently before potentially joining forces with someone else.

So relish in this phase of your life. Embrace singlehood as an opportunity for personal exploration, growth, and empowerment. Seize the chance to create a fulfilling life script that reflects who you truly are and what you want to achieve. By reframing alone time, you can lay the groundwork for a future filled with happiness, success, and authentic relationships.

Building a strong sense of self is crucial during singlehood in your twenties. This phase of life offers an invaluable opportunity to delve deep into self-reflection and self-discovery. By taking the time to understand yourself on a deeper level, you can lay a solid foundation for personal growth and future relationships.

Start by asking yourself important questions about your values, interests, passions, and goals. Reflect on what truly matters to you and what brings you joy and fulfillment. Take the time to explore different hobbies and interests, trying new experiences and pushing yourself out of your comfort zone. This will help you gain a better understanding of who you are and what makes you unique.

During this process, it's essential to be honest with yourself and not be influenced solely by external factors or societal expectations. What matters is that you are true to yourself and align your choices with your own values and aspirations. Don't rush into a romantic relationship simply because it seems like the norm or because you feel pressured to be in one. Embrace singlehood as an opportunity to focus on your personal growth and building a strong foundation for your future.

By developing a strong sense of self, you enter into potential relationships with a clearer understanding of who you are and what you want. This not only helps you make better choices but also ensures that you are entering into relationships from a place of strength rather than dependency.

Remember, being in a relationship should enhance your life, not define it. By building a strong sense of self in your twenties, you set yourself up for healthier, more fulfilling relationships in the future. So take this time to invest in yourself, discover your passions, pursue your goals, and build the life you truly desire.

Establishing healthy boundaries is crucial not only in romantic relationships but also in all areas of life. During singlehood in your twenties, it is even more important to learn how to set boundaries with family, friends, colleagues, and potential partners. By establishing and maintaining healthy boundaries, you can protect your mental and emotional well-being, maintain your sense of self, and foster healthier and more fulfilling relationships.

One common challenge that young adults face when it comes to boundary-setting is the fear of disappointing or upsetting others. It's essential to recognize that setting boundaries is not selfish or mean; it is an act of self-care and self-respect. You have the right to prioritize your needs, emotions, and values.

To establish healthy boundaries, consider the following tips:

1. Identify your limits: Reflect on what is acceptable and unacceptable behavior for you in various relationships. Consider how much time and energy you are willing to invest in different areas of your life. Understanding your own limits will help you communicate them clearly to others.
2. Communicate assertively: Clearly express your needs, desires, and limits with confidence and respect. Use "I" statements to express how a certain behavior makes you feel or what you need from others. Remember that open communication is key to establishing healthy boundaries.
3. Learn to say no: It's okay to say no when something doesn't align with your values, interests, or priorities. Practice saying no respectfully and without guilt. Remember, saying no to one thing means saying yes to yourself and your well-being.
4. Recognize red flags: Be aware of any signs of manipulation, disrespect, or crossing of boundaries from others. Trust your instincts and take necessary measures to protect yourself from toxic relationships.
5. Practice self-care: Prioritize self-care activities that help you recharge and rejuvenate. Make time for activities that bring you joy, peace, and relaxation. Taking care of yourself enables you to be more present and engaged in your relationships.

While establishing healthy boundaries can be challenging, remember that it is an ongoing process. Be patient with yourself and others as you navigate this journey. Revisit and reassess your boundaries regularly as your needs and circumstances may change. By setting healthy boundaries in all areas of your life, you can cultivate healthier relationships, protect your well-being, and create a balanced and fulfilling life during singlehood in your twenties.

Maximizing Alone Time for Personal Growth: This section explores the importance of making the most out of alone time during singlehood in one's twenties. It emphasizes the value of engaging in self-care activities, pursuing hobbies and interests, setting personal goals, and exploring new experiences.

When individuals are single, they have the freedom and flexibility to focus on their own personal growth and development. This period offers a unique opportunity for self-discovery and self-improvement. By utilizing their alone time effectively, young adults can build a strong foundation for future success and fulfillment.

Engaging in self-care activities is crucial during singlehood. Taking care of one's physical, emotional, and mental well-being is essential for overall happiness and success. This can involve practicing regular exercise, maintaining a healthy diet, getting enough sleep, and managing stress. Additionally, dedicating time for relaxation, mindfulness practices, and self-reflection can promote personal growth and inner peace.

Pursuing hobbies and interests is another beneficial way to maximize alone time. Exploring new hobbies or immersing oneself in existing passions allows individuals to cultivate new skills, expand their knowledge, and discover hidden talents. Whether it's painting, writing, playing an instrument, or engaging in outdoor activities, embracing these hobbies can bring joy and fulfillment to one's life.

Setting personal goals is an important aspect of utilizing alone time effectively. By defining specific objectives and creating actionable plans, individuals can work towards achieving their aspirations and dreams. Whether it's pursuing higher education, starting a business, or traveling the world, setting goals provides motivation and direction in life.

Exploring new experiences is also encouraged during singlehood. Trying new things expands horizons, broadens perspectives, and fosters personal growth. This can involve traveling to different places, volunteering for meaningful causes, or participating in workshops and seminars. Each new experience brings valuable lessons and insights that contribute to personal development.

Lastly, managing loneliness and finding fulfillment in one's own company is a key aspect of maximizing alone time during singlehood. It's important to remember that being single does not equate to being lonely or unhappy. By cultivating self-love, self-acceptance, and self-compassion, individuals can truly enjoy their own company and embrace the benefits of solitude. Engaging in activities that bring joy, practicing gratitude, and nurturing healthy relationships with oneself are all ways to find fulfillment and happiness while single.

By engaging in self-care activities, pursuing hobbies and interests, setting personal goals, exploring new experiences, and finding fulfillment in one's own company, young adults can maximize their alone time and utilize this period for personal growth and development. Singlehood can be a transformative phase filled with valuable opportunities if approached with a positive mindset and a commitment to self-improvement.

Singlehood in Your Twenties: Reframing Alone Time

Navigating Dating and Relationships: This section dives into the intricacies of dating and establishing relationships during one's twenties. It offers practical advice on navigating the dating scene, recognizing red flags, and building healthy romantic relationships.

One crucial aspect of successful dating and relationships is effective communication. Young adults often face challenges when it comes to expressing their needs, desires, and boundaries clearly. This section provides insights and strategies for developing strong communication skills, such as active listening, expressing emotions effectively, and resolving conflicts in a healthy manner.

Recognizing red flags is another essential skill that young adults should cultivate when entering into romantic relationships. This section explores common warning signs of unhealthy relationships, such as lack of trust, controlling behavior, and manipulation. By being aware of these red flags, readers can make informed decisions about whether to pursue or continue a relationship.

Fostering emotional intimacy is also crucial for building fulfilling relationships. This section delves into the importance of vulnerability, empathy, and emotional openness in cultivating deep connections with a partner. It provides guidance on how to create a safe and supportive environment where both individuals can express their emotions and needs authentically.

Maintaining a healthy balance between personal growth and romantic partnerships is emphasized throughout this section. It highlights the significance of continuing personal development and pursuing individual goals while being in a relationship. It encourages readers to nurture their own passions, interests, and friendships alongside their romantic partnership.

By addressing these key points in the chapter, "Singlehood in Your Twenties: Reframing Alone Time," provides valuable guidance on navigating the complexities of dating and relationships during this transformative phase of life.

Part 5:
Health and
Wellness

Chapter 1

Prioritizing Physical Fitness: Your Body's Best Decade

*****

The Key Role of Physical Fitness

Physical fitness plays a crucial role in the lives of individuals in their twenties. This phase of life is often referred to as "your body's best decade" due to the natural strength and vitality that accompanies youth. By prioritizing physical fitness, young adults can lay the foundation for a healthy and active lifestyle that will benefit them in the long run.

One key reason why physical fitness is important during this phase is that it sets the tone for future health and well-being. Building healthy habits in your twenties can have a significant impact on your overall health as you age. Engaging in regular exercise and maintaining a nutritious diet can help prevent chronic diseases such as heart disease, diabetes, and obesity. By taking care of your physical health now, you are investing in a healthier future.

In addition to the long-term health benefits, prioritizing physical fitness in your twenties also has immediate advantages. Regular exercise boosts energy levels and improves mood by releasing endorphins, the "feel-good" hormones. This can greatly enhance your overall quality of life and help you cope with the stresses and challenges that may arise during this phase.

Moreover, physical fitness can provide an opportunity for personal growth and self-discovery. Trying out different forms of exercise and physical activities allows you to explore your interests and passions. From yoga to kickboxing, hiking to swimming, there is a wide range of options available to suit every individual's preferences. Exploring these activities not only keeps you physically fit but also helps you develop new skills, build confidence, and discover hidden talents.

It is worth noting that physical fitness goes beyond just appearances. While it may be tempting to focus solely on achieving a certain body shape or size, true physical fitness encompasses various aspects, including cardiovascular endurance, strength, flexibility, and body composition. By adopting a holistic approach to fitness, you can ensure that you are nurturing all aspects of your body's well-being.

Overall, prioritizing physical fitness in your twenties is essential for maintaining a healthy, active, and fulfilling life. By understanding the importance of physical fitness and incorporating it into your lifestyle, you are setting yourself up for a future filled with vitality and well-being. So seize this opportunity to invest in yourself, prioritize your health, and lay the groundwork for a lifetime of physical success.

Understanding Your Body's Needs in Your Twenties:

During your twenties, your body undergoes significant physical changes and experiences a boost in metabolism. Understanding these changes and the different components of physical fitness is essential for prioritizing your physical well-being during this decade.

Firstly, let's explore the physical changes that occur in your twenties. This is often regarded as the peak time for physical fitness, as your body is at its most vibrant and resilient. However, it's important to note that each individual may experience these changes differently.

Metabolism plays a key role in your body's functions and determines how efficiently you burn calories. In your twenties, your metabolism is typically faster compared to other stages of life. This means that your body processes food more quickly, giving you more energy and making it easier to maintain a healthy weight.

In addition to metabolism, there are several components of physical fitness that require attention. These include cardiovascular endurance, strength, flexibility, and body composition.

Cardiovascular endurance refers to the ability of your heart and lungs to supply oxygen to your muscles during physical activity. It is crucial for maintaining a healthy cardiovascular system and overall stamina. Engaging in activities such as running, cycling, swimming, or dancing can help improve cardiovascular endurance.

Strength training is important for building muscle mass and increasing overall strength. It not only enhances physical performance but also provides long-term health benefits such as improved bone density and the prevention of age-related muscle loss. Incorporating resistance exercises using weights, resistance bands, or bodyweight exercises into your fitness routine can help develop strength.

Flexibility is another vital component of physical fitness. As we age, our muscles naturally become less flexible, leading to reduced range of motion. Stretching exercises and activities like yoga or Pilates can help improve flexibility and prevent injuries.

Lastly, body composition refers to the proportion of fat, muscle, bone, and other tissues in your body. Achieving a healthy body composition involves maintaining a balance between muscle mass and body fat. Regular exercise, along with a balanced diet, can contribute to a healthy body composition.

Understanding these different components of physical fitness will allow you to tailor your exercise routine to meet your specific needs and goals. Whether you prioritize cardiovascular endurance, strength training, flexibility, or a combination of all three, developing a well-rounded fitness regimen in your twenties will set the foundation for a lifetime of good health.

By grasping the unique physical changes and needs specific to your twenties, you can make informed decisions regarding your fitness journey. Remember that everyone's body is different, so it's essential to listen to your body and consult with healthcare professionals or certified trainers if needed. With this knowledge, you can embark on a physical fitness journey that aligns with your personal goals and ensures a strong and healthy foundation for the years to come.

Setting Fitness Goals and Creating a Plan:

In order to prioritize physical fitness during your twenties, it is essential to set specific, measurable, achievable, relevant, and time-bound (SMART) fitness goals. By doing so, you can establish a clear vision for what you want to achieve and create a plan that will help you reach those goals.

When setting fitness goals, it is important to be realistic and consider your current level of fitness. Start by identifying what you want to accomplish, whether it's improving cardiovascular endurance, building strength, increasing flexibility, or achieving a specific body composition. Once you have a clear goal in mind, break it down into smaller, more manageable milestones that can be achieved within a set timeframe.

Creating an individualized fitness plan is crucial to ensure that your workouts are effective and tailored to your specific needs and preferences. Incorporating both cardiovascular exercises and strength training into your routine is key for overall fitness and achieving balanced results.

For cardiovascular exercise, consider activities that you enjoy and that get your heart rate up. This could include running, swimming, cycling, dancing, or participating in group fitness classes. Aim for at least 150 minutes of moderate-intensity aerobic activity or 75 minutes of vigorous-intensity aerobic activity each week.

Strength training is equally important as it helps build muscle strength and endurance. Include exercises that target major muscle groups such as squats, lunges, push-ups, pull-ups, and weightlifting. Aim for at least two days of strength training per week, allowing for recovery time in between sessions.

Remember to start gradually and listen to your body as you progress. It's important to find a balance between pushing yourself to improve and avoiding overexertion or injury. Varying your workouts and incorporating different types of exercises can help prevent boredom and keep you motivated.

Consider consulting with a fitness professional or personal trainer who can assess your current fitness level and help create a personalized plan based on your goals and preferences. They can also provide guidance on proper form, technique, and progression to ensure that you are working out safely and effectively.

By setting SMART fitness goals and creating an individualized plan that incorporates both cardiovascular exercises and strength training, you can maximize the benefits of physical fitness during your twenties. This will not only improve your overall health and well-being but also lay a strong foundation for a lifetime of fitness and wellness.

Incorporating Exercise into Your Routine:

To prioritize physical fitness in your twenties, it's important to find activities or exercises that align with your personal interests and preferences. By choosing activities that you genuinely enjoy, you are more likely to stick with them and make exercise a regular part of your routine.

Here are some tips for incorporating exercise into your daily routines:

1. Morning Workouts: Consider starting your day with a workout to energize yourself and set a positive tone for the rest of the day. Whether it's hitting the gym, going for a run, or practicing yoga, find a morning exercise routine that invigorates you and kick-starts your metabolism.

2. Lunchtime Walks: If you have a busy work schedule, use your lunch break as an opportunity to get moving. Take a brisk walk around your office building or find a nearby park where you can enjoy some fresh air while stretching your legs. Not only will this help you stay active, but it can also serve as a midday mental refresher.

3. After-Work Fitness Classes: Joining fitness classes after work can be a great way to stay motivated and meet like-minded individuals. Whether it's dancing, kickboxing, cycling, or any other activity that piques your interest, signing up for scheduled classes can provide structure and make exercise a social experience.

4. Explore Outdoor Activities: Take advantage of the great outdoors by engaging in outdoor activities that double as exercise. This could be hiking, swimming, cycling, playing sports with friends, or even joining recreational leagues or clubs. By including nature and social interactions in your exercise routine, you'll find added enjoyment and motivation.

5. Find Accountability Partners: Consider partnering up with friends or family members who share similar fitness goals. Having someone to exercise with can provide accountability and make workouts more enjoyable. You can plan regular workout sessions together, cheer each other on, and celebrate achievements along the way.

Remember, the key is to make physical activity a consistent part of your routine. Find activities that excite you, make it a priority in your schedule, and create a habit that supports your overall well-being. By incorporating exercise into your daily life, you'll not only enhance your physical fitness but also experience increased energy levels, improved mental clarity, and a greater sense of overall happiness.

Maintaining Motivation and Overcoming Obstacles:

Staying motivated and committed to a regular exercise routine can be challenging, especially when faced with various obstacles. However, developing strategies to overcome these obstacles is crucial for long-term success in prioritizing physical fitness. In this section, we will explore techniques and solutions to help you stay motivated and overcome common barriers.

1. Find Your Motivation:

✓ Reflect on your personal motivations for prioritizing physical fitness. Whether it's improving your overall health, boosting your energy levels, or achieving specific fitness goals, understanding your "why" can provide a powerful source of motivation.

✓ Set meaningful and achievable goals that align with your values and aspirations. By having clear objectives, you can track your progress and celebrate small victories along the way.

2. Create a Support System:

✓ Surround yourself with like-minded individuals who prioritize their physical well-being. Join fitness classes, sports teams, or online communities where you can connect with others who share similar goals.

✓ Seek out an accountability partner, whether it's a friend, family member, or personal trainer. Having someone to share your progress, challenges, and successes can provide encouragement and support.

3. Make Exercise Enjoyable:

✓ Choose activities that you genuinely enjoy. Find exercises that align with your interests and preferences. This could be anything from dancing, hiking, swimming, or team sports.

✓ Vary your workouts to prevent boredom and maintain excitement. Incorporate different forms of exercise such as cardio workouts, strength training, yoga, or Pilates into your routine.

4. Prioritize Time Management:

- ✓ Schedule dedicated time for exercise in your daily or weekly routine. Treat it as an important appointment that cannot be missed.
- ✓ Be flexible and adaptable. If unexpected commitments or emergencies arise, find alternative ways to squeeze in shorter workouts or modify your exercise plans instead of skipping them altogether.

5. Overcome Resource and Equipment Limitations:

- ✓ Look for cost-effective or free fitness options such as local community centers, public parks, or online workout videos.
- ✓ Explore bodyweight exercises that require minimal or no equipment. These exercises utilize your body's weight to build strength and improve cardiovascular fitness.

6. Deal with Plateaus and Setbacks:

- ✓ Plateaus are a normal part of any fitness journey. Instead of getting discouraged, use them as an opportunity to reassess your routine and make necessary adjustments.
- ✓ Seek professional guidance from personal trainers or fitness experts who can provide specialized advice tailored to your needs and goals.
- ✓ Embrace setbacks as learning experiences rather than failures. Maintain a positive mindset and focus on progress rather than perfection.

By implementing these techniques and solutions, you can maintain motivation and overcome obstacles that may arise on your path to prioritizing physical fitness. Remember, consistency is key, and small steps taken every day will lead to significant improvements in your overall well-being.

Chapter 2

Mental Health Basics: Understanding Stress and Anxiety

****

Mental Health Basics: Understanding Stress and Anxiety

In this section, we will delve into the fundamental aspects of stress and anxiety, providing a clear understanding of their definitions and differentiating between normal levels and chronic disorders. By exploring the impact that stress and anxiety can have on our mental and physical health, readers will gain crucial insights into the importance of managing these conditions effectively.

Firstly, let's define stress and anxiety. Stress can be described as the body's response to external pressures or demands, whether they are physical, psychological, or emotional in nature. On the other hand, anxiety refers to feelings of unease, worry, or fear that can arise in response to specific situations or as a general state of being.

It is important to note that experiencing some level of stress and anxiety is a normal part of life. In fact, short-term stress can even be beneficial as it can motivate us to meet deadlines, accomplish goals, or overcome challenges. However, when stress or anxiety becomes chronic or overwhelming, it can significantly impact our well-being.

Chronic stress and anxiety disorders, such as generalized anxiety disorder (GAD), panic disorder, or post-traumatic stress disorder (PTSD), can interfere with daily functioning and quality of life. These conditions may require professional intervention and treatment.

The impact of stress and anxiety extends beyond our mental health; it can also take a toll on our physical well-being. Prolonged periods of high stress can lead to increased blood pressure, weakened immune function, digestive problems, sleep disturbances, and a higher risk of developing chronic conditions such as heart disease or diabetes.

By understanding the definition of stress and anxiety and recognizing the difference between normal levels and chronic disorders, readers will be able to assess their own experiences more accurately. This knowledge serves as an essential foundation for implementing effective strategies to manage stress and anxiety in their lives.

In this section, we will delve deeper into identifying personal stress and anxiety triggers. It is important to recognize that each individual's triggers may vary, but there are common factors that can contribute to stress and anxiety in most people's lives.

One significant trigger is work or school pressure. The demands of deadlines, performance expectations, and the need to constantly excel can create overwhelming stress and anxiety. It is crucial to be aware of how these pressures affect you personally and to develop strategies for managing them effectively.

Relationships, both romantic and platonic, can also be a source of stress and anxiety. Conflicts, misunderstandings, or unmet expectations in relationships can weigh heavily on one's emotional well-being. Understanding the dynamics within your relationships and learning effective communication skills can help alleviate stress in this area.

Financial worries can be a significant trigger for stress and anxiety, especially during early adulthood when financial independence is often being established. Concerns about debt, bills, or meeting financial obligations can cause a great deal of stress. Developing healthy money management habits and creating a budget can help alleviate some of these anxieties.

Other common triggers include major life changes such as moving, starting a new job or school, or dealing with significant loss or trauma. These events can disrupt your sense of stability and security, leading to increased stress and anxiety levels. By recognizing the impact of these changes on your well-being, you can take proactive steps to manage them effectively.

To identify your personal stress and anxiety triggers, it is essential to practice self-awareness. Pay attention to situations or circumstances that consistently cause you to feel stressed or anxious. Keep a journal or use a tracking app to monitor your moods and emotions throughout the day, noting any specific triggers that may arise.

By identifying these triggers, you gain the power to address them head-on. You can then develop personalized strategies for managing stress and anxiety in specific situations. Remember that everyone's triggers are unique, so it is crucial to approach this exploration with an open mind and a commitment to self-reflection.

In the next section, we will discuss coping strategies for managing stress and anxiety, providing you with practical techniques to implement in your daily life.

Coping Strategies for Managing Stress and Anxiety:

In this section, we will delve into various coping strategies that can effectively manage stress and anxiety. These techniques provide practical tools for readers to incorporate into their daily lives, helping them reduce stress levels and improve their overall well-being.

1. Relaxation techniques:

One of the most effective ways to combat stress and anxiety is through relaxation techniques. Deep breathing exercises are simple yet powerful tools that can be done anywhere, anytime. Encourage readers to take slow, deep breaths, inhaling through the nose and exhaling through the mouth. This practice helps activate the body's relaxation response, calming the mind and reducing stress.

Progressive muscle relaxation is another technique that involves tensing and then releasing different muscle groups in the body. By systematically relaxing each muscle group, readers can release built-up tension and experience a sense of relaxation and calmness.

Meditation is a mindfulness practice that allows individuals to focus their attention on the present moment while cultivating a nonjudgmental and accepting mindset. There are various meditation techniques such as guided meditations, loving-kindness meditations, or silent meditation. Encourage readers to explore different forms of meditation and find one that resonates with them.

2. Incorporating mindfulness practices into daily routines:

Mindfulness involves intentionally bringing one's attention to the present moment without judgment. It is a powerful practice for reducing stress and anxiety by promoting awareness and acceptance of thoughts and emotions.

Readers can integrate mindfulness into their daily routines by practicing activities such as mindful eating, where they pay close attention to the taste, texture, and sensations of their food. Mindful walking or engaging in other mindful movements can help individuals cultivate a sense of calmness and connection with their bodies.

Encourage readers to set aside dedicated time for mindfulness practice, whether through meditation or engaging in mindful activities. By incorporating these practices into their daily lives, readers can strengthen their ability to manage stress and anxiety.

3. Engaging in physical activities to reduce stress and anxiety:

Regular physical activity is not only beneficial for physical health but also plays a crucial role in managing stress and anxiety. Encourage readers to engage in activities they enjoy, such as yoga, exercise, dancing, or walking. These activities help release endorphins, which are natural mood-boosting chemicals in the brain. By participating in physical activities, individuals can reduce stress levels, improve sleep quality, and enhance overall well-being.

4. Journaling as a therapeutic tool for emotional expression and reflection:

Writing in a journal can be a therapeutic tool for managing stress and anxiety. Encourage readers to dedicate time each day to reflect on their thoughts, emotions, and experiences. By putting their thoughts onto paper, individuals can gain clarity, process their emotions, and identify patterns that may be contributing to their stress or anxiety.

Suggest different journaling techniques such as gratitude journaling, where readers write down things they are grateful for each day, or stream-of-consciousness writing, where they allow their thoughts to flow freely without judgment. By incorporating journaling into their routine, readers can develop a deeper understanding of themselves and find solace in expressing their feelings.

By integrating these coping strategies into their lives, readers can effectively manage stress and anxiety during their twenties. It's important to remind them that these techniques may require practice and consistency but can greatly contribute to their overall well-being. With these tools at their disposal, readers will be better equipped to handle the challenges that arise during this pivotal stage of life.

Building Resilience to Combat Stress and Anxiety:

Resilience plays a crucial role in managing stress and anxiety effectively. It refers to the ability to bounce back from setbacks, adapt to change, and maintain a positive mindset even in challenging situations. Developing resilience empowers individuals to navigate stress and anxiety with strength and confidence. In this section, we will explore various strategies for building resilience and fostering optimism, adaptability, and problem-solving skills.

One important aspect of building resilience is recognizing the power of healthy coping mechanisms. Instead of resorting to harmful habits or avoidance strategies when faced with stress and anxiety, it is essential to develop positive ways of dealing with these challenges. This can include engaging in activities that bring joy and relaxation, such as hobbies, exercise, or spending time in nature. By incorporating these activities into daily routines, individuals can create a strong foundation for resilience.

Fostering optimism is another key component of building resilience. Optimistic thinking involves focusing on the positive aspects of a situation and maintaining hope for the future. This mindset enables individuals to see setbacks as temporary obstacles rather than permanent failures. Strategies for fostering optimism include practicing gratitude, reframing negative thoughts into more positive ones, and surrounding oneself with positive influences.

Adaptability is also vital in managing stress and anxiety. Being able to adapt to new circumstances and changes helps individuals navigate uncertain situations more effectively. Cultivating adaptability involves developing flexibility in thinking and embracing new perspectives. Seeking opportunities for growth and learning can enhance adaptability, as it allows individuals to expand their skillset and knowledge.

Problem-solving skills are another crucial aspect of resilience. By developing the ability to analyze challenges, identify potential solutions, and take decisive action, individuals can address stressors head-on. Problem-solving skills involve breaking down complex problems into manageable steps and seeking support or guidance when needed. Building problem-solving skills empowers individuals to take control of their circumstances and find effective solutions.

Lastly, seeking support from trusted friends, family, or mental health professionals is vital in building resilience. Talking about stress and anxiety with supportive individuals can provide valuable insights, guidance, and reassurance. Additionally, professional help can offer specialized techniques and strategies tailored to specific stress and anxiety disorders. Seeking support is not a sign of weakness but rather a proactive step towards building resilience.

By implementing these strategies, individuals can strengthen their resilience and effectively combat stress and anxiety. Building resilience empowers individuals to navigate the challenges of their twenties with grace, confidence, and a positive mindset. Remember, resilience is not something that develops overnight but rather through consistent practice and intentional effort.

Creating a Self-Care Plan for Mental Well-being:

In this section of "Mental Health Basics: Managing Stress and Anxiety," we explore the importance of prioritizing self-care activities for maintaining optimal mental well-being. Taking care of yourself is essential, especially during times of stress and anxiety. By implementing a personalized self-care plan, you can ensure that your mental health remains a top priority.

Firstly, it is crucial to identify activities that promote relaxation, pleasure, and self-reflection. Engaging in activities that bring you joy and allow you to unwind can significantly reduce stress and anxiety levels. Whether it's spending time in nature, reading a good book, practicing a hobby, or listening to music, find what resonates with you and make it a regular part of your routine.

Establishing healthy boundaries is another key aspect of self-care. Learning to say no when necessary and setting limits on your commitments can prevent burnout and overwhelm. Recognize your limitations and ensure that you are focusing on your well-being by setting boundaries with work, relationships, and other aspects of your life.

Designing a personalized self-care plan involves creating a roadmap for activities and practices that support your mental health consistently. Consider incorporating relaxation techniques such as deep breathing exercises, guided meditation apps, or practicing mindfulness into your daily routine. Experiment with different strategies and find what works best for you.

It is also important to conduct regular self-check-ins to assess your mental well-being. Schedule time to reflect on how you're feeling emotionally and mentally. This self-awareness will help you recognize any signs of stress or anxiety early on so that you can address them promptly. Adjust your self-care plan as needed based on these check-ins to ensure it remains effective.

Remember, self-care is an ongoing practice that requires commitment and dedication. It is not selfish but rather essential for maintaining overall well-being. By prioritizing self-care activities, identifying personal triggers, establishing healthy boundaries, and designing a personalized self-care plan, you can better manage stress and anxiety, promoting a healthier and more fulfilling life.

Nutrition plays a vital role in maintaining overall health and well-being, particularly during the demanding twenties. It is essential to understand the profound impact that nutrition has on various aspects of our lives, including energy levels, productivity, mental clarity, and physical vitality.

Proper nutrition provides our bodies with the necessary fuel to function optimally. By fueling ourselves with nutritious foods, we can enhance our energy levels, allowing us to tackle the demands of our busy lives with vigor and enthusiasm. The nutrients obtained from a balanced diet help support bodily functions, promote cell growth and repair, aid in metabolism, and strengthen the immune system. When we prioritize nutrition, we provide our bodies with the tools they need to perform at their best.

Furthermore, nutrition influences our cognitive abilities and mental well-being. Research has shown that certain nutrients, such as omega-3 fatty acids and antioxidants found in fruits and vegetables, can improve brain function, enhance memory, and boost mood. Conversely, a diet high in processed foods and added sugars has been linked to cognitive decline, increased risk of mental health disorders, and decreased overall well-being.

In addition to physical and mental health benefits, proper nutrition also supports our physical appearance. A diet rich in vitamins, minerals, and antioxidants helps maintain healthy skin, hair, and nails. By nourishing our bodies from within, we can enhance our external appearance, promoting confidence and self-esteem.

Given the numerous benefits of nutrition for overall health and well-being, it is crucial for busy twenty-somethings to prioritize their nutritional needs. By making mindful choices when it comes to food, young adults can optimize their energy levels, improve cognitive function, support physical appearance, and lay the groundwork for long-term health. Investing in good nutrition now sets the stage for a healthy and thriving future.

The Fundamentals of a Healthy Diet:

To live a healthy and vibrant life, it is essential to understand the fundamentals of a balanced diet. This section will provide an in-depth overview of the key components necessary for optimal nutrition. It will cover macronutrients, micronutrients, portion control, and mindful eating habits.

Macronutrients are the primary nutrients that our bodies require in large amounts. They include carbohydrates, proteins, and fats. Carbohydrates are our main source of energy and are found in foods such as grains, fruits, and vegetables. Proteins are crucial for cell repair and growth and can be obtained from sources like lean meats, fish, legumes, and dairy products. Fats are vital for hormone production, insulation, and protecting organs. It is important to focus on healthy fats such as avocados, nuts, seeds, and oily fish while limiting saturated and trans fats found in processed foods.

Micronutrients are essential vitamins and minerals that our bodies need in smaller quantities but play a significant role in various bodily functions. These include vitamins like vitamin C, vitamin D, vitamin B12, and minerals like iron, calcium, and zinc. Consuming a variety of fruits, vegetables, whole grains, nuts, and seeds ensures an adequate intake of these essential micronutrients.

Portion control is another critical aspect of a healthy diet. It involves being mindful of the quantity of food we consume to maintain a balanced calorie intake. Understanding appropriate portion sizes can prevent overeating and promote weight management. Tools like measuring cups or visual references can help estimate appropriate portions for different food groups.

Mindful eating habits involve being present and aware while consuming meals. It means slowing down to fully appreciate and savor the flavors, textures, and aromas of our food. Practicing mindful eating helps us recognize when we are full and prevents mindless or emotional eating. It allows us to tune into our body's hunger and satiety cues, promoting a healthy relationship with food.

Incorporating these fundamentals of a healthy diet into our everyday lives can have a profound impact on our overall well-being. By understanding the importance of macronutrients and micronutrients, practicing portion control, and adopting mindful eating habits, we can fuel our bodies with the nutrition they need to thrive. Remember, a well-nourished body is the foundation for a successful life at any age.

Practical Tips for Healthy Eating on a Busy Schedule:

1. Meal Planning: One of the most effective ways to ensure healthy eating habits on a busy schedule is through meal planning. Dedicate some time each week to plan your meals and snacks in advance. Consider your schedule, upcoming events, and the nutritional needs of your body. Plan balanced meals that include a variety of fruits, vegetables, lean proteins, whole grains, and healthy fats.

2. Grocery Shopping: Make a grocery list based on your meal plan and stick to it while shopping. This will help you avoid impulse purchases of unhealthy foods. Choose fresh, whole foods whenever possible and opt for minimally processed options. Stock up on nutritious pantry staples such as whole grains, canned beans, nuts, seeds, and spices to create quick and easy meals.

3. Preparing Meals in Advance: When you have some free time, take advantage of it by preparing meals in advance. Cook large batches of grains, proteins, and vegetables that can be easily stored and reheated throughout the week. Use containers to portion out your meals for grab-and-go convenience. You can also prepare healthy snacks like cut-up fruits and vegetables or homemade energy bars to have on hand when hunger strikes.

4. Grab-and-Go Options: Keep your kitchen stocked with healthy grab-and-go options for those days when you're short on time. Purchase pre-washed salad greens or pre-cut vegetables to make quick salads or stir-fries. Pack single-serving portions of yogurt, cottage cheese, or hummus for easy snacking. Keep a supply of portable snacks like nuts, trail mix, protein bars, or fresh fruit that you can take with you on the go.

5. Utilize Kitchen Gadgets: Invest in helpful kitchen gadgets that can make healthy cooking faster and easier. A slow cooker or Instant Pot can be a lifesaver for busy individuals. You can throw ingredients into the pot in the morning and come home to a delicious, home-cooked meal. A blender or food processor can also be handy for making quick and nutritious smoothies, soups, or sauces.

6. Healthy Takeout Options: Recognize that there will be times when cooking isn't possible, and you'll need to rely on takeout or dining out. However, this doesn't mean you have to sacrifice nutrition. Look for healthier options on menus such as grilled protein with steamed vegetables or a salad with lean protein. Opt for smaller portion sizes or split meals with a friend to avoid overeating.

7. Stay Hydrated: Don't forget the importance of staying hydrated throughout the day. Keep a reusable water bottle with you at all times and aim to drink at least 8 cups (64 ounces) of water daily. You can also infuse your water with slices of fruits or herbs for added flavor.

By implementing these practical tips into your busy lifestyle, you can ensure that healthy eating becomes an achievable goal. With proper planning and preparation, you can nourish your body with nutritious meals even when time is limited. Remember, small steps towards healthier eating habits can have a significant impact on your overall well-being.

Chapter 3

Nutrition for the Busy Twenty-Something

****

Nutrition for the Busy Twenty-Something: Nutrition for Stress Management

Here- we will investigate furthe-r the bond betwee-n nourishment and stress administration. We will inve-stigate how certain sustenance-s can either intensify or lighte-n stress levels and passionate-swings. By including sustenances that diminish stress into your e-very day eating regime-n, you can outfit yourself with the device-s to more productively confront the difficultie-s and weights of your twenties.

Stress is a common aspect of life, particularly during this phase when we are juggling multiple responsibilities and facing various uncertainties. However, what we eat can greatly influence our ability to cope with stress. Certain foods have been found to trigger stress responses in the body, while others can help promote relaxation, enhance mood, and reduce anxiety.

While it is important to compre-hend how distinct nourishment assortments influe-nce our mental prosperity whe-n battling pressure, one should re-member that a adjusted e-ating routine rich in supplements is most gainful. For instance-, exorbitant admission of caffeine, sugar, and handle-d sustenances may prompt more e-levated amounts of tension and une-asiness. Then again, consolidating foods wealthy in supple-ments, for example, e-ntire grains, natural products and vegetable-s, lean proteins, and sound fats can help control pre-ssure and upgrade emotional we-ll-being. A scope of nutritious decisions give-s the body the suppleme-nts it needs to work productively and fe-el revived.

There- are several me-thods one can utilize to help de-crease tension through nourishme-nt. One approach is to incorporate foods wealthy in vitamins B and C into your me-als and snacks. These nutrients play an e-xtremely significant part in regulating pre-ssure hormones and advancing psychological prosperity. Foods like- oranges, berries, le-afy greens, avocados, and nuts are supe-rb wellsprings of these fundame-ntal supplements. By reme-mbering them when you e-at consistently, you can build your body's toughness against pressure-.

Furthermore-, mindful eating practices can moderate-ly contribute to stress manageme-nt. Taking a few extra minutes to truly taste- your meals, consuming them gradually and delibe-rately, lets you totally appreciate- and value the sustenance- you're giving yourself. Mindful eating not just assists with ke-eping you from overindulging yet in addition pe-rmits you to tune in to your body's cravings and fulfillment markers, advancing a more- adjusted association with sustenance. While- mindful eating has advantages, it is important to not take too much time- with meals to avoid creating additional stress or worrie-s.

Beside-s concentrating on specific stress-re-ducing foods, maintaining a harmonious and diverse diet as a whole- is extremely important. A nourishme-nt plan abundant in organic products, vegetables, e-ntire grains, lean proteins, and sound fats give-s your body the fundamental suppleme-nts expected to work at its ide-al. When you give your body the corre-ct fuel through such a balanced diet, it can all the- more successfully overse-e pressure and advance- psychological wellness. A sound body furnished with an assortme-nt of supplements is bette-r ready to adapt.

It's worth noting that nutrition is just one piece of the puzzle when it comes to managing stress. Taking a holistic approach to stress management involves not only mindful eating but also incorporating other lifestyle factors into your daily routine. Regular exercise, adequate sleep, and practicing self-care activities are equally important in stress reduction.

As you navigate the- difficulties of your twenties, ke-ep in mind that what nourishment you choose to consume- can considerably influence your capacity to de-al with stress. By intentionally sele-cting foods that reduce strain in your eating re-gimen and cultivating mindful eating practices, you can be-tter outfit yourself to manage the- pressures of this period of life-. Giving nutrition first priority as piece of your gene-ral wellbeing will permit you to succe-ed and accomplish achieveme-nt both personally and expertly.

Beyond Food: Holistic Approach to Nutrition

Here- we will take a brief look into the- significance of adopting a comprehensive- perspective re-garding nourishment and its effect on ge-neral prosperity. Without a doubt, dietary choice-s are pivotal, however the-re are differe-nt way of life components that assume a critical part in ke-eping up a solid lifestyle. Factors, for e-xample, exercise-, rest, pressure the- executives, social conne-ctions and environmental ele-ments can all add to or undermine we-llbeing. Considering all parts of an individual's life e-mpowers a more strong and maintainable way to de-al with wellbeing advanceme-nt.

Staying physically active is vital for bodily we-ll-being, muscle tone, and he-art wellness. It assists not just with weight mainte-nance yet additionally encourage-s psychological prosperity by decreasing pre-ssure and boosting disposition. Including activity into your everyday sche-dule can be as uncomplicated as going for a stroll amid your lunch se-parate, joining a wellness class, or discove-ring an entertainment you appre-ciate, for example, moving or swimming. Exe-rcise gives advantageous advantage-s for both actual and mental wellbeing.

Ensuring adequate- rest is another crucial part of a complete- method towards nourishment. Not getting e-nough sleep can result in he-ightened degre-es of stress bodily hormones, diminishe-d intellectual function, a weake-ned resistant system, and pote-ntial weight attain. Developing a consiste-nt bedtime schedule- and cultivating a calming nightly ritual can significantly enhance both the quality and amount of your slumbe-r.

Taking care of one-'s mental condition is just as essential in sustaining a balance-d way of life. Long-term anxiety and psychological mise-ry can have harmful impacts on both bodily and psychological prosperity. Participating in stress-re-ducing practices like meditation, private- journaling, or being mindful can assist in alleviating anxiety le-vels and endorsing total psychological well-be-ing. Looking for therapy or guidance when re-quired is in addition a helpful instrument in ove-rseeing psychological health difficultie-s.

Rephrase Furthermore-, examining supplements and the-ir role in assisting ideal nourishment is prude-nt. While supplements must not substitute- a balanced diet, they can offe-r added assistance for particular nutrient inade-quacies or certain wellbe-ing conditions. Seeing a medicinal se-rvices proficient or enliste-d dietitian before including any supple-ments into your everyday practice- is vital to ensure wellbe-ing and viability. It is significant that any supplements are safe-guarded and successful.

While focusing on nourishing food se-lections provides an esse-ntial foundation for wellness, taking a broader vie-wpoint that incorporates additional lifestyle factors can significantly e-nhance your health and happiness now and late-r in life. Making physical activity, sufficient rest, stre-ss management, and suppleme-ntation when neede-d core priorities supports achieving a balance-d and energized e-xistence. Reme-mber, optimal well-being e-merges from consistently caring for your e-ntire being, not mere-ly what sustains you physically but also how you tend to your mental, emotional and spiritual ne-eds each day. A holistic regime- nurtures the whole pe-rson from within.

Chapter 4

The Benefits of Sleep:
Rest for Success
*****

The Importance of Sleep

In today's fast-paced world, it can be tempting to sacrifice sleep in favor of productivity or socializing. However, adequate sleep is crucial for overall well-being and success. In this chapter, we will explore the importance of sleep in maintaining physical health, mental clarity, and emotional stability.

Quality sleep plays a vital role in maintaining our physical health. During sleep, our bodies undergo important restorative processes that promote healing and repair. Without enough sleep, our immune system becomes compromised, making us more susceptible to illnesses and infections. Lack of sleep has also been linked to weight gain and an increased risk of chronic conditions such as diabetes and heart disease. By prioritizing sleep, we can support our bodies' natural healing abilities and ensure long-term health.

Sleep deprivation has a profound impact on cognitive function and productivity. When we don't get enough sleep, our ability to focus and concentrate diminishes significantly. We may find ourselves struggling to stay alert during important tasks or unable to retain information effectively. Sleep-deprived individuals are also more prone to errors and poor decision-making, which can have serious consequences in both personal and professional settings. By giving ourselves the gift of sufficient sleep, we can optimize our cognitive abilities and perform at our best.

Furthermore, quality sleep is essential for memory consolidation and learning. During periods of deep sleep, our brains process and integrate the information we have acquired throughout the day. This process strengthens our memories and improves our ability to recall information accurately. Adequate sleep has been shown to enhance creativity, problem-solving skills, and critical thinking abilities. By valuing our sleep, we can unlock our full potential for learning and intellectual growth.

In conclusion, sleep is not just a luxury; it is a necessity for personal growth and success. By recognizing the significance of adequate sleep in maintaining physical health, mental clarity, and emotional stability, we can prioritize rest and reap the benefits it offers. In the next sections of this chapter, we will explore the science behind sleep and strategies for improving sleep quality. Together, let's embark on a journey towards better sleep habits and ultimate success.

Understanding the Science Behind Sleep:

Sleep is a fundamental biological process that plays a crucial role in our overall well-being and success. To fully appreciate the benefits of sleep, it's important to understand the science behind it. In this section, we will explore the sleep cycle, the role of neurotransmitters, and the effects of circadian rhythms on sleep quality.

The sleep cycle consists of four stages: NREM (non-rapid eye movement) stage 1, NREM stage 2, NREM stage 3, and REM (rapid eye movement) sleep. During NREM stage 1, which occurs when you first fall asleep, your brain waves slow down, and you may experience light sleep. NREM stage 2 is characterized by slower brain waves with occasional bursts of rapid waves known as sleep spindles. This stage accounts for approximately 50% of total sleep time.

NREM stage 3 is often referred to as deep sleep or slow-wave sleep. It is during this stage that the body repairs and regenerates tissues, boosts immune function, and strengthens the immune system. Delta waves dominate the brain activity during this phase.

Finally, REM sleep is the stage where most dreaming occurs. The brain becomes highly active, resembling wakefulness in many aspects. REM sleep is essential for memory consolidation, learning, and emotional regulation. It is worth noting that REM sleep cycles become longer as the night progresses.

Neurotransmitters such as melatonin and serotonin play vital roles in regulating sleep patterns. Melatonin, often referred to as the "sleep hormone," is produced by the pineal gland in response to darkness. It helps regulate the body's internal clock and signals that it's time to sleep. Serotonin, on the other hand, promotes wakefulness and alertness during daylight hours.

Circadian rhythms are natural internal processes that regulate our sleep-wake cycles over a 24-hour period. These rhythms are primarily influenced by environmental cues, such as light and darkness. Light exposure stimulates the release of cortisol, a hormone that promotes wakefulness, while darkness triggers the production of melatonin, inducing sleepiness.

Disruption of circadian rhythms, such as those caused by irregular sleep schedules or exposure to artificial light at night, can significantly impact sleep quality. It can lead to difficulties falling asleep or staying asleep, resulting in sleep deprivation and its associated negative effects on cognitive function, productivity, and overall well-being.

By understanding the science behind sleep, you can gain insight into the importance of maintaining a consistent sleep schedule and creating a sleep-friendly environment. Implementing strategies that align with the natural sleep-wake cycle can help optimize your sleep quality and enhance your overall success in life.

Benefits of sleep for personal growth and professional achievement:

Adequate sleep holds immense value when it comes to personal growth and professional achievement. By getting sufficient sleep, individuals can experience a range of benefits that directly contribute to their success in various aspects of their lives.

One key benefit of quality sleep is improved focus, concentration, and attention span. When we are well-rested, our minds are more alert and able to concentrate on tasks at hand. This heightened focus allows us to be more productive, accomplish goals efficiently, and excel in our professional endeavors. Whether it's tackling complex projects or studying for exams, a well-rested brain is better equipped to absorb information and retain knowledge.

Furthermore, quality sleep has been found to enhance creativity, innovation, and critical thinking skills. During the various stages of sleep, our brains undergo processes that help us consolidate memories and make connections between different pieces of information stored in our minds. This cognitive process known as memory consolidation is vital for creative problem-solving, as it enables us to draw upon past experiences and knowledge to come up with innovative solutions. By prioritizing sleep, individuals can unlock their creative potential and approach challenges with fresh ideas and perspectives.

In addition to improving cognitive functions, restful sleep plays a pivotal role in managing stress, supporting emotional well-being, and building mental resilience. When we are sleep-deprived, our bodies produce higher levels of stress hormones such as cortisol. Elevated levels of cortisol can lead to increased anxiety, mood swings, and decreased emotional stability. On the other hand, a good night's sleep helps regulate these hormones, promoting emotional balance and reducing the negative impact of stress. This emotional stability translates into greater resilience when facing setbacks or navigating challenging situations, both personally and professionally.

In summary, prioritizing quality sleep is essential for personal growth and professional achievement. By ensuring sufficient rest, individuals can reap the benefits of improved focus, enhanced creativity and critical thinking skills, and better stress management. Incorporating healthy sleep habits into daily routines sets the foundation for success, allowing individuals to thrive mentally, emotionally, and professionally.

Strategies for improving sleep quality:

1. Create a conducive sleep environment:
- ✓ Optimize lighting: Use blackout curtains or blinds to block out external light sources that may disrupt sleep. Consider using low-wattage bulbs or warm-toned lights in the bedroom to create a calming atmosphere.
- ✓ Control temperature: Keep the room cool, ideally between 60-67°F (15-19°C), as a cooler environment promotes better sleep. Experiment with different bedding materials and adjust the thermostat to find the optimal temperature for your comfort.

✓ Manage noise levels: Minimize disruptive noises by using earplugs or investing in a white noise machine to drown out background sounds. Additionally, consider using a fan or a sound machine to provide soothing ambient noise.

2. Establish a consistent sleep schedule:

✓ Set a regular sleep routine: Go to bed and wake up at the same time each day, even on weekends, to regulate your body's internal clock. Consistency reinforces healthy sleep patterns and helps improve overall sleep quality.

✓ Wind down before bed: Develop pre-sleep rituals that signal relaxation and prepare the mind for rest. Engage in calming activities such as reading, taking a warm bath, or practicing gentle stretching exercises to promote a sense of calm.

3. Incorporate relaxation techniques:

- Practice meditation: Set aside dedicated time before bed to engage in mindfulness meditation or guided meditation practices. Focus on deep breathing, relaxing each part of your body, and letting go of any tension or racing thoughts.

- Deep breathing exercises: Incorporate deep breathing techniques into your pre-sleep routine. Take slow, deep breaths in through your nose, hold for a few seconds, then exhale slowly through your mouth. This helps activate the body's natural relaxation response.

Remember that everyone's sleep needs and preferences may vary, so it is important to experiment and find what works best for you individually. By implementing these strategies, you can create a sleep environment conducive to optimal rest and improve the quality of your sleep.

Overcoming common obstacles to obtaining sufficient sleep:

Addressing technology distractions:

In today's digital age, technology has become an integral part of our lives. However, excessive screen time, particularly before bedtime, can disrupt our sleep patterns. The blue light emitted by electronic devices inhibits the production of melatonin, the hormone responsible for regulating sleep. To overcome this obstacle, it is essential to establish a technology-free zone or a digital curfew before bed. Switch off electronic devices at least an hour before sleep and engage in relaxing activities instead, such as reading a book or practicing mindfulness exercises.

Managing shift work:

For individuals who work shifts or irregular hours, maintaining consistent sleep patterns can be challenging. Our body's natural sleep-wake cycle, also known as the circadian rhythm, functions best when we have a regular sleep routine. To manage shift work effectively, create a schedule that allows for adequate rest between shifts. Prioritize quality sleep during your off days by establishing a relaxing bedtime routine and creating a conducive sleep environment. Consider using blackout curtains to darken your room during daylight hours and wearing earplugs or using white noise machines to block out external disturbances.

Coping with anxiety:

Anxiety and stress can significantly impact our ability to fall asleep and maintain restful slumber. Racing thoughts, worries, and overactive minds can make it difficult to relax and find peace before bedtime. If anxiety is interfering with your sleep, consider incorporating stress management techniques into your daily routine. This may include practicing mindfulness or meditation, engaging in physical exercise, or seeking support from a therapist or counselor. Establishing a pre-sleep ritual that includes relaxation activities, such as taking a warm bath or listening to calming music, can also help alleviate anxiety and promote better sleep.

Prioritizing self-care:

One of the biggest obstacles to obtaining sufficient sleep is neglecting self-care. Many individuals in their twenties juggle multiple responsibilities and commitments, often putting their own well-being on the back burner. However, prioritizing self-care is crucial for maintaining a healthy sleep routine. By recognizing and addressing your own needs, you are better equipped to establish and maintain healthy sleep habits. Set boundaries, learn to say no when necessary, and allocate time for rest and relaxation. Practice good sleep hygiene by creating a sleep-friendly environment, setting consistent bed and wake times, and investing in a comfortable mattress and pillow.

By addressing these common obstacles to obtaining sufficient sleep, readers can overcome challenges that may disrupt their sleep patterns. Implementing strategies for managing technology distractions, shift work, anxiety, and prioritizing self-care will enable readers to establish healthy sleep habits and reap the numerous benefits of quality rest. Remember, making sleep a non-negotiable aspect of your daily routine is an investment in your overall well-being and future success.

Introduction to the importance of self-care in maintaining physical and mental well-being during the formative years of one's twenties.

In the hustle and bustle of our daily lives, it is easy to overlook our own needs and well-being. We often prioritize our work, relationships, and external obligations, leaving little time or energy for taking care of ourselves. However, self-care is not a luxury; it is a vital component of a healthy and fulfilling life.

During the transformative phase of our twenties, when we are shaping our identities and exploring new paths, practicing self-care becomes even more critical. This is a time when we are faced with numerous challenges and uncertainties that can take a toll on our physical and mental health. By prioritizing self-care, we can build resilience, maintain balance, and develop a strong foundation for personal growth and success.

Self-care encompasses various aspects that contribute to our overall well-being, including exercise, nutrition, sleep, and stress management. Each of these components plays a crucial role in supporting our physical and mental health. By incorporating them into our daily routines, we can cultivate sustainable habits that promote long-term well-being.

Exercise is not just essential for maintaining physical fitness; it also has significant mental health benefits. Engaging in regular physical activity releases endorphins, which boost mood and reduce stress levels. Finding enjoyable forms of exercise that align with your interests and schedule can make it easier to incorporate this self-care practice into your daily life.

Nutrition is another key aspect of self-care that is often overlooked. The food we consume directly impacts our energy levels, cognitive function, and overall health. By making informed food choices and creating a balanced diet, we can nourish our bodies and enhance our well-being.

Quality sleep is essential for optimal physical and mental functioning. Yet, many young adults struggle with establishing healthy sleep habits due to busy schedules or distractions. Creating a relaxing bedtime routine, implementing strategies to manage sleep disruptions, and prioritizing sufficient rest can significantly improve our overall well-being.

Stress is an inevitable part of life, especially during our twenties when we are juggling various responsibilities and facing significant transitions. However, managing stress effectively is crucial for maintaining our physical and mental well-being. Incorporating stress management techniques such as mindfulness exercises, relaxation techniques, and engaging in self-care activities can help us navigate challenges and maintain a sense of balance.

Developing a sustainable self-care routine requires self-reflection and self-awareness. It involves understanding our individual needs and adjusting our habits accordingly. By consistently practicing self-care and prioritizing our well-being, we can enhance our productivity, improve our overall health, and experience greater fulfillment in all areas of our lives.

In the following chapters, we will delve deeper into each component of a sustainable self-care routine, providing practical strategies and tips for incorporating these practices into your busy twenties. By investing time and effort in your self-care journey, you are taking a powerful step towards building a solid foundation for success and achieving long-term well-being.

The Importance of Self-care

Understanding the different components of a sustainable self-care routine is crucial for maintaining physical and mental well-being during the formative years of one's twenties. This chapter explores various aspects of self-care, including exercise, nutrition, sleep, and stress management, providing practical strategies for incorporating these elements into a busy lifestyle.

Exercise plays a vital role in maintaining overall health and well-being. Finding enjoyable physical activities that align with personal interests can make it easier to incorporate exercise into a busy schedule. Time management techniques, such as scheduling workouts and prioritizing physical activity, can help ensure regular exercise becomes a habit. Whether it's joining a sports team, practicing yoga, or simply going for a jog, finding an activity that brings joy and fits seamlessly into one's routine is essential for long-term success.

Nutrition is another key component of a sustainable self-care routine. Recognizing the importance of balanced meals and making informed food choices supports optimal health. Creating a diverse diet that includes fruits, vegetables, whole grains, lean proteins, and healthy fats ensures that the body receives necessary nutrients. Understanding portion sizes and practicing mindful eating can also contribute to a healthier relationship with food and overall well-being.

Quality sleep is often overlooked but is crucial for both physical and mental health. Establishing healthy sleep habits can significantly impact one's well-being. Creating a relaxing bedtime routine that includes winding down before bed, engaging in calming activities such as reading or taking a warm bath, can promote better sleep quality. Additionally, managing sleep disruptions, such as limiting caffeine intake and minimizing exposure to screens before bed, can contribute to improved sleep patterns.

Stress management is essential for maintaining balance and preventing burnout. Incorporating stress-reducing activities into daily routines can have lasting benefits. Mindfulness exercises, such as meditation or deep breathing techniques, can help calm the mind and reduce stress levels. Engaging in hobbies or activities that bring joy and relaxation can also alleviate stress. By incorporating self-care activities into daily routines, individuals can proactively manage stress and promote overall well-being.

It is important to develop healthy coping mechanisms to navigate challenges and setbacks effectively. Building resilience and emotional well-being is crucial during the formative years of one's twenties. Engaging in self-reflection and self-awareness practices helps identify individual needs and adjust habits accordingly. By understanding personal triggers, individuals can develop strategies to cope with stress, setbacks, and uncertainties that may arise.

While time constraints or societal pressures may act as barriers to practicing self-care, practical solutions exist to overcome these obstacles. Prioritizing self-care should be viewed as an essential investment in long-term success and well-being. Small, intentional changes can lead to significant improvements over time. By setting realistic goals and creating a supportive environment, individuals can establish a sustainable self-care routine that works for them.

By prioritizing self-care early on in life, individuals can reap the long-term benefits. Regular exercise improves physical fitness, boosts mood, and enhances cognitive function. A balanced diet provides necessary nutrients for optimal health and energy levels. Quality sleep supports overall well-being, including improved focus and increased productivity. Effective stress management techniques contribute to better mental health and emotional resilience. By investing in self-care throughout their twenties, individuals can lay a solid foundation for a fulfilling and successful future.

Practical strategies for incorporating exercise into a busy schedule:

In today's fast-paced world, finding time for exercise can be challenging, especially for young adults in their twenties who are juggling multiple responsibilities. However, prioritizing physical activity is crucial for maintaining overall health and well-being. Here are some practical strategies to help you incorporate exercise into your busy schedule:

1. Time management techniques: Start by evaluating how you currently spend your time and identify areas where you can carve out small pockets of time for exercise. Look for opportunities to maximize your efficiency, such as combining exercise with other tasks. For example, you can listen to educational podcasts or audio books while going for a walk or jog.

2. Set realistic goals: Instead of aiming for lengthy workouts, focus on short bursts of high-intensity exercises or quick workout routines that can be done in as little as 10-15 minutes. This way, you can fit exercise into even the busiest days without feeling overwhelmed.

3. Incorporate physical activities you enjoy: Find activities that align with your interests and passions. Whether it's dancing, hiking, playing a team sport, or practicing yoga, choosing activities you genuinely enjoy will make exercising feel like less of a chore and more like a fun and rewarding experience.

4. Make use of available resources: Explore the numerous fitness apps, online workout videos, or YouTube channels that offer guided exercises and routines. These resources often provide flexible options that can be done at home or on-the-go, eliminating the need for expensive gym memberships or specific equipment.

5. Utilize breaks effectively: If your schedule doesn't allow for dedicated exercise time, take advantage of breaks throughout the day. Use your lunch break to go for a brisk walk or do a quick workout in your office or nearby park. Even small bouts of physical activity can add up and contribute to your overall fitness.

6. Incorporate exercise into daily routines: Look for opportunities to add movement to your everyday activities. For instance, take the stairs instead of the elevator, walk or bike to nearby destinations instead of driving, or opt for active hobbies like gardening or cleaning.

Remember, consistency is key when it comes to exercise. Aim for at least 150 minutes of moderate-intensity aerobic activity or 75 minutes of vigorous-intensity aerobic activity each week, along with muscle-strengthening activities on two or more days. By implementing these practical strategies and finding creative ways to stay active, you can successfully incorporate exercise into your busy schedule and prioritize your physical well-being.

Chapter 5

Developing a Sustainable
Self-Care Routine

****

Developing a Sustainable Self-Care Routine:

In this section of "Build Your Character at Twenty: Writing the Life Success Script at the Age of 20," we delve into the importance of nutrition and its impact on overall health. Creating a balanced diet and making informed food choices are essential components of a sustainable self-care routine during your formative years.

Nutrition plays a crucial role in maintaining physical well-being and fueling your body for optimal performance. It provides the necessary nutrients, vitamins, and minerals that support various bodily functions, including immune system function, cognitive abilities, and energy levels. By prioritizing nutrition, you can enhance your overall health and vitality.

Creating a balanced diet involves incorporating a variety of food groups into your meals. Aim to include fruits, vegetables, whole grains, lean proteins, and healthy fats. These food groups offer a range of nutrients that are vital for your body's growth, repair, and maintenance.

Making informed food choices is about understanding the impact of different foods on your body. It involves reading food labels, considering portion sizes, and being mindful of added sugars, sodium, and unhealthy fats. By developing a basic understanding of nutrition principles, you can make choices that align with your health goals.

One way to make informed food choices is to prioritize whole, unprocessed foods. These include fresh fruits and vegetables, whole grains, lean meats, and nuts. These foods are rich in nutrients and provide the fuel your body needs to thrive.

Additionally, learning to cook simple, nutritious meals can make a significant difference in your overall well-being. Developing basic cooking skills allows you to have greater control over what goes into your meals and enables you to experiment with different flavors and ingredients. It can also be a fun and creative outlet.

It's important to note that while nutrition is essential, it's also crucial to cultivate a healthy relationship with food. Avoid falling into restrictive diets or labeling certain foods as "good" or "bad." Instead, focus on moderation, mindful eating, and listening to your body's hunger and fullness cues.

By prioritizing nutrition and making informed food choices, you are investing in your long-term health and well-being. It sets the foundation for a sustainable self-care routine that supports your physical and mental health throughout your twenties and beyond. Remember, nourishing your body with nutritious food is a powerful act of self-care.

Developing a Sustainable Self-Care Routine:

Discussing the significance of quality sleep and providing tips for establishing healthy sleep habits, including creating a relaxing bedtime routine and managing sleep disruptions.

Quality sleep is essential for maintaining physical and mental well-being, especially during the formative years of one's twenties. However, many young adults struggle to establish healthy sleep habits due to busy schedules, stress, or technological distractions. In this section, we will explore the importance of quality sleep and provide practical tips for developing a sustainable sleep routine.

Creating a relaxing bedtime routine is key to preparing both your mind and body for a restful night's sleep. Start by establishing a regular sleep schedule, aiming to go to bed and wake up at the same time every day, even on weekends. This helps regulate your internal body clock and promotes better sleep quality.

In addition to consistent bedtimes, it is crucial to create a calm and soothing environment in your bedroom. Consider dimming the lights, playing soft music, or using aromatherapy to create a peaceful ambiance. Avoid engaging in stimulating activities close to bedtime, such as intense workouts or screen time, as these can interfere with your ability to relax and fall asleep.

Managing sleep disruptions is another vital aspect of developing a sustainable self-care routine. If you struggle with falling or staying asleep, try implementing relaxation techniques before bed. Deep breathing exercises, progressive muscle relaxation, or guided meditation can help calm your mind and prepare your body for slumber.

It is also important to address any potential factors that may be interfering with your sleep quality. Evaluate your sleep environment for noise disturbances or uncomfortable bedding that may disrupt your rest. Consider investing in a supportive mattress and pillows that promote spinal alignment and comfort. Additionally, minimize exposure to blue light from electronic devices before bed, as it can suppress the production of melatonin, the hormone responsible for regulating sleep.

If you consistently struggle with getting sufficient sleep despite implementing these strategies, it may be beneficial to consult a healthcare professional. They can help identify any underlying medical conditions or sleep disorders that may be affecting your sleep and provide appropriate treatments or recommendations.

By prioritizing the quality of your sleep and implementing these tips for establishing healthy sleep habits, you can pave the way for improved physical and mental well-being. Remember, adequate rest is not a luxury but a vital component of self-care that supports your overall health and success in all aspects of life.

Techniques for managing stress effectively are essential components of a sustainable self-care routine. By incorporating mindfulness exercises and relaxation techniques into daily routines, individuals can effectively reduce stress levels and promote overall well-being.

Mindfulness exercises, such as meditation or deep breathing exercises, are powerful tools for managing stress. By focusing on the present moment and cultivating a non-judgmental awareness of thoughts and emotions, individuals can reduce anxiety and increase mental clarity. Regular practice of mindfulness can also improve emotional regulation and resilience, enabling individuals to navigate challenges with greater ease.

In addition to mindfulness exercises, incorporating relaxation techniques into daily routines can also help manage stress levels. Activities such as taking a warm bath, engaging in gentle stretching exercises, or practicing progressive muscle relaxation can promote relaxation and relieve tension in the body. These techniques provide an opportunity for individuals to unwind and recharge, fostering a sense of calmness and inner peace.

Furthermore, integrating self-care activities into daily routines can be highly effective in managing stress. Engaging in activities that bring joy and fulfillment, such as pursuing hobbies, spending time in nature, or connecting with loved ones, can serve as powerful stress-reducing practices. By prioritizing self-care and making time for activities that nourish the mind, body, and soul, individuals can cultivate a sense of balance and resilience in the face of stressors.

It is important to note that each individual's approach to managing stress may vary, as what works for one person may not work for another. It is crucial to explore different techniques and find what resonates with personal preferences and needs. Regular self-reflection and self-awareness are vital in identifying effective stress management strategies unique to each individual.

By incorporating these techniques into a sustainable self-care routine, individuals can effectively manage stress levels, enhance their overall well-being, and promote long-term physical and mental health. Building a strong foundation of stress management during the twenties sets the stage for a healthier and more fulfilling life.

Encouraging the development of healthy coping mechanisms is essential for individuals in their twenties to navigate challenges and setbacks, promoting resilience and emotional well-being. The formative years of one's twenties often come with various pressures and uncertainties, making it crucial to have effective strategies in place to cope with difficulties.

One key aspect of developing healthy coping mechanisms is understanding the importance of self-awareness and self-reflection. By taking the time to understand oneself and identify individual needs, individuals can better navigate challenging situations and respond in a way that aligns with their values and goals. Self-awareness allows individuals to recognize their emotions, thoughts, and behaviors, providing a solid foundation for implementing effective coping strategies.

Another important element is mindfulness. Practicing mindfulness exercises can help individuals stay present in the moment, reducing stress and anxiety. Mindfulness techniques such as deep breathing, meditation, or yoga can be incorporated into daily routines to promote relaxation and foster emotional well-being. Regular practice can enhance focus, reduce negative thinking patterns, and improve overall mental health.

Engaging in regular self-care activities is also vital for maintaining emotional well-being. This can involve engaging in hobbies or activities that bring joy and fulfillment. Whether it's pursuing artistic endeavors, spending time in nature, or enjoying quality time with loved ones, these activities replenish energy levels and serve as a source of rejuvenation during challenging times.

Building a support network is another essential aspect of developing healthy coping mechanisms. Surrounding oneself with positive and supportive individuals helps foster resilience and provides a support system during difficult moments. It's important to cultivate relationships that uplift and inspire, where individuals can share their struggles openly and receive encouragement.

While setbacks are unavoidable, reframing them as opportunities for growth and learning can be a powerful coping mechanism. Rather than viewing failures as obstacles, individuals can choose to see them as stepping stones toward personal development. Embracing a growth mindset allows individuals to bounce back from setbacks more easily and persevere in the face of challenges.

Incorporating self-care into daily routines should be seen as a priority, not as a luxury. By actively practicing healthy coping mechanisms, individuals can enhance their emotional well-being, reduce stress, and build resilience. Taking time to develop effective coping strategies during this critical phase of life sets the foundation for navigating future challenges with grace and strength.

Developing a Sustainable Self-Care Routine:

In order to create and maintain a sustainable self-care routine, it is crucial to engage in self-reflection and cultivate self-awareness. This entails taking the time to understand your own individual needs and adjusting your habits accordingly. By being attuned to what truly nourishes and revitalizes you, you can tailor your self-care practices to effectively support your physical and mental well-being throughout your twenties.

Self-reflection involves looking inward and gaining insight into your thoughts, emotions, and behaviors. It allows you to identify the areas of your life that may be causing stress or imbalance, as well as the activities and practices that bring you joy and fulfillment. By actively reflecting on your experiences and thought patterns, you can gain a deeper understanding of what self-care practices resonate with you personally.

Self-awareness goes hand in hand with self-reflection, as it involves being conscious of your needs, boundaries, strengths, and limitations. When you are aware of what makes you thrive and what depletes your energy, you are better equipped to make choices that align with your well-being. Developing self-awareness requires paying attention to how different activities, relationships, and environments impact your mood, energy levels, and overall sense of happiness.

Once you have gained insight through self-reflection and cultivated self-awareness, it is important to adjust your habits accordingly. This may involve incorporating new self-care practices into your daily routine or modifying existing ones to better suit your needs. For example, if you discover that spending time alone rejuvenates you, you can prioritize carving out moments of solitude in your schedule. On the other hand, if you find that certain commitments or activities drain your energy, it may be necessary to reassess and make changes that align with your well-being.

By incorporating self-reflection and self-awareness into your journey towards developing a sustainable self-care routine, you will be able to create habits that truly nourish and support your physical and mental health. Remember, self-care is not a one-size-fits-all approach. It is a deeply personal and individualized practice that requires ongoing exploration, experimentation, and adjustment. Your twenties provide the perfect opportunity to invest in yourself and cultivate habits that will carry you towards a lifetime of well-being and fulfillment.

Addressing common barriers to practicing self-care, such as time constraints or societal pressures, and offering practical solutions to overcome these obstacles is crucial for maintaining a sustainable self-care routine. In the fast-paced world of the twenties, it can often feel like there's never enough time to prioritize self-care. However, by recognizing and addressing these barriers head-on, individuals can make meaningful changes to improve their well-being.

One common barrier to practicing self-care is the perception that it takes too much time. Many young adults feel overwhelmed by their responsibilities, whether it's work, school, or personal commitments. As a result, self-care often gets pushed to the bottom of the priority list. However, it's important to remember that taking care of oneself is not a luxury but a necessity.

To overcome this time constraint, it's essential to shift our mindset about self-care. Instead of viewing it as an indulgence or a time-consuming activity, think of it as an investment in your overall well-being and productivity. Start by carving out small pockets of time each day dedicated solely to self-care. It could be as simple as setting aside 15 minutes in the morning for meditation or incorporating short exercise breaks throughout the day.

Another barrier to practicing self-care is societal pressure and the fear of being perceived as selfish or lazy. Society often glorifies busyness and productivity, making it challenging for individuals to prioritize their own needs without feeling guilty. However, neglecting self-care can lead to burnout and negatively impact every aspect of life.

To overcome societal pressures, it's important to recognize that taking care of oneself is not selfish but essential for long-term success and happiness. Remind yourself that you deserve love and care just as much as anyone else. Surround yourself with supportive individuals who understand and value the importance of self-care.

It's also crucial to set boundaries and learn to say no when necessary. Prioritize activities that align with personal values and bring genuine joy. Remember that self-care looks different for everyone, and what works for others may not work for you. Find activities that resonate with your unique interests and needs to make self-care a fulfilling and enjoyable part of your daily routine.

In conclusion, addressing common barriers to practicing self-care is vital for establishing a sustainable self-care routine in your twenties. By shifting your mindset, carving out dedicated time, overcoming societal pressures, and setting boundaries, you can overcome these obstacles and make self-care a priority in your life. Remember, investing in your well-being now will pay off in the long run, leading to increased productivity, improved overall health, and enhanced well-being.

the long-term benefits of prioritizing self-care early on in life, including increased productivity, improved overall health, and enhanced well-being.

Developing a sustainable self-care routine at the age of twenty is not only crucial for immediate well-being but also lays the groundwork for a lifetime of success and fulfillment. By prioritizing self-care early on, individuals can reap numerous long-term benefits that extend far beyond their twenties.

One of the key advantages of establishing a sustainable self-care routine is increased productivity. Taking the time to care for oneself physically and mentally allows for greater focus, concentration, and energy levels. When individuals prioritize activities that nurture their well-being, they are better equipped to tackle tasks and responsibilities with efficiency and effectiveness. With a clear mind and heightened energy levels, they can accomplish more in less time, leading to increased productivity in both personal and professional endeavors.

Furthermore, implementing consistent self-care practices contributes to improved overall health. Engaging in regular exercise, consuming a balanced diet, getting quality sleep, and managing stress all play pivotal roles in maintaining physical well-being. By incorporating these components into a sustainable routine, individuals can boost their immunity, reduce the risk of chronic diseases, and enhance their physical fitness. A healthy body serves as a solid foundation for pursuing one's goals and dreams without being hindered by frequent illness or fatigue.

In addition to physical health benefits, prioritizing self-care also leads to enhanced well-being. Taking time to engage in activities that bring joy, relaxation, and fulfillment contributes to emotional and mental well-being. By engaging in hobbies, spending time with loved ones, practicing mindfulness techniques, or pursuing interests outside of work or studies, individuals can cultivate a sense of balance and contentment. This emotional well-being fosters resilience in the face of challenges and setbacks throughout life.

By highlighting the long-term benefits of prioritizing self-care early on, individuals are encouraged to make it an integral part of their daily lives. The advantages of increased productivity, improved overall health, and enhanced well-being serve as strong motivations to establish and maintain a sustainable self-care routine throughout their twenties and beyond. By investing in oneself at this formative stage, individuals set the stage for a lifetime of success, fulfillment, and resilience.

Part 6:
Financial
Independence

Chapter 1

Budgeting Basics: Planning for the Present and Future

****

Understanding the Importance of Budgeting:

Budgeting is a fundamental financial skill that is crucial for individuals in their twenties who are striving for financial stability and independence. It provides a roadmap for managing income, expenses, and savings effectively. By understanding the importance of budgeting, readers can lay a solid foundation for their future financial success.

One of the key reasons why budgeting is essential is that it enables individuals to track their income. By knowing exactly how much money is coming in each month, individuals can make informed decisions about how to allocate their resources. This knowledge gives them a sense of control over their finances, allowing them to prioritize their needs and wants accordingly.

Furthermore, budgeting helps individuals keep tabs on their expenses. Tracking expenses allows individuals to see where their money is going and identify areas where they may be overspending. By having a clear picture of their spending habits, individuals can make necessary adjustments to ensure they are living within their means and avoiding debt.

Moreover, budgeting promotes savings. By setting aside a portion of their income for savings, individuals can build an emergency fund, save for future goals, and establish a financial safety net. Savings not only provide peace of mind in times of unexpected expenses or emergencies but also create opportunities for investments and long-term wealth accumulation.

Budgeting also encourages wise spending decisions. When individuals have a budget in place, they can evaluate their spending choices more consciously. They can distinguish between what they truly need versus what is merely a want. This mindfulness empowers individuals to make informed financial choices aligned with their goals and values.

In addition, budgeting helps individuals plan for the future. By tracking income and expenses, individuals can create a realistic projection of their financial situation in the coming months or years. This foresight enables them to anticipate potential challenges or opportunities and make proactive decisions to optimize their financial well-being.

Ultimately, understanding the importance of budgeting sets the stage for building a strong financial foundation. By tracking income, controlling expenses, promoting savings, and making wise spending decisions, individuals can gain control over their finances and work towards their short-term and long-term financial goals. In the following sections, we will delve deeper into the practical steps involved in budgeting and how to assess your current financial situation to create a comprehensive budget that aligns with your unique circumstances and aspirations.

Assessing Current Financial Situation:

In order to effectively manage your finances and create a solid budget, it is essential to first assess your current financial situation. This process involves gathering all the necessary information about your income, expenses, debts, and assets to create a comprehensive snapshot of your financial health.

Start by examining your sources of income. This includes your salary or wages, any side jobs or freelance work, investments, and any other sources of money coming in. Be sure to calculate your income after taxes and deductions to get an accurate understanding of how much you have available to budget.

Next, take a close look at your expenses. Categorize them into fixed expenses, such as rent/mortgage payments, utility bills, and loan repayments, and variable expenses, such as groceries, transportation costs, and entertainment. It's important to be thorough and include even the smallest expenses to get a clear picture of where your money is going.

Don't forget to assess your debts as well. This includes student loans, credit card debt, car loans, or any other outstanding loans you may have. Make note of the interest rates, minimum monthly payments, and remaining balances for each debt.

Lastly, evaluate your assets. This could be the value of any properties you own, savings accounts, investments, or any other valuable possessions that can contribute to your overall financial health.

By gathering all this information and creating a detailed overview of your financial situation, you will gain insights into your current financial standing. This will serve as the foundation for creating an effective budgeting plan that aligns with your goals and aspirations. It will also enable you to make informed decisions about how to allocate your income towards different categories such as savings, debt repayment, and discretionary spending.

Remember, being aware of your financial situation is the first step towards taking control of your finances and building a strong foundation for future success. Take the time to assess your current financial situation thoroughly, and you will be well-equipped to make the necessary adjustments and achieve your financial goals.

Setting Financial Goals: In this section, readers will explore the significance of setting clear and specific financial goals in their twenties. While budgeting is essential for managing finances, having a goal-oriented approach provides direction and motivation for saving, investing, and making smart financial decisions.

The chapter begins by emphasizing the importance of defining short-term and long-term objectives. Short-term goals may include saving for emergencies, paying off student loans, or building an emergency fund. Long-term goals could involve investing in retirement, buying a home, or starting a business. By clearly identifying these goals, readers can allocate their resources and make informed choices that align with their financial aspirations.

To effectively set financial goals, it is crucial to prioritize them based on urgency and long-term impact. Readers are encouraged to reflect on their values, needs, and desires to determine which goals hold the most significance for them personally. By prioritizing goals, individuals can create a realistic timeline that accounts for their income, expenses, and savings capacity.

Once goals are identified and prioritized, this section provides practical tips for establishing measurable targets. By setting specific dollar amounts or percentages to achieve within a given timeframe, readers can track their progress toward each goal. This allows for better accountability and motivation throughout the process.

Importantly, this chapter also highlights the value of flexibility in goal setting. As circumstances change, it is vital to reevaluate and adjust financial goals accordingly. Life events such as career changes, unexpected expenses, or new opportunities may require modifications to the original plan. By regularly reassessing goals and adjusting timelines if needed, readers can ensure their financial plans remain relevant and attainable.

Throughout this section, real-life examples and success stories provide inspiration and showcase the transformative power of setting financial goals in one's twenties. By taking proactive steps towards achieving these goals early on, young adults can lay a solid foundation for future financial stability and independence.

Creating a Monthly Budget:

Creating and sticking to a monthly budget is an essential step towards achieving financial stability and independence. By allocating income towards different categories, individuals can effectively manage their expenses, save for the future, and avoid unnecessary debt. In this section, we will explore the step-by-step process of creating a monthly budget and provide practical strategies for budgeting with irregular income or fluctuating expenses.

1. Determine your income:

The first step in creating a monthly budget is to determine your total monthly income. This includes any regular paychecks, freelance work, passive income, or other sources of revenue. Be sure to consider any taxes or deductions that may be taken out of your income.

2. Identify essential expenses:

Next, identify your essential expenses, which are the costs necessary for maintaining a basic standard of living. This includes housing (rent or mortgage payments), utilities (electricity, water, internet), transportation (car payments, gas, public transportation), groceries, and insurance. These expenses should be given priority in your budget.

3. Allocate discretionary spending:

After accounting for essential expenses, allocate a portion of your income towards discretionary spending. This category includes entertainment, dining out, shopping, vacations, and other non-essential expenses. It's important to be realistic and mindful of your spending habits when allocating funds for discretionary purposes.

4. Plan for debt repayment:

If you have any outstanding debts, such as student loans or credit card balances, allocate a portion of your income towards debt repayment. Consider your minimum monthly payments and aim to pay off higher-interest debts first. Prioritizing debt repayment in your budget will help you reduce interest charges and become debt-free sooner.

5. Save for the future:

Saving for the future is crucial for financial security. Allocate a portion of your income towards savings and investments. Aim to build an emergency fund that can cover at least three to six months' worth of expenses. Additionally, consider saving for long-term goals, such as retirement or major purchases.

6. Adjust for irregular income or fluctuating expenses:

If you have irregular income, such as from freelance work or commission-based jobs, budgeting can be more challenging. In this case, it's important to estimate your average monthly income based on past earnings. Create a budget based on this estimated income while also setting aside a portion for savings during high-income months. When planning for fluctuating expenses, such as utility bills or seasonal expenses, take an average of the highest expected costs and include them in your budget.

7. Track your expenses:

Once you have created your monthly budget, it's crucial to track your actual expenses to ensure you're staying on track. Use budgeting apps or spreadsheets to record your expenditures and compare them to your planned budget. This will help you identify areas where you may be overspending and make necessary adjustments.

8. Make adjustments as needed:

As circumstances change, be prepared to make adjustments to your budget. Life events like job changes, salary increases, or unexpected expenses may require modifications to your allocation of funds. Regularly review and update your budget to reflect any changes in income, expenses, or financial goals.

By creating a monthly budget and sticking to it, you'll gain control over your finances and be better equipped to achieve your financial goals. Budgeting allows you to prioritize spending, save for the future, and avoid unnecessary debt. Remember, the key to successful budgeting is consistency and discipline. Stay committed to your financial plan and make adjustments when necessary. Your future self will thank you for it!,Monitoring and Adjusting the Budget: The final section of this chapter emphasizes the importance of regularly monitoring and adjusting the budget as circumstances change. It is crucial for individuals to stay proactive and vigilant when it comes to managing their finances. By regularly reviewing their budget, individuals can ensure that they are on track to achieving their financial goals.

One practical tip for tracking expenses is to utilize budgeting apps or online tools that can automatically categorize expenses and provide visual representations of spending habits. These tools make it easy to see where money is being allocated and can help identify areas where adjustments can be made.

Managing cash flow is another important aspect of budgeting. Individuals should have a clear understanding of when income is expected and plan their expenses accordingly. This includes setting aside money for fixed expenses such as rent or mortgage payments, utilities, and loan repayments. By prioritizing these essential expenses, individuals can avoid financial stress and ensure that they are meeting their obligations.

Staying accountable to financial goals is key to maintaining a successful budget. One effective way to do this is by regularly reviewing progress and making adjustments as needed. This may involve reallocating funds from one category to another or finding ways to cut back on discretionary spending. By staying disciplined and motivated, individuals can continue to make progress towards their financial goals.

It is also important to acknowledge that unexpected expenses or financial setbacks may occur. However, having a well-monitored and adjusted budget can help individuals navigate these challenges more effectively. It is recommended to establish an emergency fund to handle unexpected expenses or create a plan for addressing financial setbacks. This may involve temporarily adjusting spending or seeking additional sources of income.

Overall, monitoring and adjusting the budget are ongoing processes that require consistent effort and discipline. By staying proactive, individuals can maintain control over their finances and make informed decisions to ensure long-term financial stability and success.

Chapter 2

Debt Management: Student Loans and Credit Cards

***

Understanding the Impact of Student Loans:

While pursuing post-se-condary qualifications is hugely impactful for one's prospective- career prospects and financial outcome-s, attaining such education frequently re-quires sizeable mone-tary investments. Loans for students are- pivotal in financing higher learning for many, permitting pe-ople to chase their scholarly aspirations. That be-ing said, it is extremely important to be- cognizant of the long-term conseque-nces and duties linked with taking on de-bt to fund your education. Carefully considering the- costs involved today versus potential e-arnings later can help make informe-d decisions about student borrowing.

To begin, allow's e-xamine the numerous kinds of scholar loans acce-ssible. Federal loans, like- Direct Subsidized Loans and Direct Unsubsidize-d Loans, are issued by way of the gove-rnment and provide aggressive- hobby quotes and versatile re-payment options. Those loans are a top notch option for most colle-ge students due to the- fact they feature low inte-rest and flexible re-payment plans. Private loans, at the same- time as, are rece-ived thru banks or credit unions and regularly include- higher hobby quotes. In assessme-nt, those loans frequently lack the- client-friendly terms provide-d by means of the fede-ral executive. While- non-public loans can assist in covering prices now not covere-d through federal help, colle-ge students nee-d to cautiously weigh the hobby charges and te-rms prior to accepting them.

While mulling ove-r student loans, it is extreme-ly vital to cautiously assess the particulars and provisions relate-d with each loan choice. Look past the quick advantage-s and consider components, for example-, financing costs, reimbursement de-signs, and postponement choices. Compre-hending these subtle- elements will assist you with se-ttling on educated choices with re-gards to which loans best accommodate your monetary circumstance-.

Taking out student loans is an important financial de-cision that requires careful conside-ration of various factors. Here are a fe-w tips that may help when choosing student loans: Care-fully research your loan options to understand re-payment terms, intere-st rates, and total costs. Federal stude-nt loans usually offer

It's important to thoroughly investigate- the numerous loan possibilities available-: dedicate the time-required to examine- and contrast the diverse loan package-s and loan providers. Comprehend the-ir rates of interest, costs, provisions, and payme-nt schedules. See-king advice from a financial consultant can likewise furnish e-xtra direction. While exploring your choice-s, look closely at interest charge-s and extra fees, fixe-d or variable rates, penaltie-s for prepayment, and the total cost ove-r the life of the loan. Ge-tting personalized recomme-ndations from someone knowledge-able about current programs can help e-nsure you choose an option that best fits both short- and long-te-rm needs and goals.

When planning your e-ducation finances, it's important to thoughtfully consider your caree-r aspirations and future earning power. Take- time to research the- typical salaries within your intended fie-ld upon obtaining your degree. This will he-lp you estimate a realistic monthly loan re-payment budget that fits within the income- you expect to make post-graduation. Be-ing prudent now about what you can reasonably afford later will he-lp prevent debt from be-coming a burden down the road.

To dete-rmine your complete stude-nt loan amount, add up the balances from each ye-ar of your education. Knowing your total student loan debt e-arly will assist with financial planning both during school and after graduation. This total will help guide spe-nding decisions and repayment prioritization going forward.

There- are various options to consider financing your education without taking on e-xcessive student loan de-bt. Look into scholarship and grant opportunities which do not require re-payment. These can he-lp lower tuition costs. Part-time or full-time e-mployment is another choice to e-arn wages that can offset school expe-nses. Additionally, completing gene-ral education prerequisite-s at an affordable community college prior to transfe-rring to a bachelor's degree- program is a wise approach. Starting out your postsecondary path in this manner ke-eps costs down initially.

Understand the long-term financial impact: Recognize that excessive student loan debt can hinder your ability to achieve other financial goals, such as purchasing a home or starting a business. Be mindful of the financial burden you're taking on and consider whether it aligns with your long-term aspirations.

Rephrase While gaining insight into the- importance of student loans is prudent, the-re are steps one- can take to prevent be-ing overwhelmed by de-bt. Considering strategies like- only borrowing what is absolutely necessary for tuition and living e-xpenses can help ke-ep your obligations manageable long te-rm. Proactively address your loans by learning re-payment options available and creating a solid plan to tackle- amounts owed. Maintaining consistent payments is ke-y to avoiding spiraling costs. With diligence and care, your e-ducation investment can pave the- way for financial security ahead.

Rephrase Creating a Repayment Strategy for Student Loans:

To properly handle- student loan debt, deve-loping a repayment approach tailored to your e-conomic circumstance and aims is extreme-ly important. Thinking through the numerous opportunities available- and utilizing clever financial planning technique-s can assist you in smoothly moving through the repayment proce-ss and progressing towards being debt-fre-e. Whether it be- extending your term to lowe-r monthly installments or considering income-drive-n plans that base the amount due on your e-arnings, analyzing the diverse choice-s can aid in determining the most suitable- path. Mindfully tracking expenses is also ke-y to having a realistic sense of how much can re-asonably be allocated to loans each month. With dilige-nce and strategy, working step-by-ste-p to fulfill obligations is very possible.

1. Outline strategies for managing student loan debt:

Rese-arch different repayme-nt plans: Familiarize yourself thoroughly with the various re-payment options available for fede-ral student loans, such as the Standard Repayme-nt Plan, Income-Driven Repayme-nt Plans like Income-Based Re-payment and Pay As You Earn, and Graduated Repayme-nt Plans. Be sure to comprehe-nd their eligibility nee-ds, advantages, and potential negative-s. These plans can help you manage- payments in a way that aligns with your budget and financial situation.

Consider loan consolidation as it can simplify your re-payment process. When you consolidate- multiple student loans into a single loan with a fixe-d interest rate, it combine-s all your loans into one, making managing your monthly payments easie-r. This option of consolidation is worth evaluating as it streamlines re-paying your student debt.

- Carefully conside-r refinancing options if you have built a solid repayme-nt history and good credit score. Refinancing may allow se-curing a reduced intere-st rate, lowering monthly costs. Howeve-r, thoroughly evaluate pros and cons before- deciding whether re-financing suits your situation. Weighing factors like fee-s, loan terms, and long term savings can help de-termine if refinancing be-nefits outweigh potential drawbacks.
- Creating a se-nsible budget and repayme-nt plan is essential when de-aling with student loans. It's important to have a clear unde-rstanding of your loan balance and monthly payments so you can plan your finances accordingly. A re-alistic budget allows you to allocate
- Take stock of your financial circumstance-s: Consider your earnings, costs, and other mone-tary responsibilities. Grasp how much you can designate- towards paying down student loans every month without je-opardizing different basic require-ments. It's important to have a clear picture- of your finances so you can create a plan to re-pay your loans responsibly.
- Set achie-vable goals: Break down your debt into manage-able milestones base-d on your target payoff date. This helps you stay motivate-d and focused on your progress as you tackle smalle-r pieces one at a time- rather than feeling ove-rwhelmed by the whole-. Set short term targets to cross off fre-quent enough to fee-l a sense of accomplishment in chipping away at the- larger task.
- Deve-lop a thorough budget that itemizes your e-xpected earnings, costs of living, and stude-nt loan installments each month. Evaluate whe-re you can decrease- spending to free up additional

mone-y to dedicate towards paying off your loans sooner. This organizing of finance-s will help focus your funds on repayment.

- Here- are some tips for effe-ctively communicating with loan servicers and unde-rstanding available repayment assistance- programs: Be sure to contact your loan service-r if you are having trouble making payments - the-y may be able to help you e-nroll in alternative repayme-nt plans or loan forgiveness programs. Ask about income-drive-n repayment

- Maintain regular contact with your loan se-rvicer to ensure you are- informed about potential changes or update-s to your loans. This allows open communication, which can help preve-nt issues. Contact them right away if facing money trouble-s that could impact making payments. Staying in touch helps address proble-ms before they be-come larger.

- Reach out to your loan se-rvicer for guidance: Loan service-rs have valuable expe-rtise and can help you understand your re-payment choices, eligibility for loan forgive-ness programs, or the possibility to temporarily postpone- or lower payments during financially difficult times through de-ferment and forbearance-. Their advice can offer clarity on handling your loans.

- Take time- to investigate repayme-nt help programs: Become acquainte-d with conceivable advance le-niency programs or reimburseme-nt help activities particular to your vocation or conditions. Rese-arch qualification necessities and e-xpected strides to ge-t to these projects. The-se projects can potentially offe-r help paying off your credits or eve-n pardon a percentage on the- off chance that you meet the-ir prerequisites.

While de-veloping a thorough strategy to repay your stude-nt loans and adopting prudent budgeting habits can assist you in efficie-ntly handling your student debt and progressing towards financial inde-pendence, re-member that kee-ping well-informed of your options, proactively inte-racting with loan servicers, and investigating aid programs offe-red will substantially aid your endeavor to be-come debt-free-. By creating a plan for repayment that fits your circumstance-s and monitoring expenses monthly, you e-quip yourself to satisfy obligations on schedule. Additionally, maintaining ope-n lines of communication and exploring any accessible- relief helps smooth the- path ahead.

Navigating Credit Card Usage:

While cre-dit cards can serve as a useful tool whe-n handled wisely, it is important for those just starting out on the-ir own financial journey to carefully consider both the- potential benefits and risks be-fore deciding how cards may fit into their budge-t. Maintaining awareness of advantages like- rewards programs or the convenie-nce of credit over cash can e-mpower smart spending habits. At the same-time, one must acknowledge- drawbacks such as interest charges whe-n balances are not paid in full or the e-ase with which overspending may occur without vigilance-. As young adults establish themselve-s, gaining perspective on cre-dit card responsibilities through open-minde-d research and prudent de-cision making from the

To begin, le-t us examine briefly the- pros of credit cards. One key advantage- is ease of use. Cre-dit cards enable you to buy things without hauling around cash or checks. The-y likewise furnish superior se-curity versus debit cards against fraudulent activity. Furthe-rmore, numerous credit cards include-incentives programs that can return a pe-rcentage of expe-nditures as cash, travel miles, or price- cuts on select buys. Unfortunately, cre-dit cards can encourage overspe-nding if not used judiciously.

While cre-dit cards offer convenience-, there are risks to conside-r if not managed carefully. One of the- key factors is spending sensibly. Whe-n a credit limit is available, it can be e-nticing to spend beyond one's me-ans. However, it is esse-ntial to only use the card for purchases you have- the funds to pay off completely e-ach cycle. Carrying a balance month after month risks spiraling de-bt mounting due to steep inte-rest charges. Debt burde-ns grow heavier over time- as unpaid interest adds to the principal owe-d. Therefore, discipline- is important to avoid going beyond your financial means. Credit, whe-n handled prudently, provides fle-xibility but demands responsibility.

Comprehe-nding the nuances relate-d to credit cards is indispensable for making se-nsible choices. The rate-s levied for exte-nding credit, usually denoted as Annual Pe-rcentage Rates (APR), can fluctuate-markedly subject to the providing institution and your trustworthine-ss with repaying debt. It is prudent to e-valuate the differing APRs across cards and opt for one- tendering a reduce-d rate if you plan to maintain a balance over time-. Moreover, kee-p in mind any yearly charges linked to the- card and measure whethe-r the advantages outweigh the- expenses.

Whethe-r opting for a new credit card, it is prudent to conte-mplate your distinctive nece-ssities and predilections. Ce-rtain cards cater to particular interests, like- travel or eating out, proffering re-munerations geared towards those- types of expenditure-s. Assess your way of life and buying behaviors to asce-rtain which style of remunerations program will furnish the- most worth. Furthermore, ponder any e-xtra perquisites or advantages supplie-d by the card, such as purchase security or e-xtended guarantee-s. When picking, focus on cards with benefits that match your typical costs to maximize- the value you rece-ive in return.

RephraseUltimately, cre-dit cards can serve as practical monetary instrume-nts when applied judiciously. Grasping the pros and cons re-lated to credit card impleme-ntation is vital for youths to stay clear of collecting nee-dless financial obligation. By opting for an appropriate credit card, be-ing aware of costs, and repaying balances comple-tely every month, one- can successfully navigate the cre-dit card landscape while constructing a strong economic base-.

Building Healthy Credit Habits:

Having and kee-ping a good credit score is very important for financial chance-s later on. A solid credit past not just impacts your capacity to get loans or cre-dit cards however additionally influence-s intrigue rates, protection pre-miums, and potentially even e-mployment openings. To guarantee- a solid credit profile, it is basic to create- positive credit propensitie-s from a youthful age. The accompanying are a couple- functional hints to assist you with building up solid credit propensities:

1. Paying bills promptly each month is absolute-ly essential for constructing favorable cre-dit. If obligations are not satisfied by the due- date, it can dramatically damage your credit score- and perhaps lead to additional charges. To avoid this, e-stablish automatic withdrawals on the expecte-d payment date or use cale-ndar alerts to remembe-r obligations. Making certain bills are paid in a timely manne-r consistently over time is ke-y for demonstrating responsible financial habits to le-nders.

2. It's important to maintain a low credit utilization in orde-r to showcase your responsible use- of credit lines. Credit utilization is the- percentage of your total cre-dit limits that you're currently using, and it's best to ke-ep this number below 30%. Doing so illustrate-s that you don't rely heavily on borrowed funds and can e-xercise good judgment with cre-dit. A utilization rate lower than 30% signals that you have e-nough available credit remaining and are-n't overextende-d financially, which lenders view positive-ly. Aim to minimize the balances you carry month to month re-lative to your total credit limits exte-nded.

3. **Monitor Your Credit Reports:** Regularly check your credit reports from the major credit bureaus (Equifax, Experian, and TransUnion) to identify any errors or discrepancies. Disputing inaccuracies promptly can help maintain the accuracy of your credit history.

4. **Use Credit Cards Wisely:** Credit cards can be useful tools for building credit when used responsibly. Avoid carrying balances from month to month and aim to pay off your balance in full each billing cycle. If you find yourself struggling with credit card debt, develop a repayment plan and explore options such as balance transfers or negotiating lower interest rates.

While it's wise- to have different type-s of credit accounts like student loans, auto loans, or mortgage-s to build your credit history, be sure not to take- on debt you don't truly need. Maintaining a varie-ty of credit lines can provide be-nefits for your credit score by de-monstrating responsible handling of differe-nt obligations over time. Just make ce-rtain any new accounts are reasonable- commitments you're able to fulfill as agre-ed without becoming overe-xtended financially or risking missed payme-nts. Your creditworthiness is best se-rved through prudent manageme-nt of existing responsibilities rathe-r than seeking diversification at the- cost of unnecessary burden.

While it can be- advantageous to have seve-ral credit accounts, opening too numerous accounts in a brie-f timeframe should be side-stepped. Each credit inquiry and fre-shly opened account has the te-mporary effect of marginally decre-asing your credit score. It is wise to judiciously space- out applying for and establishing new credit line-s over longer periods to minimize- the impact on your credit rating.

While he-lping others access credit can be- kind, cosigning for someone brings high responsibility. As a cosigne-r, the lender se-es you as equally accountable for re-paying the debt should the primary borrowe-r default. Before ple-dging to cover another's loan or credit line-, carefully consider whethe-r you fully trust their commitment and ability to make time-ly installments. Only cosign after peace-fully confident in the other pe-rson's financial reliability. Communicating clear expe-ctations also helps protect a cosigner from unfore-seen difficulties me-eting payments, to prese-rve the credit ratings of all involve-d.

While de-bt struggles are difficult, help is available-. Nonprofit credit counseling service-s offer guidance and solutions. They can work with you to cre-ate a personalized plan for managing de-bts, sticking to a sensible budget, and taking ste-ps to enhance your credit re-port over time. See-king their assistance is worthwhile if bills fe-el overwhelming. Counse-lors have experie-nce navigating credit issues and can sugge-st proven approaches for getting finance-s on track. You do not have to handle debt alone-. Reach out - these organizations want to assist pe-ople in improving their situations.

Impleme-nting healthy credit habits can help lay the- groundwork for financial success down the road. Establishing and sustaining a strong credit score- will provide access to more favorable- loan conditions, reduced intere-st levels, and expande-d monetary potential as your journey continue-s. By cultivating positive credit practices, you prime- yourself for possibilities yet to come- such as getting approved for larger loans or cre-dit cards with higher limits. While it takes e-ffort initially, forming a track record of responsibility with credit will se-rve you well in the long-run by lowe-ring costs of borrowing and widening your options.

Balancing Student Loan Repayment with Credit Card Usage:

When it come-s to managing debt, finding the right balance be-tween student loan re-payment and credit card usage is crucial. Paying more- than the minimum due on credit cards e-ach month while also making consistent payments toward stude-nt loans can help reduce inte-rest costs over time. It's important to prioritize- high interest debt first if possible-. Consider creating a budget to stay on track with re-payment goals. Tracking expense-s can help ensure funds are- available to tackle debts e-ach payment period.

To begin tackling your financial obligations, take- inventory of the intere-st charges and timelines for your stude-nt loans and credit cards. It's usually wisest to first concentrate- on debts with higher rates, like- credit card balances which typically have pricie-r rates than student loans. By channeling e-xtra funds towards your credit cards initially, you can minimize the total amount of inte-rest you'll owe over time-. Assess each obligation to dete-rmine which will cost you most if not paid down swiftly. Getting high-rate de-bts under control first allows you to then focus on other liabilitie-s in a way that saves money across all accounts in the long haul.

There- are two main approaches to handling multiple de-bts - the debt snowball method and the- debt avalanche method. With the- debt snowball strategy, you first focus your extra payme-nts on the debt with the lowe-st balance, while still making at least minimum payme-nts on all other accounts. Once that smallest de-bt is wiped out, you roll the amount you were- paying on it to the next smallest de-bt. Rinse and repeat. This me-thod may not save the most intere-st, but can help encourage continue-d progress as you cross debts off your list one by one-. You see the de-bts melting away in order of size, giving a se-nse of accomplishment at each ste-p. The debt avalanche approach targe-ts the highest intere-st debt first regardless of size-. This usually minimizes long-term costs, but may not provide as much short-te-rm motivation from quick wins. Consider which path may work best for your situation and motivational nee-ds.

While one- approach involves tackling the smallest balance-s first for a feeling of progress, an alte-rnate route cente-rs on the debts bearing the- highest rates of intere-st. By prioritizing repayment of loans or credit cards with e-xorbitant interest, you can minimize the- amount ultimately owed through intere-st. Take time to ponder which strate-gy best fits your financial aims and what works for your circumstances, whethe-r speedily wiping out small tabs or cutting long-term costs through focusing down usurious rate-s.

It's crucial that you thoughtfully consider the- minimum payments due on your student loans e-ach month. While putting extra funds towards your credit card balance-s is wise, neglecting those- minimum loan payments could result in unnece-ssary costs. Missing or delaying those payments may le-ad to fines, surcharges, and a lower cre-dit rating. Be certain to satisfy all of your debt obligations in a time-ly way. Setting up automatic withdrawals or calendar alerts can he-lp guarantee you fulfill each minimum payme-nt requirement across all of your accounts. Taking care- of even the base-line amounts expecte-d will prevent potential pe-nalties and protect your financial standing.

While managing both stude-nt loan and credit card debt can fee-l overwhelming, do not struggle alone-. Reach out if you require aid. Contact the- servicers handling your loans and credit cards to e-xplore repayment choice-s or programs for difficult times. Speak with a monetary consultant as we-ll, who can offer customized assistance and e-ncouragement. Asking for help take-s courage, yet alleviate-s unnecessary strain. Togethe-r, solutions can be found.

While it's important to unde-rstand potential outcomes, focusing too much on conseque-nces can increase stre-ss and anxiety. It's best to take a balance-d approach. For student loans, commit to the repayme-nt plan and keep lines of ope-n communication if difficulties arise. Lende-rs want to work with borrowers, so be proactive about any change-s in your situation. Similarly, only charge what you can comfortably pay each month on credit cards. Avoid late- fees or going over the- limit by tracking expenses and paying more- than the minimum when possible. Se-ek counseling from nonprofit credit age-ncies if debt become-s overwhelming. They can he-lp work through options without jeopardizing your future. While de-fault should always be avoided, do not let "what if" sce-narios paralyze you. Take prudent ste-ps each day and week to stay on track financially.

Kee-p in mind, successfully handling your obligations necessitate-s willpower, planning a budget, and a lucid strategy for re-payment. By making debt repayme-nt a priority, examining various options for repayment, and asking for assistance- when essential, you can ade-ptly attain equilibrium betwee-n repaying your student loans and utilizing credit cards. With ste-adfastness and judicious fiscal choices, you'll be on track to a future- without any debts.

Chapter 3

Introduction to Investing: Making Your Money Work for You

****

The Importance of Financial Independence:

Achieving financial independence is a crucial step towards personal growth and long-term success. In this section, we will explore the significance of attaining financial stability early in life and how investing can play a pivotal role in this endeavor.

Financial independence provides individuals with a sense of security and freedom. It allows us to have more control over our lives and make decisions based on our aspirations, rather than being limited by financial constraints. By investing wisely, we can build wealth and create a solid foundation for the future.

One of the primary benefits of investing is the potential for significant returns. Unlike simply saving money, investing allows our money to grow over time through compound interest and capital appreciation. By investing early, we harness the power of time and allow our investments to accumulate wealth steadily.

Investing also helps us combat the eroding effects of inflation. Inflation diminishes the purchasing power of our money over time. By generating returns that outpace inflation, investing provides a means to preserve and increase our wealth in real terms.

Moreover, investing empowers us to achieve specific financial goals. Whether it's saving for retirement, buying a home, or funding further education, strategic investment allows us to allocate our resources towards these objectives. By establishing clear financial milestones and consistently investing towards them, we pave the way for achieving these aspirations.

Financial independence not only benefits us personally but also enhances our ability to support others. It enables us to contribute to causes we care about, help family members in need, and give back to our communities. By taking control of our finances through investing, we position ourselves to make a positive impact on both our own lives and the lives of those around us.

In summary, achieving financial independence is essential for personal growth and success. Investing plays a crucial role in this pursuit by providing opportunities to build wealth, secure our future, and have greater control over our finances. By recognizing the importance of financial independence and embracing the world of investing, we can unlock a pathway to long-term prosperity and fulfillment.

Understanding Risk and Return:

Investing is a key component of achieving financial independence, and understanding the concept of risk and return is crucial for making informed investment decisions. In this section, we will delve deeper into the relationship between risk and return and explore different investment options.

When it comes to investing, risk refers to the possibility of losing money or not achieving the expected return on your investment. On the other hand, return refers to the profit or gain you make from your investment over a specific period. It is important to note that higher returns often come with higher risks, as there is no guarantee of investment success.

To help mitigate risk and maximize returns, it is essential to diversify your investment portfolio. Diversification involves spreading your investments across different asset classes, such as stocks, bonds, mutual funds, and real estate. By diversifying, you can reduce the impact of any one investment performing poorly.

Let's take a closer look at some common investment options:

1. Stocks: Stocks represent ownership in a company and offer potential for high returns. However, they also come with a higher level of risk compared to other investments. Stock prices are

influenced by various factors such as market conditions, company performance, and economic trends.

2. Bonds: Bonds are debt securities issued by governments or corporations to raise capital. When you purchase a bond, you are essentially lending money to the issuer in exchange for regular interest payments and the return of the principal amount at maturity. Bonds are generally considered lower-risk investments compared to stocks.

3. Mutual Funds: Mutual funds pool money from multiple investors to invest in a diversified portfolio of stocks, bonds, or other assets. They are managed by professional fund managers who aim to achieve specific investment objectives. Mutual funds offer opportunities for diversification, but it's important to carefully assess their fees and performance before investing.

4. Real Estate: Investing in real estate involves purchasing properties with the expectation of generating income through rental payments or capital appreciation. Real estate investments can provide a stable income stream and potential tax advantages. However, they may require significant upfront capital and involve ongoing maintenance and management.

By understanding the potential risks and returns associated with different investment options, you can make more informed decisions based on your financial goals, risk tolerance, and time horizon. It's crucial to assess your own risk appetite and conduct thorough research before investing in any specific asset class. Remember, diversification is key to minimizing risk and maximizing potential returns in your investment portfolio.

Next, we will explore how to create an investment plan that aligns with your financial goals and risk tolerance. We will discuss setting investment objectives, determining asset allocation, and creating a diversified portfolio that suits your needs. Let's continue our journey towards building a solid foundation for financial success!,Creating an Investment Plan:

In this section, we will focus on guiding readers through the process of creating an investment plan that aligns with their financial goals and risk tolerance. It is essential to have a well-thought-out investment plan to ensure long-term success in building wealth and achieving financial independence.

1. Setting Investment Objectives:

- Begin by identifying your investment goals, whether it is saving for retirement, purchasing a home, or funding higher education.
- Clearly define your objectives and establish timelines for each goal.
- Consider the level of risk you are comfortable with and how it aligns with your investment goals.

2. Determining Asset Allocation:

- Asset allocation refers to how you distribute your investment portfolio across different asset classes such as stocks, bonds, and real estate.
- Assess your risk tolerance and time horizon to determine the optimal asset allocation strategy.
- Generally, younger individuals with a longer time horizon can afford to take more risks and allocate a higher percentage of their portfolio to stocks for potentially higher returns.

3. Creating a Diversified Portfolio:

- Diversification involves spreading your investments across different asset classes, industries, and geographical regions.
- By diversifying your portfolio, you can reduce the impact of any single investment's performance on your overall portfolio.
- Consider investing in a mix of stocks, bonds, mutual funds, and other assets to achieve diversification.

4. Regular Portfolio Reviews and Adjustments:

- It is crucial to regularly review your investment portfolio to ensure it continues to align with your investment objectives and risk tolerance.
- Monitor the performance of your investments and make necessary adjustments based on market conditions or changes in personal circumstances.
- Rebalancing your portfolio periodically helps maintain the desired asset allocation ratios.

Remember, creating an investment plan is not a one-time task. It requires periodic reviews and adjustments to stay on track towards achieving your financial goals. By setting clear investment objectives, determining suitable asset allocation, creating a diversified portfolio, and regularly reviewing and adjusting your investments, you can increase your chances of building wealth and securing your financial future.

(Note: This section does not cover topics discussed in other chapters, such as understanding risk and return or specific investing strategies. It solely focuses on the process of creating an investment plan.)

Investing Strategies for Beginners:

This section delves into various investing strategies that are specifically tailored for beginners. It aims to provide readers with a solid foundation of knowledge and guidance on how to effectively implement these strategies.

1. Dollar Cost Averaging:

This strategy involves consistently investing a fixed amount of money at regular intervals, regardless of the market conditions.

Advantages:

- Reduces the impact of short-term market fluctuations by spreading out investments over time.
- Allows individuals to benefit from buying more shares when prices are low and fewer shares when prices are high.

Disadvantages:

- May not maximize returns in a rapidly rising market.
- Requires discipline to stick to the investment plan even during times of market volatility.

2. Value Investing:

This strategy involves identifying undervalued stocks or assets and investing in them with the expectation that their value will increase over time.

Advantages:

- Provides the opportunity to buy assets at a discounted price, potentially leading to significant long-term returns.
- Encourages thorough analysis and research before making investment decisions.
- Disadvantages:
- Requires patience, as it can take time for the market to recognize the true value of an asset.
- Involves a higher level of risk, as there is no guarantee that the undervalued asset will appreciate in value.

3. Index Fund Investing:

- This strategy involves investing in index funds, which are passively managed funds that replicate the performance of a specific market index (e.g. S&P 500).

Advantages:

- Offers instant diversification by providing exposure to a broad range of stocks or assets within the index.
- Tends to have lower expense ratios compared to actively managed funds.

Disadvantages:

- Limits potential for outsized returns compared to actively managed funds that aim to beat the market.
- Provides exposure to both high-performing and underperforming assets within the index.

It is important for beginners to understand that each investing strategy has its own set of advantages and disadvantages. It is recommended to consider personal financial goals, risk tolerance, and time horizon when deciding which strategy to pursue. Additionally, diversification across different asset classes and regular portfolio reviews are key components of successful investing. By exploring and implementing these strategies, beginners can begin their investment journey with confidence and increase their chances of long-term financial success.

Tools and Resources for Successful Investing:

In this section of "Introduction to Investing: Making Your Money Work for You," readers are provided with a comprehensive list of tools, resources, and platforms that can assist them in their investment journey. These recommendations serve as valuable assets for young adults looking to make informed decisions and navigate the complex world of investing.

1. Financial Apps: There are numerous financial apps available today that can help individuals track their investments, monitor market trends, and manage their portfolios efficiently. Some popular examples include Mint, Personal Capital, Robinhood, Acorns, and Betterment. These apps provide users with real-time updates, personalized insights, and user-friendly interfaces.

2. Online Brokerages: Online brokerages have made investing more accessible than ever before. They offer low-cost trading options, educational resources, and robust research tools. Recommended online brokerages include Charles Schwab, Fidelity, TD Ameritrade, and E*TRADE. These platforms provide a seamless and user-friendly experience for buying and selling stocks, bonds, mutual funds, and other investment vehicles.

3. Investment Newsletters: Subscribing to reputable investment newsletters can be a valuable source of information and insights. These newsletters often provide expert analysis, investment recommendations, and market trends. Some popular investment newsletters include Morningstar, The Motley Fool, Seeking Alpha, and Bloomberg Briefs. Reading these newsletters regularly can help individuals stay informed about industry developments and identify potential investment opportunities.

4. Reputable Financial Websites: There are several reliable financial websites that offer a wealth of information for investors. These websites provide news articles, research reports, educational resources, and interactive tools. Recommended financial websites include Investopedia, Bloomberg, Yahoo Finance, CNBC, and The Wall Street Journal. Visiting these websites regularly can help individuals stay updated on global economic trends and gain insights from industry experts.

It is important to note that while these tools and resources can be valuable, they should be used in combination with thorough research and careful consideration. Individuals should evaluate the credibility of these sources and cross-reference information before making any investment decisions. Additionally, ongoing education is crucial in the ever-evolving field of investing, so readers are encouraged to stay curious, seek out additional resources, and continuously expand their knowledge.

By utilizing these recommended tools and resources, readers can enhance their investment journey and make more informed decisions. Staying informed about market trends, utilizing user-friendly platforms, and accessing expert insights will empower young adults to take control of their financial future and maximize their investment potential.

Chapter 4

Financial Goals: Buying a Home or Starting a Business

****

Understanding the Importance of Financial Goals:

Setting financial goals is crucial for individuals in their twenties as it lays the foundation for a stable and secure future. Whether it's buying a home or starting a business, having clear objectives helps create a roadmap towards achieving financial independence and success.

One of the key benefits of setting financial goals is stability. By having a target to work towards, individuals can establish stability in their personal and professional lives. Financial stability provides a sense of security, ensuring that unexpected expenses or emergencies can be handled without significant stress or burden.

Moreover, clear financial goals also contribute to personal growth. When individuals have a vision for their financial future, it motivates them to develop and refine their skills, expand their knowledge, and explore avenues for growth. Achieving financial milestones can boost confidence and self-esteem, creating a positive ripple effect across other areas of life.

Financial goals also play a crucial role in professional growth. They provide the means to invest in education, acquire valuable certifications, or start a business venture. By setting financial objectives early on, individuals can align their career choices and make strategic decisions that will enhance their long-term earning potential and career progression.

Additionally, achieving financial goals fosters independence. It provides individuals with the freedom to make choices based on their own desires and values rather than being limited by financial constraints. Whether it's pursuing a passion project or taking time off to travel, financial independence enables individuals to live life on their own terms.

In conclusion, setting financial goals is essential for individuals in their twenties as it brings stability, personal growth, and independence. By recognizing the significance of financial objectives and working towards them diligently, young adults can lay the groundwork for a fulfilling and prosperous future.

Assessing Personal Financial Situation:

When it comes to achieving financial goals, it is important to have a clear understanding of your current financial situation. By assessing your personal finances, you can gain valuable insights into your income, expenses, savings, and debts, which will help you make informed decisions about buying a home or starting a business.

To begin the assessment, gather all your financial documents, including bank statements, pay stubs, credit card bills, and loan statements. Take note of your monthly income after taxes and any additional sources of income. This will give you an idea of how much money you have available to allocate towards your financial goals.

Next, analyze your expenses by categorizing them into fixed expenses (such as rent or mortgage payments, utilities, and insurance) and variable expenses (such as groceries, entertainment, and transportation). Identifying where your money goes each month will allow you to determine areas where you may be able to cut back or save more.

In addition to expenses, evaluate your current savings and debts. Consider the amount of money you have saved in emergency funds or other savings accounts. It is important to have at least three to six months' worth of living expenses set aside in case of unexpected emergencies.

Furthermore, take stock of any outstanding debts you may have, such as student loans, credit card debt, or car loans. Understanding the total amount owed, interest rates, and minimum monthly payments will help you gauge your overall financial health.

Building a strong credit history is crucial for achieving financial goals. Check your credit score regularly and review your credit report for any errors or discrepancies. Paying bills on time, keeping credit card balances low, and minimizing new credit applications can all contribute to a favorable credit score.

By thoroughly assessing your personal financial situation, you will gain clarity on where you stand financially and identify areas for improvement or adjustment. This knowledge will provide a solid foundation for making informed decisions regarding your financial goals, whether it be buying a home or starting a business.

Evaluating the Feasibility of Buying a Home:

When considering the feasibility of buying a home, it's important to weigh the pros and cons based on individual circumstances. Homeownership offers several advantages, such as increased stability, the potential for appreciation in property value, and the opportunity to build equity over time. However, it also comes with responsibilities like maintenance and upfront costs.

The first step in evaluating the feasibility of buying a home is to assess your current financial situation. Take a thorough look at your income, expenses, savings, and debts. This will give you an idea of how much you can afford to spend on a home and help determine if homeownership is financially viable at this stage of your life.

Consider your credit score as well, as it plays a vital role in the mortgage loan approval process. Lenders use credit scores to assess borrowers' creditworthiness and determine interest rates. If your credit score is low, it's important to take steps to improve it before applying for a mortgage.

Next, conduct research on housing markets to understand price trends, availability, and other relevant factors. Evaluate different neighborhoods, taking into account proximity to amenities, transportation options, and potential for future growth. Analyzing these aspects will help you identify areas that align with your preferences and budget.

Furthermore, explore various mortgage options available in the market. Different loans have different requirements, down payment percentages, and interest rates. Familiarize yourself with options like conventional loans, FHA loans, and VA loans to make an informed decision.

It's also beneficial to explore any government or local programs designed to assist first-time homebuyers. These programs may offer grants or low-interest loans to help with down payments and closing costs. Researching and utilizing these programs can significantly impact the financial feasibility of buying a home.

As you delve into the process of buying a home, don't hesitate to seek advice from professionals such as real estate agents, mortgage lenders, and financial advisors. They can provide valuable insights tailored to your specific situation and guide you through the intricacies of the homebuying journey.

By evaluating the feasibility of buying a home based on factors like income, credit score, housing market research, and available programs, you can make an informed decision about whether homeownership is the right choice for you at this stage of your life.

Exploring Entrepreneurship and Starting a Business:

Introduce the concept of entrepreneurship as an alternative financial goal to buying a home. Many individuals in their twenties may consider starting their own business as a means to achieve financial stability and independence. Entrepreneurship offers exciting opportunities for growth, creativity, and the potential to make a lasting impact on the world.

Discuss the entrepreneurial mindset and qualities necessary for success in business. To embark on the entrepreneurial journey, aspiring entrepreneurs must possess certain characteristics such as resilience, self-motivation, adaptability, and a willingness to take calculated risks. These traits empower individuals to navigate uncertainties, overcome obstacles, and persevere in the face of challenges.

Provide practical advice for aspiring entrepreneurs on generating business ideas. Encourage readers to explore their passions, interests, and unique skills as a starting point for identifying potential business opportunities. Setting aside time for self-reflection and brainstorming can help generate innovative ideas that align with personal values and goals.

Conducting market research is crucial for any aspiring entrepreneur. Teach readers how to conduct thorough research to understand target markets, identify customer needs, and assess market demand for their proposed product or service. By gaining insights into industry trends, competition, and consumer behavior, readers can make informed decisions about the viability of their business ideas.

Guide readers in developing a business plan. Discuss the essential components of a comprehensive business plan, including an executive summary, company description, market analysis, organizational structure, marketing strategy, financial projections, and operational plans. Emphasize the importance of creating a solid foundation through strategic planning before launching a business venture.

By providing practical guidance on generating business ideas, conducting market research, and developing a business plan, this chapter equips aspiring entrepreneurs with the necessary tools to pursue their entrepreneurial dreams. It empowers young adults to embrace the world of entrepreneurship and take charge of their financial future by leveraging their unique skills and passions to create successful businesses.

Making Financial Decisions:

When it comes to making significant financial decisions like buying a home or starting a business, it is essential to carefully weigh the pros and cons. These decisions can have a profound impact on your financial situation and overall success.

Firstly, it is crucial to evaluate the risks and rewards associated with each option. Buying a home offers the stability of owning a property and the potential for appreciation in value over time. On the other hand, starting a business can provide you with the opportunity for financial independence and the fulfillment of pursuing your passions. Consider your personal goals, values, and aspirations when assessing which option aligns best with your long-term vision.

To make an informed decision, it is important to gather as much information as possible. Research the housing market if you are considering buying a home, evaluating factors such as location, pricing trends, and potential resale value. Understand the mortgage options available to you and explore any homebuying programs that may provide financial assistance.

If starting a business is your desired path, conduct thorough market research to identify potential gaps or opportunities. Evaluate competitors, target markets, and demand for your product or service. Develop a comprehensive business plan that outlines your objectives, strategies, and financial projections.

In both cases, assess the potential risks involved and devise strategies to mitigate them. For buying a home, ensure that you have a solid understanding of your financial situation, including income stability, creditworthiness, and debt obligations. Consider factors such as interest rates, property taxes, and homeowners association fees when calculating affordability. With regard to starting a business, create contingency plans for potential challenges such as competitive pressures, market fluctuations, or unforeseen expenses. Build a strong professional network that can offer guidance and support throughout your entrepreneurial journey.

Maximizing opportunities for success requires careful planning and execution. Seek advice from professionals in real estate or entrepreneurship who can provide valuable insights based on their expertise. Continuously educate yourself on financial management, investment strategies, and industry trends relevant to your chosen path.

Remember, financial decisions of this magnitude require thoughtful consideration. Take the time to assess your personal circumstances, evaluate risks, and develop a strategy that aligns with your long-term goals. By making informed choices and taking calculated risks, you can set yourself up for success whether you choose to buy a home or start a business.

Chapter 5

Saving for Retirement: Why Start in Your Twenties

***

The Importance of Starting Early:

Imagine a scenario where two individuals, Alex and Ben, both start saving for retirement at the age of 25. Alex diligently contributes $200 per month to their retirement fund for 10 years, totaling $24,000. Meanwhile, Ben decides to delay saving for retirement until the age of 35 and contributes the same amount of $200 per month for 30 years, totaling $72,000.

Assuming an average annual return of 6% on their investments, let's see how their retirement savings would fare when they turn 65. Despite contributing three times less money than Ben, Alex's retirement fund would grow significantly due to the power of compound interest. In fact, Alex's account balance would be roughly $380,000, while Ben's account balance would only reach around $260,000.

This example demonstrates the immense advantage of starting to save for retirement in your twenties. Even though Alex contributed less money overall, their contributions had more time to grow and accumulate interest. This illustrates the impact of compound interest, which allows your investment returns to generate additional returns over time.

By starting early, you are giving your money more time to work for you. The longer your money is invested in retirement accounts like 401(k)s or IRAs, the more opportunity it has to benefit from compounding returns. This means that even small contributions made in your twenties can grow significantly over several decades.

Research indicates that individuals who start saving for retirement early have a much higher chance of achieving financial security during their golden years. According to a study by Fidelity Investments, millennials who begin saving at age 25 can potentially accumulate twice as much retirement savings compared to those who wait until age 35.

Starting early also provides a safety net against unexpected hurdles that life may throw at you. By developing the habit of saving in your twenties, you establish a solid foundation for financial security. The discipline and foresight cultivated during this phase of life will serve you well when faced with unexpected expenses or financial challenges in the future.

Moreover, beginning to save for retirement in your twenties allows you to take advantage of employer-sponsored retirement plans like 401(k)s, especially if your employer offers a matching contribution. Employer matches are essentially free money that can significantly boost your retirement savings. By starting early, you increase the likelihood of being eligible for retirement plan benefits and maximizing any potential employer matches.

Remember, time is your greatest asset when it comes to saving for retirement. The earlier you start, the more time your investments have to grow and compound. Small contributions made in your twenties can lead to substantial savings down the line. By taking action now and making retirement savings a priority, you are setting yourself up for a financially secure future filled with peace of mind.

Understanding Retirement Funds and Options:

In this section, we delve into the various retirement savings options available to young adults in their twenties. Understanding these options is crucial for making informed decisions about saving for retirement.

One option is an employer-sponsored 401(k) plan. Many companies offer these plans, which allow employees to contribute a portion of their salary directly into a retirement account. Employers often match a percentage of these contributions, providing an additional boost to savings. Readers will learn about the benefits and limitations of 401(k) plans, as well as any associated tax advantages or penalties.

Individual retirement accounts (IRAs) are another common option. These accounts can be opened by individuals and offer tax advantages. Traditional IRAs allow for tax-deductible contributions, meaning that the money contributed reduces taxable income in the year it is made. Roth IRAs, on the other hand, do not provide immediate tax benefits but offer tax-free withdrawals during retirement. Readers will gain an understanding of how these different IRA options function and the implications for their retirement savings.

It's important for individuals to choose the most suitable retirement fund for their financial goals. This may involve considering factors like risk tolerance, investment preferences, and long-term plans. By providing readers with clear explanations and examples, we aim to empower them to make informed decisions regarding their retirement savings options.

By covering this important topic in the chapter on saving for retirement in your twenties, readers will gain a comprehensive understanding of the various retirement funds available to them and how they can choose the most suitable one for their financial goals. This knowledge will be vital as they begin crafting their own scripts for a financially secure future.

Creating a Budget for Retirement Savings: This section will serve as a practical guide for readers in their twenties on how to develop a budget specifically tailored for retirement savings. While budgeting may be covered in earlier chapters, this section will provide specific strategies and tips related to retirement savings.

To begin, readers will be encouraged to assess their current expenses and identify areas where they can potentially cut back or reduce spending. This may involve analyzing monthly bills, such as subscriptions or excessive dining out, and finding ways to trim unnecessary expenses. By identifying these areas, readers can redirect those funds towards retirement savings.

Next, readers will learn the importance of setting specific savings goals for retirement. This includes determining the desired retirement age and lifestyle, estimating the potential expenses during retirement, and calculating the amount needed to achieve those goals. By having a clear target in mind, readers can allocate an appropriate portion of their income towards retirement savings.

Readers will also be introduced to the concept of "paying themselves first." This means prioritizing retirement savings by automatically setting aside a percentage of each paycheck before allocating funds for other expenses. Setting up automatic transfers or contributions to retirement accounts can help ensure consistency in saving for retirement and reduce the temptation to spend those funds elsewhere.

Additionally, this section will address common challenges faced by individuals in their twenties when it comes to saving for retirement. For instance, some readers may feel that they have limited income or are burdened with student loan debt. Strategies will be provided on how to overcome these obstacles, such as exploring opportunities for increasing income through side hustles or seeking higher-paying job prospects. Moreover, readers will be encouraged to tackle debt head-on by devising a plan to pay it off efficiently, thus freeing up more resources for retirement savings.

Finally, this section will emphasize the importance of regularly reviewing and adjusting the budget as circumstances change. Life events such as promotions, career changes, or starting a family may require modifications to the retirement savings plan. By staying actively engaged with their budget, readers can ensure they are on track to achieve their retirement savings goals.

By covering these specific points in the chapter on creating a budget for retirement savings, readers will gain practical strategies and tips on how to allocate their income towards retirement, overcome common challenges, and stay motivated on their journey towards financial security.

Investment Strategies for Retirement:

In this section, we will explore different investment strategies specifically tailored to individuals in their twenties who are looking to build a robust retirement fund. While previous chapters have touched on the importance of budgeting and saving for retirement, this chapter will focus specifically on investment options and strategies that can help maximize growth and wealth accumulation over time.

One important concept to understand when it comes to investing for retirement is diversification. Diversifying your investments means spreading your money across different asset classes such as stocks, bonds, mutual funds, and exchange-traded funds (ETFs). By diversifying your portfolio, you can reduce the impact of any single investment performing poorly and increase the likelihood of overall growth.

When considering investment options, it's important to assess your risk tolerance. Risk tolerance refers to your ability and willingness to endure fluctuations in the value of your investments. Generally, younger individuals with a longer time horizon until retirement can afford to take on more risk because they have more time to recover from market downturns. However, it's crucial to strike a balance between risk and reward that aligns with your personal comfort level.

Stocks are one of the most common types of investments for long-term growth. Investing in individual stocks allows you to own shares of specific companies and potentially benefit from their success. However, individual stocks can be volatile and come with higher risks. It's important to thoroughly research and analyze companies before investing in their stock.

Bonds are another investment option that offers a more conservative approach compared to stocks. When you invest in bonds, you are essentially loaning money to a government or corporation in exchange for periodic interest payments and the return of your principal investment when the bond matures. Bonds are generally considered less risky than stocks but offer lower potential returns.

Mutual funds pool money from multiple investors to invest in a diversified portfolio of stocks, bonds, or other securities. They are managed by professional fund managers who make investment decisions on behalf of the investors. Mutual funds are a convenient option for individuals who want exposure to a variety of investments without the need for active management.

Exchange-traded funds (ETFs) are similar to mutual funds but trade on stock exchanges like individual stocks. ETFs offer diversification, low fees, and flexibility in buying and selling shares throughout the trading day. They are an increasingly popular investment option for those looking to build a diversified portfolio.

Regardless of the investment options you choose, it is important to regularly review and adjust your investment portfolio. This ensures that your investments continue to align with your financial goals, risk tolerance, and market conditions. Rebalancing your portfolio periodically helps maintain diversification and keeps your investments on track.

It's worth noting that investing always comes with some level of risk. The value of investments can fluctuate, and there is no guarantee of future returns. As with any investment decision, it's essential to do thorough research, seek professional advice if needed, and stay updated on market trends.

By understanding the potential risks and rewards associated with different investment options, individuals in their twenties can develop an investment strategy that aligns with their long-term financial goals. Remember, building a robust retirement fund requires consistency, discipline, and periodic evaluation to ensure continued growth and financial security in the future.

Overcoming Barriers and Staying Motivated:

In this final section, we address common barriers that may discourage young adults from saving for retirement in their twenties. It is essential to acknowledge these obstacles and develop strategies to overcome them, ensuring long-term financial security.

One major barrier many individuals face is competing financial priorities. In our twenties, we often have numerous financial obligations, such as student loans, rent, and daily expenses. It can be challenging to allocate funds for retirement amidst these immediate needs.

To overcome this barrier, it's crucial to evaluate your spending habits and identify areas where you can cut back or save money. Consider creating a budget that includes a specific allocation for retirement savings. By prioritizing your future financial well-being and making conscious choices with your money, you can gradually increase your retirement contributions.

Another significant challenge is the perception of having limited income during this phase of life. Many young adults are just starting their careers or still in school, resulting in lower salaries or irregular income. This mindset may lead them to believe that saving for retirement is not feasible.

However, it's important to remember that even small contributions made early on can have a significant impact due to the power of compound interest. Aim to save a percentage of your income regardless of its amount. No contribution is too small when it comes to building a solid financial future.

If you find it difficult to spare any additional funds, consider finding ways to increase your income. Explore opportunities for side hustles or part-time jobs that can provide extra cash flow. Additionally, focus on improving your earning potential through continuous education, skill-building, and career advancement.

Reducing debt is another crucial step towards overcoming barriers to saving for retirement. High-interest debts, such as credit card balances or personal loans, can hinder your ability to accumulate savings. Develop a debt repayment plan by prioritizing high-interest debts first and consistently making payments towards reducing your outstanding balances.

Seeking professional guidance can provide invaluable support in overcoming barriers and establishing a clear path towards retirement savings. Financial advisors can offer tailored strategies, recommend suitable investment options, and help you navigate complex financial decisions. Their expertise can ensure that your efforts are aligned with your long-term goals.

Above all, maintaining motivation and consistency is crucial in this journey. Saving for retirement is a long-term commitment, and it's vital to remain focused on the future benefits and peace of mind that come with financial independence. Celebrate small milestones along the way to stay motivated, revisit your goals regularly, and remind yourself of the importance of prioritizing your financial well-being.

By acknowledging common barriers, implementing practical strategies, and staying motivated, young adults can overcome obstacles and start building a solid foundation for their retirement. Remember, starting early and being consistent are key ingredients for achieving financial security and enjoying a comfortable retirement in the future.

Part 7:
Life Skills and
Practicalities

Chapter 1

Mastering Time Management: Work-Life Balance at Twenty

***

Understanding the Importance of Time Management:

It is often said that time is one of the most valuable resources we have, and effective time management is crucial for achieving personal and professional goals. When we manage our time well, we can optimize our productivity, reduce stress, and maintain a healthy work-life balance.

Proper time management allows us to prioritize tasks, allocate our energy efficiently, and make the most of each day. By effectively managing our time, we can accomplish more in less time, leaving us with additional opportunities to pursue our passions and enjoy leisure activities.

Moreover, efficient time management contributes to reduced stress levels. When we have a clear plan and know how to allocate our time wisely, we can minimize the feeling of being overwhelmed by deadlines and responsibilities. This enables us to approach our tasks with focus and clarity, leading to higher quality work and a greater sense of accomplishment.

In addition to personal benefits, mastering time management is also essential for maintaining a healthy work-life balance. In today's fast-paced world, it can be easy for work to consume our lives if we do not establish boundaries. Proper time management allows us to dedicate adequate time to our careers while still nurturing relationships, pursuing hobbies, and taking care of our physical and mental well-being.

Understanding the significance of work-life balance is crucial for maintaining overall well-being. It ensures that we have time for self-care, relaxation, and engaging in activities outside of work. By setting aside time for ourselves and our loved ones, we can recharge, foster deeper connections, and find fulfillment beyond our professional accomplishments.

In "Mastering Time Management: Work-Life Balance at Twenty," readers will delve further into strategies for effective time management, including assessing personal priorities, setting SMART goals, organizing schedules, and finding a balance between work and personal life. By mastering these skills, young adults in their twenties can ensure they are making the most of their time, optimizing their performance in all areas of life, and setting themselves up for long-term success and happiness.

Assessing Personal Priorities and Setting Goals:

In order to master time management and achieve a healthy work-life balance, it is crucial to first assess your personal priorities and set goals that align with your values and aspirations. By taking the time to identify what truly matters to you, you can ensure that your time and energy are invested in the areas that will bring you the most fulfillment and success.

Start by considering all aspects of your life, including career aspirations, relationships, health, and personal development. Reflect on what you envision for each area and determine which ones hold the most significance for you. Ask yourself questions such as:

- What are my long-term career goals? How can I break them down into smaller, achievable milestones?
- What kind of relationships do I want to cultivate? How can I invest more time and effort into nurturing these connections?
- How can I prioritize my physical and mental well-being? What steps can I take to improve my health and overall happiness?
- What personal development goals do I have? How can I continue learning, growing, and acquiring new skills?

Once you have identified your priorities, it is important to turn them into actionable goals. Use the SMART (Specific, Measurable, Achievable, Relevant, Time-bound) criteria to create clear and attainable objectives. For example:

- **Career Aspirations:** Instead of setting a vague goal like "advance in my career," make it specific by stating "obtain a management position within my current company within the next two years." This goal is measurable as it has a time frame, relevant to your career aspirations, and achievable with a clear action plan.
- **Relationships:** Rather than saying "improve my relationships," set a goal such as "schedule regular quality time with loved ones by planning weekly family dinners or monthly outings with friends." This goal is specific, measurable, achievable, and time-bound.
- Health: Instead of aiming to "be healthier," set a goal like "exercise for at least 30 minutes five times a week and incorporate a balanced diet with more fruits and vegetables." This goal is specific, measurable, and achievable.
- Personal Development: Rather than having a general goal of "self-improvement," set a specific target such as "complete an online course in a subject I'm passionate about within the next six months." This goal is specific, time-bound, achievable, and relevant to your personal growth.

To create a personalized goal-setting system and action plan, consider using tools and techniques that work best for you. This may include keeping a journal, using a digital task manager or calendar app, or creating vision boards. Regularly review and update your goals as needed to ensure they remain aligned with your evolving priorities and aspirations.

By assessing your personal priorities and setting SMART goals, you will have a clear roadmap for how to effectively manage your time and prioritize tasks. This will allow you to make intentional choices that align with your values, ensuring that you are investing your time and energy in the areas of life that truly matter to you.

Techniques for Efficient Time Organization:

In this section, we will dive deeper into popular time management methods and provide practical tips for creating effective schedules, calendars, and to-do lists to optimize productivity. We will also explore strategies for prioritizing tasks, managing distractions, and overcoming procrastination.

1. Introduction to popular time management methods:

- The Pomodoro Technique: Discuss the concept of breaking work into 25-minute intervals, known as pomodoros, followed by short breaks. Explain how this method can help improve focus and productivity.

Eisenhower Matrix: Introduce this matrix that categorizes tasks based on their urgency and importance. Guide readers on how to prioritize tasks accordingly and avoid procrastination.

- Time Blocking: Explain the concept of allocating specific blocks of time for different activities or tasks. Demonstrate how to create a visual schedule to enhance organization and efficiency.

2. Creating effective schedules, calendars, and to-do lists:

- Provide tips on using digital or physical tools to plan and visualize one's schedule effectively. Discuss the benefits of using calendars or planners with reminders and notifications.
- Guide readers in creating daily, weekly, and monthly to-do lists that are both realistic and achievable. Emphasize the importance of breaking down larger tasks into smaller, manageable ones.

3. Prioritizing tasks and managing distractions:

- Teach readers how to assess task urgency and importance using the Eisenhower Matrix, allowing them to focus on high-priority items first.
- Discuss techniques for minimizing distractions, such as turning off social media notifications, setting designated workspaces, and implementing "do not disturb" periods.

4. Overcoming procrastination:

- Explore common causes of procrastination and provide strategies for overcoming this habit. These may include breaking tasks into smaller steps, setting deadlines with accountability partners or mentors, or utilizing positive reinforcement techniques.

By incorporating these techniques into their daily lives, readers will be better equipped to manage their time efficiently, stay organized, and overcome obstacles that hinder productivity.

Balancing Work and Personal Life:

In order to achieve a healthy work-life balance, it is essential to establish clear boundaries between your professional and personal life. This ensures that you have adequate time for relaxation, hobbies, and social activities, ultimately promoting overall well-being and preventing burnout.

To effectively balance your work and personal life, consider implementing the following strategies:

1. Set Boundaries: Clearly define your working hours and communicate them with your colleagues, supervisors, and clients. Establishing these boundaries will help prevent work from encroaching on your personal time.
2. Prioritize Self-Care: Make self-care a non-negotiable part of your routine. This includes activities such as exercise, meditation, getting enough sleep, and engaging in hobbies or activities that bring you joy and relaxation. Remember, taking care of yourself allows you to show up fully in both your personal and professional life.
3. Practice Effective Multitasking: Inevitably, there will be times when you have multiple responsibilities vying for your attention. By practicing effective multitasking, you can make the most of your time and accomplish tasks efficiently. For example, listening to educational podcasts during your commute or catching up on emails during your lunch break.
4. Learn to Delegate: Recognize that you don't have to do everything on your own. Delegate tasks or seek assistance when necessary, both in your professional and personal life. Whether it's asking a colleague for help at work or enlisting the support of family or friends for household chores, sharing the load can alleviate stress and create more time for leisure activities.
5. Embrace Technology: Leverage technology tools that can help streamline tasks and save time. For instance, using productivity apps or project management software can help you stay organized and efficiently complete assignments. However, be mindful of setting boundaries with technology usage to avoid overworking or blurring the line between work and personal life.
6. Foster a Supportive Network: Surround yourself with individuals who understand the importance of work-life balance and support your efforts to achieve it. This can include friends, family members, mentors, or colleagues who can provide guidance, motivate you, and hold you accountable.
7. Practice Stress Management Techniques: Chronic stress can have detrimental effects on both your physical and mental well-being. Incorporate stress management techniques into your daily routine, such as mindfulness meditation, deep breathing exercises, or engaging in activities that help you unwind and relax.

Remember, achieving a healthy work-life balance is an ongoing process that requires conscious effort and regular evaluation. By setting boundaries, prioritizing self-care, practicing effective multitasking, and managing stress, you can maintain a fulfilling and harmonious life that encompasses both professional success and personal happiness.

Adapting Time Management Skills in Different Areas of Life:

Applying effective time management principles is not limited to just work or academic settings. In fact, mastering time management skills can greatly impact various aspects of life, including education, career, relationships, and personal growth. By learning how to manage your time efficiently, you can find a balance between different commitments and ensure success in all areas.

When it comes to education or work, applying time management techniques becomes essential for meeting deadlines and completing assignments or projects on time. Start by creating a schedule or a to-do list that outlines all the tasks and responsibilities you need to accomplish within a specific timeframe. Prioritize the most important or urgent tasks and allocate sufficient time for each one. Break larger tasks into smaller, manageable chunks to make them more achievable.

It's also important to recognize your most productive times of the day and schedule your study or work sessions accordingly. If you're an early bird, consider allocating mornings for focused work or studying.

Alternatively, if you're a night owl, designating evenings for productivity might work best for you. By aligning your work or study sessions with your natural energy levels, you can maximize your productivity and efficiency.

Managing social commitments is another area where time management skills prove invaluable. It's important to strike a balance between maintaining healthy relationships and finding time for self-care and personal growth. Set boundaries and communicate your availability with friends and loved ones. You can block off certain times in your schedule specifically for socializing or spending quality time with others, ensuring that you're still able to pursue your own personal goals as well.

Additionally, finding time for self-improvement activities is crucial for personal growth. Whether it's reading, learning a new skill, exercising, or engaging in hobbies, dedicating time to activities that nourish your mind and body is vital. Incorporate these activities into your schedule and treat them as non-negotiable commitments.

Remember, adapting time management skills to different areas of life requires a proactive mindset and a willingness to prioritize. By implementing the tips mentioned above and tailoring them to suit your specific circumstances, you'll be able to make the most of your time and achieve success in all aspects of your life.

Chapter 2

Learning to Cook: An Essential Skill for Independence

*****

The Importance of Cooking Skills for Independence

In this chapter, we explore the significance of learning to cook as a young adult and the benefits it brings for achieving independence and self-reliance. While many individuals in their twenties may rely on takeout or dining out, developing cooking skills can have a transformative impact on various aspects of one's life.

One of the primary advantages of learning to cook is the ability to save money. Dining out or ordering takeout regularly can quickly drain a budget, especially for individuals living on a tight income during this phase of life. By cooking at home, young adults can significantly reduce their expenses and allocate those saved funds towards other financial goals, such as paying off student loans, saving for future investments, or pursuing personal passions.

Additionally, cooking at home allows individuals to adopt a healthier lifestyle. Many restaurant meals are laden with excessive salt, unhealthy fats, and added sugars. By preparing meals from scratch, young adults have control over the ingredients used and can prioritize fresh produce, whole grains, lean proteins, and healthy fats. This not only improves overall well-being but also reduces the risk of chronic diseases in the long run.

Furthermore, learning to cook fosters creativity in meal planning. Young adults can experiment with different flavors, cuisines, and ingredients to create unique dishes tailored to their preferences. This creative exploration not only enhances culinary skills but also encourages self-expression and enjoyment in the process of cooking.

By emphasizing the importance of cooking skills for independence, this chapter aims to empower young adults to take charge of their nutrition, finances, and personal growth. With an understanding of the benefits that cooking at home brings, readers are encouraged to embark on a journey of exploration in the kitchen, ultimately fostering a sense of self-reliance and achievement.

Basic Cooking Techniques and Kitchen Essentials

In this section, we will explore the fundamental cooking techniques that every aspiring chef should master. By understanding these techniques and having the right kitchen tools and equipment at hand, readers can confidently tackle any recipe and create delicious meals.

1. Sautéing: Sautéing involves cooking food quickly in a small amount of oil or fat over high heat. It is commonly used to cook vegetables, meats, and seafood. To sauté effectively, heat a pan over medium-high heat, add oil or butter, and then add your ingredients. Stir them frequently to ensure even cooking and prevent burning.

2. Boiling: Boiling is a simple yet essential cooking technique used to cook ingredients such as pasta, rice, and vegetables. To boil effectively, bring a pot of water to a rolling boil and add your ingredients. Cook until they are tender but still firm to the bite. Remember to salt the water for better flavor absorption.

3. Baking: Baking involves cooking food in an oven using dry heat. It is commonly used for baking bread, pastries, casseroles, and roasted dishes. To bake effectively, preheat your oven to the specified temperature, place your dish in the oven, and allow it to cook for the designated time.

4. Grilling: Grilling is a popular cooking technique that imparts a smoky flavor to food while giving it a charred exterior. It is ideal for cooking meats, vegetables, and even fruits. To grill effectively, preheat your grill to the desired temperature, brush the grates with oil to prevent sticking, and place your food on the grill. Flip it occasionally for even cooking.

When it comes to kitchen tools and equipment, certain essentials are necessary for a well-equipped kitchen:

1. Pots and Pans: Invest in a sturdy set of pots and pans in various sizes. A saucepan, a frying pan, and a stockpot are versatile options that will cover most of your cooking needs.
2. Knives: A set of high-quality knives is essential for precise cutting. Look for a chef's knife, a paring knife, and a serrated knife to handle various tasks efficiently.
3. Cutting Boards: Having separate cutting boards for fruits, vegetables, meats, and seafood prevents cross-contamination and maintains hygiene in the kitchen.
4. Measuring Utensils: Accurate measurements are crucial in cooking. Invest in measuring cups and spoons to ensure consistent results in your recipes.

By understanding these basic cooking techniques and having the essential kitchen tools and equipment, readers can confidently embark on their culinary journey. With practice, they will be able to create delicious meals that not only nourish their bodies but also bring joy and satisfaction to their taste buds.

Building a Pantry and Grocery Shopping Tips

One of the most crucial aspects of learning to cook and becoming independent in the kitchen is building a well-stocked pantry. By having essential ingredients on hand, you can easily whip up delicious meals without constantly running to the grocery store. Here are some tips for stocking your pantry and making efficient grocery shopping trips:

1. Essential Pantry Ingredients:

Canned goods: Stock up on canned tomatoes, beans, broth, and vegetables. They have a long shelf life and can be used in a variety of recipes.

- Grains and legumes: Keep a selection of rice, pasta, quinoa, lentils, and other whole grains in your pantry. These versatile ingredients serve as a base for many dishes.
- Oils and vinegars: Olive oil, vegetable oil, and vinegar (such as balsamic, red wine, and apple cider) are staples for cooking and dressing salads.
- Herbs and spices: Build a collection of commonly used herbs and spices like salt, black pepper, garlic powder, paprika, cumin, oregano, and basil. They add flavor to your dishes and allow for experimentation with different cuisines.
- Baking essentials: Flour, sugar, baking powder, baking soda, and vanilla extract are necessary for baking homemade treats.
- Condiments: Stock up on essentials like ketchup, mustard, mayonnaise, soy sauce, hot sauce, and salad dressings.

2. Organizing Your Pantry:

- **Group similar items together:** Arrange your pantry shelves so that similar items are kept together. For example, place all canned goods in one section and grains in another.
- **Use clear containers:** Transfer items like flour, rice, and pasta into clear airtight containers to keep them fresh and easily visible.
- **Label everything:** Labeling shelves or containers helps maintain organization and makes it easier to find what you need.

3. Efficient Grocery Shopping:

- **Create a shopping list:** Plan your meals for the week and create a shopping list based on the ingredients needed. This helps you stay focused and prevents impulse buying.
- Compare prices: Look for sales and compare prices between different brands or stores to get the best deals.
- **Choose fresh produce:** When selecting fruits and vegetables, opt for those that are in season and look fresh. Avoid bruised or damaged produce.
- Shop with a budget in mind: Set a budget for your grocery shopping and stick to it. This helps you prioritize essential items and avoid overspending.
- **Consider bulk purchases:** Certain pantry staples like rice, pasta, and beans can be more cost-effective when bought in bulk.

By building a well-stocked pantry and practicing efficient grocery shopping, you can save time, money, and unnecessary stress. Having essential ingredients readily available empowers you to prepare delicious meals whenever inspiration strikes, leading to a greater sense of independence in the kitchen.

Easy and Healthy Recipes for Beginners

In this section, we will present a variety of simple yet nutritious recipes that are perfect for beginner cooks. Each recipe will include step-by-step instructions and explanations of the cooking methods used. These recipes are designed to help young adults develop their cooking skills while also providing them with delicious and healthy meals.

1. Vegetable Stir-Fry

Ingredients:

- Assorted vegetables (such as bell peppers, broccoli, carrots, and snap peas)
- Garlic cloves (minced)
- Soy sauce or tamari
- Sesame oil
- Olive oil

Instructions:

1. Heat olive oil in a pan over medium heat.
2. Add minced garlic and sauté for a minute.
3. Add the chopped vegetables to the pan.
4. Stir-fry the vegetables until they are tender-crisp.
5. Add soy sauce or tamari and sesame oil for flavor.
6. Continue cooking for another minute, then remove from heat.
7. Serve as a side dish or with rice or noodles.

2. Quinoa Salad

- Ingredients:
- Cooked quinoa
- Cherry tomatoes (halved)
- Cucumber (diced)
- Red onion (thinly sliced)
- Fresh parsley (chopped)
- Lemon juice
- Olive oil
- Salt and pepper to taste

Instructions:

1. In a bowl, combine cooked quinoa with cherry tomatoes, cucumber, red onion, and fresh parsley.
2. In a separate bowl, whisk together lemon juice, olive oil, salt, and pepper to make the dressing.
3. Pour the dressing over the quinoa salad and toss to combine.
4. Adjust seasoning if needed and refrigerate for at least 30 minutes before serving.

3. Baked Chicken with Roasted Vegetables

- Ingredients:
- Chicken breast
- Assorted vegetables (such as potatoes, carrots, and Brussels sprouts)
- Olive oil
- Garlic powder
- Paprika
- Salt and pepper to taste

Instructions:

1. Preheat the oven to 400°F (200°C).
2. Place the chicken breast on a baking sheet lined with parchment paper.

3. Drizzle olive oil over the chicken, then season with garlic powder, paprika, salt, and pepper.
4. Arrange the chopped vegetables around the chicken on the baking sheet.
5. Drizzle olive oil over the vegetables and season with salt and pepper.
6. Bake for approximately 20-25 minutes or until the chicken is cooked through and the vegetables are tender.

These recipes are just a starting point for beginner cooks. Feel free to experiment with different ingredients and flavors to suit your taste preferences. Remember, cooking is both an art and a science, so don't be afraid to get creative in the kitchen!

Advancing Culinary Skills and Exploring Different Cuisines

Building on the foundation of basic cooking techniques and kitchen essentials discussed earlier in this chapter, it's time to take your culinary skills to the next level. By exploring different cuisines and experimenting with new ingredients and flavors, you can expand your cooking repertoire and bring excitement to your meals.

One way to advance your culinary skills is by trying out recipes from different cuisines. Each culture has its own unique culinary traditions, ingredients, and cooking methods. By exploring these diverse cuisines, you not only broaden your knowledge of global flavors but also enhance your ability to create exciting and delicious meals.

To explore different cuisines, consider starting with popular ones such as Italian, Mexican, Chinese, Indian, or Thai. Each of these cuisines offers a wide array of dishes that are relatively easy to make and can introduce you to new ingredients and techniques. Look for cookbooks or online recipes that focus on these specific cuisines to guide you in your culinary journey.

Cookbooks are an excellent resource for learning about different cuisines. They often provide comprehensive guides to traditional ingredients, cooking techniques, and cultural contexts. Additionally, many cookbooks include step-by-step instructions and beautiful photos that can inspire and guide you through the cooking process. Visit your local library or bookstore to browse through a variety of cookbooks available or search for recommendations online.

In addition to cookbooks, there are numerous online resources dedicated to sharing recipes from around the world. Websites, food blogs, and social media platforms offer a vast collection of recipes that cater to various skill levels. You can explore new cuisines by following recipe websites or subscribing to YouTube channels featuring international chefs who share their expertise.

If you're looking for a more hands-on approach to developing your culinary skills, consider taking cooking classes. Many culinary schools and community centers offer courses specifically designed for amateur cooks looking to expand their repertoire. These classes not only provide practical knowledge but also offer the opportunity to interact with instructors and fellow cooking enthusiasts.

Attending food festivals, joining cooking clubs or groups, and participating in culinary events can also expose you to different cuisines. These experiences allow you to taste authentic dishes, engage with cultural traditions, and connect with individuals who share a passion for food.

As you venture into exploring different cuisines, remember to approach it with an open mind and a willingness to try new ingredients and flavors. Don't be afraid to experiment or adapt recipes according to your taste preferences. Cooking is a creative process, and by embracing this creativity, you can develop your own unique culinary style.

By expanding your culinary skills and exploring different cuisines, you not only enhance your ability to create delicious meals but also broaden your cultural understanding and appreciation. Embrace the richness and diversity of global flavors as you continue on your journey towards independence in the kitchen.

Chapter 3

Home Maintenance and DIY: The Fundamentals

****

Home Maintenance

Home maintenance is a crucial aspect of homeownership that often goes overlooked, especially for young adults just starting out. In this chapter, we will explore the importance of home maintenance in ensuring safety, comfort, and preserving property value.

First and foremost, home maintenance plays a pivotal role in the safety of your living space. Regularly inspecting and maintaining key areas of your home can help identify potential hazards and address them before they become major issues. From checking smoke detectors to ensuring proper functioning of electrical systems, these routine tasks can greatly reduce the risk of accidents or emergencies.

Additionally, home maintenance is essential for maintaining a comfortable living environment. By regularly cleaning and servicing HVAC systems, you can ensure consistent heating and cooling throughout the year. Proper insulation and sealing of windows and doors can also improve energy efficiency and reduce utility costs. Taking care of these tasks proactively will contribute to a more comfortable and enjoyable home.

Furthermore, performing regular maintenance on your property helps preserve its value. Neglected homes tend to depreciate in value over time, while well-maintained properties often appreciate in value. Simple tasks like painting the exterior, maintaining the landscaping, and cleaning gutters can go a long way in maintaining curb appeal and protecting your investment.

The DIY (Do It Yourself) approach to home maintenance offers numerous benefits beyond just saving money on professional services. It provides an opportunity to learn new skills, gain self-sufficiency, and take pride in being able to care for your own home. By taking charge of your home's maintenance, you can develop valuable skills that will benefit you throughout your life.

In conclusion, home maintenance is a critical responsibility for homeowners of all ages. By prioritizing regular upkeep and addressing any issues promptly, you can ensure the safety, comfort, and longevity of your home. Embracing the DIY approach not only saves money but also empowers you to take control of your living space and develop valuable skills along the way.

Essential Tools and Equipment:

To effectively tackle home maintenance tasks, it's essential to have the right tools and equipment on hand. Here is a detailed list of basic tools that every homeowner should have in their arsenal, along with an explanation of their purposes and tips for purchasing high-quality tools within a budget.

1. Screwdriver Set: A versatile tool used for tightening or loosening screws. Invest in a set that includes both flathead and Phillips head screwdrivers to handle various types of screws commonly found around the house.
2. Hammer: An essential tool for driving nails into walls, assembling furniture, or making repairs. Look for a hammer with a comfortable grip and a weight that feels balanced in your hand.
3. Adjustable Wrench: Also known as a crescent wrench, this tool is used for tightening or loosening nuts and bolts of different sizes. Opt for an adjustable wrench that can accommodate various sizes to minimize the number of tools you need.
4. Pliers: A multipurpose tool used for gripping, bending, cutting wires, or holding objects firmly in place. Invest in a pair of slip-joint pliers that can be adjusted to fit different sizes.
5. Tape Measure: A must-have tool for accurately measuring dimensions when planning renovation projects or buying new furniture. Look for a sturdy tape measure with clear markings and a lock feature to keep your measurements in place.

6. Level: Used to ensure that pictures, shelves, and other items are perfectly straight. Choose a level with multiple vials for horizontal and vertical measurements.
7. Utility Knife: A versatile cutting tool used for opening packages, trimming materials, or performing small precision cuts. Opt for a utility knife with a retractable blade for safety and durability.
8. Cordless Drill: An indispensable power tool for drilling holes and driving screws efficiently. Look for a cordless drill with adjustable speed settings and interchangeable drill bits to handle various materials.
9. Ladder: Depending on the size of your home, invest in a sturdy ladder to safely reach heights when performing repairs or cleaning gutters. Consider a multipurpose ladder that can be adjusted into different positions for added versatility.
10. Safety Gear: Always prioritize safety when working on home maintenance tasks. Invest in safety glasses, work gloves, and a dust mask to protect your eyes, hands, and respiratory system.

When purchasing tools, consider both quality and affordability. While it's tempting to opt for the cheapest option available, investing in high-quality tools will ensure durability and longevity. Look out for sales, discounts, or consider buying second-hand tools from reputable sources to save money without compromising on quality.

By having these essential tools at your disposal, you'll be well-equipped to handle basic home maintenance tasks and make minor repairs when needed. Remember to follow safety guidelines and consult professional assistance when necessary for complex or potentially dangerous projects.

Basic Home Repairs:

In this section, we will delve into step-by-step instructions for common DIY home repairs that are frequently encountered. By gaining the knowledge and skills needed to tackle basic repairs, readers can save money on professional services, increase self-sufficiency, and maintain a safe and comfortable living environment.

1. Fixing Leaky Faucets:

- Begin by turning off the water supply to the affected faucet.
- Disassemble the faucet handle and inspect the components for any damage or wear.
- Replace faulty parts such as washers, O-rings, or cartridges.
- Reassemble the faucet and test for leaks.

2. Unclogging Drains:

- Start by using a plunger to create suction and dislodge the clog.
- If that doesn't work, try using a drain snake or auger to physically remove the blockage.
- For stubborn clogs, consider using a chemical drain cleaner as a last resort.
- Flush the drain with hot water to ensure it is clear.

3. Replacing Light Fixtures:

- Make sure the power is turned off at the circuit breaker before starting any electrical work.
- Remove the existing light fixture by unscrewing the screws or nuts holding it in place.
- Disconnect the wiring from the old fixture, making note of which wires are connected to each other.
- Install the new light fixture following the manufacturer's instructions and connect the wiring accordingly.
- Secure the fixture in place and restore power to test its functionality.

It is important to note that certain repairs may require professional assistance or specialized knowledge. For example, electrical, plumbing, or structural repairs should be handled by professionals to ensure safety and compliance with building codes. It's crucial to assess your own capabilities and seek help when necessary.

Throughout all DIY repairs, it is essential to prioritize safety. Always turn off power sources, wear protective gear, and follow proper procedures. Additionally, if a repair seems too complex or you feel uncomfortable taking it on, don't hesitate to consult a professional. Your safety and the integrity of your home should always be the top priority.

By understanding and practicing these basic home repairs, readers will become more confident in their ability to handle common household issues. This newfound knowledge will not only save money but also provide a sense of accomplishment and self-sufficiency. Remember, with each successful repair, your skills will continue to grow, allowing you to take on more advanced projects in the future.

Home Maintenance Schedule:

Creating a personalized home maintenance schedule is a crucial aspect of responsible homeownership. By staying organized and proactive, you can prevent future issues and ensure that your home remains safe and in good condition. In this section, we will discuss the importance of a home maintenance schedule, outline seasonal tasks, and provide tips on prioritizing your tasks based on urgency and available time.

Importance of a Home Maintenance Schedule:

A home maintenance schedule serves as a roadmap for keeping your property in excellent shape. It helps you stay on top of routine tasks and allows you to identify potential problems before they become major issues. By adhering to a schedule, you can save money on costly repairs and extend the lifespan of various components in your home.

Seasonal Maintenance Tasks:

Different seasons bring specific maintenance requirements for your home. By understanding these seasonal tasks, you can plan accordingly and ensure that your property is well-prepared for any changes in weather or environmental conditions. Here are some examples of seasonal tasks to include in your schedule:

1. Spring:

- Inspect and clean gutters and downspouts.
- Check for any signs of roof damage or leaks.
- Service air conditioning units and prepare them for summer.
- Test smoke detectors and carbon monoxide alarms.

2. Summer:

- Maintain your lawn by mowing, watering, and fertilizing regularly.
- Inspect and clean outdoor decks, patios, and fences.
- Check and repair any cracks or gaps in windows and doors to improve energy efficiency.
- Clean and maintain outdoor furniture and equipment.

3. Fall:

- Rake leaves and clear debris from gutters to prevent clogging.
- Inspect and service heating systems to ensure they are functioning properly.
- Seal gaps around windows and doors to prevent drafts.
- Test and replace batteries in smoke detectors and carbon monoxide alarms.

4. Winter:

- Protect outdoor faucets and pipes from freezing temperatures.
- Remove snow and ice from driveways, walkways, and roofs.
- Check insulation in attics and walls to prevent heat loss.
- Inspect and clean chimneys and fireplaces before regular use.

Tips for Prioritizing Tasks:

When creating your home maintenance schedule, it's important to consider factors such as urgency and available time. Here are some tips to help you prioritize your tasks effectively:

1. Start with safety-critical tasks first. Address any issues that could pose a risk to your safety or cause further damage if left unattended.
2. Consider the seasonality of tasks. Focus on the current season's maintenance needs but also plan ahead for future tasks.
3. Break down larger tasks into manageable sub-tasks. This will make it easier to fit them into your schedule and track progress.
4. Allocate time based on task complexity and urgency. Some tasks may require more time or immediate attention, so plan accordingly.

5. Take advantage of weekends or vacation days for longer or more time-consuming projects.

By incorporating these tips into your home maintenance schedule, you'll be able to effectively manage your household upkeep while ensuring that you have ample time for other commitments.

As you create your personalized home maintenance schedule, remember that it's not set in stone. Adapt it as needed based on your changing circumstances or any unforeseen repairs that may arise. Regularly reviewing and updating your schedule will help you stay organized and maintain a well-functioning home for years to come.

Troubleshooting and Problem-solving Techniques:

- Identification of common household problems, such as squeaky doors, stuck windows, or a malfunctioning HVAC system.
- While some common household problems may have been briefly mentioned in previous chapters, this section will delve deeper into the specific issues that can arise in homes and provide detailed troubleshooting tips.
- Step-by-step troubleshooting guide to diagnose issues and find appropriate solutions.
- This step-by-step guide will walk readers through the process of identifying the root cause of common household problems and finding effective solutions. It will include detailed instructions and diagrams where necessary to ensure clarity.
- Resources, websites, and books for further learning on advanced DIY home repairs.
- This section will provide a list of reputable resources, websites, and books that readers can consult to deepen their knowledge and skills in advanced DIY home repairs. It will include recommendations for online tutorials, forums, and books written by experts in the field.

By providing practical guidance on troubleshooting and problem-solving techniques, readers will gain the confidence to tackle common household issues on their own. The step-by-step approach ensures that they can diagnose problems effectively and find appropriate solutions, saving time and money by avoiding unnecessary professional assistance. Moreover, the recommended resources will empower readers to continue expanding their knowledge beyond the basics, enabling them to handle more complex repairs in the future.

Chapter 4

Traveling on a Budget: Cultivating a Global Mindset

*****

The Importance of Travel:

Traveling is much more than just a fun way to escape the realities of everyday life—it is an essential aspect of personal growth and cultivating a global mindset. When we venture beyond our familiar surroundings and immerse ourselves in new cultures, we open ourselves up to a world of possibilities and experiences that can profoundly shape our worldview.

One of the primary benefits of travel is its ability to broaden our perspective. By exposing ourselves to different people, traditions, and lifestyles, we begin to understand that our way of life is not the only way. We learn to appreciate diversity and embrace the richness that comes from encountering different perspectives.

Travel also increases cultural awareness. When we visit other countries, we are exposed to unique customs, traditions, and ways of life. We have the opportunity to witness firsthand how people from various backgrounds navigate their daily lives, celebrate their heritage, and overcome challenges. This exposure fosters empathy and understanding, as we develop a deeper appreciation for the complexities of the human experience.

In addition to providing personal growth opportunities, travel can also be a catalyst for positive change in the world. Through responsible tourism practices, travelers can support local economies and contribute to sustainable development in host communities. By engaging with locals and learning about their culture, travelers can promote cross-cultural understanding and bridge cultural divides.

Moreover, when we expose ourselves to new environments and experiences, we develop skills such as adaptability, resourcefulness, and problem-solving. These skills are essential not only for navigating unfamiliar territories but also for thriving in an ever-changing globalized society.

It is important to note that travel doesn't necessarily mean embarking on extravagant adventures or visiting far-flung destinations. Even exploring our own cities or neighboring towns can provide valuable insights and opportunities for personal growth. The key is to approach travel with an open mind and a willingness to step out of our comfort zones.

By making travel a priority, even on a limited budget, we can cultivate a global mindset that values diversity, promotes empathy, and embraces new experiences. Whether it's a weekend road trip or a backpacking adventure across continents, each journey has the potential to expand our horizons and transform us into more compassionate, informed, and culturally sensitive individuals.

Planning and Researching:

In this section, we will delve into practical tips and strategies for planning a trip on a budget. It is crucial to prioritize your travel expenses and make informed decisions when choosing destinations and activities. By following these tips, you can ensure an exciting and fulfilling travel experience without breaking the bank.

1. Finding Affordable Airfare:

- Start by researching different airlines and comparing prices. Consider using flight comparison websites or apps to find the best deals.
- Be flexible with your travel dates and times. Flying during off-peak seasons or midweek can often result in significant savings.
- Take advantage of airline rewards programs or frequent flyer miles. Accumulate points through credit card purchases or loyalty programs to use towards discounted or free flights.

2. Accommodation Options on a Budget:

- Look beyond traditional hotels and explore alternative accommodation options such as hostels, guesthouses, or vacation rentals. These options often offer lower rates while providing unique experiences.
- Consider staying in less touristy areas or suburbs instead of city centers. Accommodation prices tend to be more affordable in these areas.
- Utilize online booking platforms that offer discounts or cash-back rewards for accommodations. Read reviews and compare prices to find the best value for your money.

3. Creating a Travel Budget:

- Start by determining how much you can allocate towards your trip. Consider your income, expenses, and savings goals.
- Break down your budget into categories such as transportation, accommodation, meals, attractions, and souvenirs.
- Research the cost of living in your destination to get an idea of daily expenses such as meals, transportation, and activities.
- Leave room in your budget for unexpected expenses or emergencies.

4. Utilizing Online Resources for Deals and Discounts:

- Subscribe to travel deal websites, newsletters, and social media accounts that specialize in finding discounted flights, accommodations, and activities.
- Use price comparison websites to compare prices across different platforms. This can help you find the best deals for flights, accommodations, and rental cars.
- Take advantage of online travel communities and forums where travelers share their experiences, tips, and recommendations for budget-friendly destinations and activities.

Remember, thorough planning and research can significantly impact the overall cost of your trip. By utilizing these strategies, you can make informed decisions that align with your budget while still enjoying a fulfilling travel experience.

Saving Money While Traveling:

In this section, readers will discover various strategies and tips for saving money while exploring new destinations. Traveling on a budget doesn't mean sacrificing experiences or missing out on the best attractions. By implementing these practical suggestions, readers can make their travel funds stretch further and have a fulfilling trip without breaking the bank.

1. Finding Affordable Meals:

- Seek out local markets and street food vendors: Eating at local markets and street food stalls not only offers a taste of authentic cuisine but also tends to be more affordable than dining at touristy restaurants.
- Embrace self-catering options: Consider booking accommodations with kitchen facilities, enabling you to prepare your own meals. This can significantly cut down on food expenses, especially for breakfast and lunch.

2. Utilizing Public Transportation:

- Research transportation options in advance: Look into the local public transportation systems, such as buses, trams, or subways, and familiarize yourself with routes and ticket prices. Opting for public transportation over taxis or private transfers can save a substantial amount of money.
- Walk or rent bikes: Exploring destinations on foot or renting bicycles can be an inexpensive and enjoyable way to get around, particularly in compact cities or scenic areas.

3. Seeking Free or Low-Cost Attractions and Activities:

- **Take advantage of city passes and tourist cards:** Many cities offer discounted passes that provide access to multiple attractions at a reduced price. Research and compare these options before your trip.
- Explore parks, gardens, and public spaces: Nature is often free to enjoy, so make the most of beautiful parks, botanical gardens, and other outdoor spaces that offer relaxation and photo opportunities.

- Look for free cultural events and festivals: Check local event calendars for free concerts, art exhibitions, or cultural celebrations during your visit. These events offer a chance to experience the local culture without spending extra money.

4. Packing Smart:

- Pack versatile clothing items: Choose clothes that can be mixed and matched to create multiple outfits. This allows you to pack lighter and avoid excess baggage fees.
- Bring a reusable water bottle and snacks: Having a refillable water bottle and some snacks on hand can save you from purchasing expensive drinks and snacks at touristy locations.

5. Negotiating for Better Prices:

- Hone your bargaining skills: In many countries, haggling is a common practice. Don't be afraid to negotiate prices for souvenirs or services, but always be respectful and polite.
- Consider local currency: Familiarize yourself with the local currency and exchange rates. Using cash instead of credit cards may give you more opportunities for negotiation.

By implementing these money-saving strategies, readers can make their travel experiences more affordable without compromising on enjoyment. Remember, traveling on a budget encourages resourcefulness, creativity, and the ability to fully immerse oneself in the local culture.```,Traveling on a Budget: Cultivating a Global Mindset

Section: Traveling Off the Beaten Path

In this section, we encourage readers to step out of their comfort zones and explore lesser-known destinations. While popular tourist spots can be wonderful, there is something magical about venturing off the beaten path and discovering hidden gems that are often overlooked by the masses. By embracing the concept of slow travel and immersing oneself in local communities and cultures, travelers can truly gain a deeper understanding of the world and themselves.

One of the key benefits of traveling off the beaten path is the opportunity to engage with locals on a more personal level. By visiting less touristy areas, you're more likely to encounter genuine interactions with locals who are eager to share their culture, traditions, and stories. This can lead to meaningful connections and friendships that transcend borders and last a lifetime.

Another advantage of exploring lesser-known destinations is the chance to witness authentic cultural practices and traditions. Away from the influence of mass tourism, these communities often preserve age-old customs that provide valuable insights into their history and way of life. Whether it's participating in a traditional ceremony, learning traditional crafts, or trying local cuisine, these experiences can enrich your understanding of different cultures and foster respect for diverse ways of living.

Traveling off the beaten path also allows for a more sustainable and responsible approach to tourism. Popular destinations can sometimes suffer from overtourism, leading to overcrowding, environmental degradation, and strain on local resources. By choosing lesser-known destinations, travelers can contribute to the preservation of natural landscapes and support local economies that rely on sustainable and ethical practices.

When venturing off the beaten path, it's important to embrace a sense of adventure and open-mindedness. These destinations may not have all the amenities and luxuries of popular tourist spots, but they offer unique experiences that are worth every bit of effort. It's essential to be respectful of local customs, traditions, and beliefs, and to always prioritize the well-being of local communities and the environment.

By choosing to explore lesser-known destinations, you not only avoid the crowds but also create memorable experiences that will stay with you long after your journey ends. The world is vast and filled with hidden treasures waiting to be discovered. So, go off the beaten path, embrace the unknown, and let your adventurous spirit guide you towards a deeper understanding of our diverse and beautiful world.

Cultivating a Global Mindset: This final section explores how travel can contribute to personal development and the cultivation of a global mindset. It emphasizes the importance of embracing diversity, learning from different cultures, and challenging one's own preconceptions. Traveling on a budget can provide unique opportunities for personal growth and expanding one's worldview. By immersing oneself in new environments, engaging with locals, and trying new experiences, readers can develop a deeper understanding and appreciation for different cultures and perspectives.

Embracing Diversity: One of the most significant benefits of travel is the opportunity to encounter diverse cultures, traditions, and ways of life. By immersing oneself in unfamiliar surroundings, readers can gain valuable insights into the richness and complexity of the world we live in. Engaging with people from different backgrounds and perspectives fosters empathy, understanding, and tolerance. It challenges our own assumptions and biases, allowing us to develop a more inclusive and open-minded attitude towards others.

Learning from Different Cultures: Travel provides a unique opportunity to learn from different cultures firsthand. By observing and participating in local customs, traditions, and practices, readers can gain insights into alternative ways of thinking and living. Whether it's exploring ancient temples in Asia, tasting exotic cuisine in South America, or witnessing traditional ceremonies in Africa, each experience offers valuable lessons about the diversity and beauty of human expression.

Challenging Preconceptions: Traveling on a budget often means venturing off the beaten path and exploring places that may not be typical tourist destinations. This encourages readers to challenge their preconceived notions about certain countries or regions. By experiencing the reality of a place beyond stereotypes or media portrayals, readers can form their own opinions based on direct experience. This allows for a more nuanced understanding of different cultures and can help break down barriers and misconceptions.

Engaging with Locals: One of the most rewarding aspects of travel is connecting with locals. Interacting with people from different backgrounds and cultures fosters cross-cultural understanding and creates opportunities for genuine human connection. By engaging in conversations, sharing stories, and immersing oneself in local communities, readers can gain new perspectives and forge meaningful relationships that transcend borders.

Trying New Experiences: Traveling on a budget often requires resourcefulness and adaptability. It encourages readers to step out of their comfort zones and try new experiences. Whether it's hiking through lush rainforests, learning to cook traditional dishes, or participating in local festivals, each new experience offers an opportunity for personal growth and self-discovery. Stepping into the unknown and embracing discomfort can lead to transformative moments that shape our worldview and broaden our horizons.

In conclusion, traveling on a budget can be a powerful tool for personal development and cultivating a global mindset. Embracing diversity, learning from different cultures, challenging preconceptions, engaging with locals, and trying new experiences are key components of this transformative journey. By venturing beyond familiar surroundings and exploring the world, readers can develop a deeper appreciation for the richness of human existence and forge connections that transcend geographical boundaries.

Chapter 5

Civic Engagement: Being an Informed and Active Citizen

****

Civic Engagement

Civic engagement plays a crucial role in the personal growth and development of individuals, as well as in the progress of communities and democracies. By actively participating in society and taking an interest in the issues that affect us all, we not only contribute to positive change but also gain a sense of fulfillment and purpose.

One of the key benefits of civic engagement is the opportunity to build social connections and form relationships with like-minded individuals. Through volunteering, attending community events, or joining advocacy groups, we meet people who share our values and passions. These connections can lead to long-lasting friendships, mentorships, and collaborations, opening doors to new opportunities for personal and professional growth.

Engaging in civic activities also allows us to develop empathy and broaden our understanding of diverse perspectives. By stepping outside of our comfort zones and interacting with individuals from different backgrounds, we gain a deeper appreciation for the challenges others face and can work towards building a more inclusive and compassionate society. This empathy not only strengthens our relationships with others but also enhances our own personal growth by expanding our worldview.

Furthermore, civic engagement fosters a sense of fulfillment by allowing us to make a meaningful impact on our communities. Whether it's through supporting local initiatives, advocating for important causes, or participating in democratic processes, we have the power to create positive change. This active involvement gives us a sense of purpose and satisfaction, knowing that our actions are contributing to the betterment of society.

By recognizing the importance of civic engagement and actively participating in it, young adults can reap the benefits of personal growth, community development, and democracy. Building social connections, developing empathy, and gaining a sense of fulfillment are just some of the rewards that come with being an informed and active citizen.

Understanding the Structures and Processes of Governance:

To truly be an informed and active citizen, it is essential to have a solid understanding of the structures and processes of governance. This knowledge allows individuals to navigate the complexities of political systems, understand how policies are created, and effectively engage with their government at various levels.

Different forms of government exist, ranging from local municipalities to state and national institutions. Each level has its own roles and responsibilities, which vary depending on the country or region. By familiarizing oneself with these different levels of government, individuals can better grasp how decisions are made and which entities hold decision-making power.

It is also crucial to understand the branches of government and their functions. Most democratic systems consist of three main branches: the executive, legislative, and judicial branches. The executive branch, led by elected officials such as mayors, governors, or presidents, is responsible for implementing policies and managing day-to-day affairs. The legislative branch, comprising elected representatives or lawmakers, creates and passes laws. Finally, the judicial branch interprets laws and ensures their constitutionality through court proceedings.

By comprehending these fundamental aspects of governance, individuals can actively participate in their communities in a more informed and impactful way. They can follow the decision-making processes that affect their lives directly, voice their concerns to the appropriate governing bodies, and work towards positive change within established frameworks.

Developing this understanding also helps citizens recognize the importance of their role in holding elected officials accountable. By knowing how policies are created and implemented, individuals can assess whether their representatives are acting in the best interest of their constituents. Informed citizens are better equipped to evaluate policy proposals critically and actively engage in dialogue with elected officials when necessary.

Additionally, understanding the structures of governance allows individuals to identify opportunities for participation within their communities. It enables them to join advisory committees, attend public hearings or council meetings, or even run for office themselves. By actively participating in these processes, individuals can contribute to shaping policies and decisions that align with their values and priorities.

Overall, having a solid understanding of the structures and processes of governance is essential for anyone looking to be an informed and active citizen. By familiarizing themselves with these concepts, individuals can navigate political systems effectively, engage with their elected officials, and work towards positive change within their communities.

Becoming an Informed Citizen:

In today's fast-paced and digital world, it is essential for young adults to become informed citizens. This section focuses on the role of media and emphasizes the importance of obtaining news from diverse and reliable sources. By being proactive in seeking out accurate information, readers can make informed decisions and contribute meaningfully to their communities.

Understanding the Role of Media:

Media plays a crucial role in providing information and shaping public opinion. However, it is important to approach media with a critical lens. Not all sources are created equal, and it is vital to distinguish between reliable news outlets and sensationalized or biased sources. Encourage readers to explore a variety of news sources, including reputable newspapers, independent publications, and verified fact-checking organizations.

Evaluating Information Critically:

Critical evaluation is an essential skill when consuming media. Readers should be encouraged to consider the source's credibility, examine the evidence provided, and assess potential biases or conflicts of interest. Fact-checking is a valuable tool to separate truth from misinformation or propaganda. Remind readers to verify information before accepting it as fact and to consult multiple reliable sources to ensure accuracy.

Identifying Biases:

Biases can subtly influence the way news is reported, affecting our understanding and perspective on important issues. It is crucial for readers to develop their ability to recognize and analyze biases. They should be encouraged to question the framing, language, and tone used in news articles and to consider alternative viewpoints to gain a more comprehensive understanding.

Staying Updated on Current Events and Social Issues:

To be informed citizens, young adults should strive to stay up-to-date on current events and social issues that affect their communities and society as a whole. Regularly reading news articles, following credible news outlets on social media, and participating in discussions can help broaden their knowledge and perspectives. By staying informed, they can actively contribute to conversations and engage in meaningful dialogue with others.

By highlighting the importance of media literacy, critical evaluation, and staying informed, this section empowers readers to become active participants in their communities. It equips them with the necessary tools to navigate the vast media landscape and make well-informed decisions that promote positive change in society.

Taking Action: Volunteering and Advocacy:

Getting involved in our communities through volunteering for nonprofit organizations or participating in grassroots movements is an essential part of civic engagement. This section discusses the various ways in which individuals can take action and make a positive impact in their communities.

Volunteering is a powerful way to contribute to causes that align with our personal values and passions. By dedicating our time and skills to nonprofit organizations, we can address pressing issues, support vulnerable populations, and create lasting change. Whether it's volunteering at a local food bank, mentoring underprivileged youth, or organizing community clean-up events, there are numerous opportunities to make a difference.

When considering volunteer opportunities, it's important to find causes that resonate with us on a deeper level. By aligning our values and interests with the mission of the organization, we are more likely to feel fulfilled and motivated to contribute. For example, if environmental conservation is a priority, joining a local sustainability organization or participating in tree planting initiatives can be a meaningful way to get involved.

In addition to volunteering, advocacy is another powerful avenue for civic engagement. Advocacy involves using our voices and taking action to promote positive change in society. There are various channels through which we can advocate for causes we care about. Writing letters or emails to elected officials expressing our concerns or supporting specific policies can have a significant impact. Attending town hall meetings and engaging in peaceful protests are other effective ways to amplify our voices and raise awareness about important issues.

When engaging in advocacy, it's crucial to be well-informed about the topics we are advocating for. This means staying updated on current events, researching reliable sources of information, and fact-checking before taking a stance. By understanding the nuances of the issues we care about, we can better articulate our positions and engage in constructive conversations with others.

Volunteering and advocacy go hand in hand when it comes to civic engagement. While volunteering allows us to directly contribute to causes, advocacy amplifies our impact by promoting systemic change. By combining these two approaches, we can create a ripple effect that goes beyond individual actions and fosters a culture of civic responsibility.

In the next section, we will explore strategies for sustaining long-term civic engagement and overcoming challenges that may arise along the way.

Sustaining Civic Engagement for Long-Term Impact:

Consistent and long-term civic engagement goes beyond sporadic involvement. It requires a commitment to staying active and involved in your community over time. Here are some strategies for maintaining long-term engagement:

1. Join Community Organizations:

One way to sustain civic engagement is by becoming a member of community organizations that align with your interests and values. These organizations provide ongoing opportunities to contribute to important causes and make a difference.

2. Run for Public Office:

If you have a passion for public service and want to have a direct impact on your community, consider running for public office. By becoming an elected official, you can actively shape policies, advocate for change, and represent the interests of your constituents.

3. Volunteer Regularly:

Consistent volunteering is an excellent way to stay engaged and maintain an active role in your community. Find volunteer opportunities that resonate with your values and allow you to utilize your skills and interests effectively.

4. Attend Local Meetings and Town Halls:

Stay informed about local issues by attending town hall meetings, city council meetings, or other community gatherings. By participating in these events, you can voice your concerns, ask questions, and contribute to meaningful discussions.

5. Utilize Online Platforms for Advocacy:

In today's digital age, social media and online platforms provide avenues for sustained advocacy. Use these channels to raise awareness about important causes, share information, and engage with like-minded individuals.

While sustaining civic engagement is crucial, it is essential to acknowledge that challenges and obstacles may arise along the way. Here are some tips for overcoming them:

1. Time Management:

Balancing work, personal life, and civic engagement can be challenging. Prioritize your commitments and create a schedule that allows you to devote time to your civic activities without neglecting other responsibilities.

2. Burnout Prevention:

Sustained civic engagement can be emotionally and physically demanding. Take care of yourself by practicing self-care, setting boundaries, and recognizing when you need to take a step back to avoid burnout.

3. Building Support Networks:

Surround yourself with like-minded individuals who share your passion for civic engagement. Joining or creating support networks can provide encouragement, accountability, and opportunities for collaboration.

4. Adapting to Changing Circumstances:

Life circumstances may change, requiring adjustments to your level of involvement. Stay flexible and be willing to adapt your engagement strategies as needed.

By following these strategies and overcoming potential obstacles, you can sustain your civic engagement efforts and make a lasting impact on your community. Remember, long-term commitment is key to effecting meaningful change and contributing to the betterment of society.

Part 8:
Challenges and
Overcoming Adversity

Chapter 6

Coping with Failure:
Lessons on Bouncing Back

****

Failure as a Path to Success

Understanding the Role of Failure: This section delves into the concept of failure and its importance in personal growth and development. It highlights the common misconceptions surrounding failure, emphasizing that it is a natural and inevitable part of life. By reframing their mindset towards failure, readers can begin to see it as an opportunity for learning, self-improvement, and resilience.

Many individuals view failure as a negative outcome or a sign of incompetence. However, this narrow perspective hinders personal growth and limits potential. In reality, failure is a valuable teacher that can provide invaluable lessons and insights.

This section encourages readers to embrace failure as a necessary stepping stone towards success. It helps them understand that failure is not an indication of worth or ability but rather a temporary setback that can lead to new opportunities. By shifting their mindset, readers can reframe failure as a catalyst for growth and cultivate a positive attitude towards adversity.

Through engaging anecdotes and real-life examples, readers will gain a deeper understanding of how successful individuals have embraced failure as a fundamental part of their journey. They will be inspired by stories of renowned entrepreneurs, athletes, and artists who experienced multiple failures before achieving greatness. These narratives serve as powerful reminders that failure is not an endpoint but rather a stepping stone towards future success.

By exploring the role of failure in personal growth and development, this section equips readers with the tools to embrace failure with resilience and determination. It empowers them to reframe their mindset, extract valuable lessons from setbacks, and ultimately use failure as fuel for their journey towards success.

Analyzing Failure: In this section, readers are guided on how to effectively analyze their failures. It is crucial to take a step back and evaluate the reasons behind each failure in order to learn from them and avoid repeating the same mistakes. By conducting a thorough analysis, readers can gain a deeper understanding of the factors that contributed to their setbacks.

One effective strategy for analyzing failure is to identify any patterns or recurring mistakes. By examining past failures, readers can start to recognize common themes or behaviors that may have led to their lack of success. This can include factors such as poor time management, lack of preparation, or ineffective communication.

Practical exercises will be provided to help readers develop analytical skills and self-awareness. These exercises may involve reflecting on specific instances of failure and identifying the key factors that played a role. Readers will be encouraged to ask themselves questions such as:

- What were the specific actions or decisions that led to the failure?
- Were there any external factors beyond their control that contributed to the outcome?
- Were there any warning signs or red flags that were overlooked?
- Were there any missed opportunities or alternative approaches that could have been considered?

Case studies will also be included to provide real-life examples of individuals who faced failure and successfully analyzed their setbacks. By examining these case studies, readers can gain valuable insights into different strategies and approaches to analyzing failure.

Overall, this section aims to equip readers with the necessary tools and mindset for effectively analyzing their failures. By developing analytical skills and self-awareness, readers will be better equipped to learn from their mistakes and make more informed decisions in the future.

Resilience and Acceptance: This section delves into the importance of building resilience and developing acceptance towards failure. It emphasizes the need for readers to cultivate a growth mindset, which involves viewing failures as opportunities for learning and growth. By adopting this mindset, individuals can bounce back stronger after experiencing setbacks.

One strategy for building resilience is practicing self-compassion. It is essential for readers to acknowledge their feelings of disappointment or frustration when facing failure, but also to treat themselves with kindness and understanding. This self-compassion allows individuals to recover from failure without dwelling on it excessively or allowing it to negatively impact their self-esteem.

Embracing failure as a stepping stone towards success is another key aspect of resilience and acceptance. By reframing the way failures are perceived, readers can recognize that every setback is an opportunity to learn, improve, and develop new strategies. Embracing failure as a natural part of life helps individuals maintain a positive mindset while navigating challenges.

Accepting one's failures without dwelling on them excessively is crucial for moving forward. Rather than focusing on past mistakes, individuals should shift their attention towards the lessons learned and the growth achieved. This ability to accept and let go of failures allows individuals to stay focused on their goals and continue striving for success.

By implementing strategies to build resilience and foster acceptance towards failure, readers will be better equipped to bounce back from setbacks. They will develop the emotional strength and mindset needed to persevere through challenges and ultimately achieve long-term success.

Learning from Failure: This section delves into the valuable lessons that can be learned from failure. It recognizes that failures can often provide unique opportunities for growth, innovation, and self-improvement. By embracing failure as a natural part of the journey towards success, individuals can extract valuable insights and use them as stepping stones towards achieving their goals.

One technique for extracting lessons from failures is through reflection exercises. By taking the time to reflect on what went wrong and why, individuals can gain a deeper understanding of their own actions, decisions, and thought processes. Through guided prompts and questions, readers are encouraged to explore their failures from different angles and uncover valuable insights about themselves and their approach to challenges.

Seeking feedback from trusted mentors, peers, or professionals is another effective method for learning from failure. By seeking input from others who have experience or expertise in the relevant area, individuals can gain new perspectives and identify areas for improvement. Feedback provides an external viewpoint that can help individuals see blind spots they may have missed on their own.

Analyzing successful individuals who have overcome failure can also offer valuable lessons. By studying the stories and experiences of those who have faced similar setbacks but ultimately achieved success, readers can gain inspiration and guidance on how to navigate their own paths. Understanding the strategies, mindset shifts, and actions taken by these individuals can provide a roadmap for turning failures into triumphs.

In addition to these techniques, it is important to approach failure with a growth mindset. Embracing the belief that abilities and intelligence can be developed through effort and learning, rather than being fixed traits, allows individuals to see failures as opportunities for growth. By reframing failure as a temporary setback rather than a reflection of one's worth or capabilities, individuals can cultivate resilience and bounce back stronger.

By incorporating these techniques and adopting a mindset of continuous learning and growth, readers can extract valuable lessons from their failures. They will develop the ability to analyze their mistakes, seek feedback, and find inspiration in the stories of others. Through this process of learning from failure, individuals can turn setbacks into stepping stones towards their desired success.

Moving Forward: The final section of "Coping with Failure: Lessons on Bouncing Back" provides practical tips for moving forward after experiencing failure. It offers guidance on goal setting, developing an action plan, and leveraging newfound knowledge and insights gained from failures.

Readers will learn how to use their failures as motivation to persevere, set new goals, and ultimately achieve success in various aspects of their lives. By reflecting on the lessons learned from failure, readers can gain clarity on what steps they need to take to move forward in a positive direction.

Setting specific and achievable goals is crucial for progress. This section will guide readers in setting meaningful goals that align with their values and aspirations. By breaking down these goals into smaller, actionable steps, readers can create a clear roadmap for their future success.

Developing an action plan is essential for translating goals into tangible results. This section will provide practical strategies for organizing tasks, managing time effectively, and staying motivated throughout the process. Readers will learn about the power of consistency and perseverance in overcoming setbacks and achieving long-term success.

Leveraging newfound knowledge and insights gained from failure requires self-reflection and a growth mindset. This section will encourage readers to analyze their failures objectively and extract valuable lessons from them. By understanding what went wrong and why, readers can avoid repeating past mistakes and make better decisions moving forward.

Incorporating these strategies into their lives, readers will be able to use their failures as stepping stones toward personal growth and achievement. With a renewed sense of purpose and determination, they can embrace new opportunities, set higher goals, and overcome obstacles with confidence.

Chapter 7

Overcoming Fear of Rejection: Building Confidence

Fear of Rejection:

Understanding the Fear of Rejection: In this section, readers are introduced to the concept of fear of rejection and its impact on self-confidence. It is natural for individuals to feel a sense of fear or anxiety when faced with the possibility of rejection, whether it be in relationships, career aspirations, or personal endeavors. Understanding why rejection can be so intimidating is the first step towards building confidence and overcoming this fear.

Research-backed insights and relatable examples are provided to help readers gain a deeper understanding of the psychological and emotional factors at play. The fear of rejection often stems from a fear of failure, judgment, or not being accepted by others. It can manifest as self-doubt, feeling unworthy, or a lack of belief in one's abilities.

Readers learn that fear of rejection can hold them back from pursuing their goals and dreams. It may prevent them from taking risks, seeking new opportunities, or expressing themselves authentically. By acknowledging and understanding the fear of rejection, readers can begin to identify its presence in their lives and take steps towards building confidence.

Through relatable anecdotes and research findings, readers recognize that fear of rejection is a common experience shared by many. They are encouraged to reflect on their own experiences and how this fear has influenced their decisions and actions. This self-reflection serves as a starting point for personal growth and building resilience.

By exploring the roots of the fear of rejection, readers can gain insight into their own thought patterns and beliefs. They will realize that rejection does not define their worth or abilities. Understanding that rejection is often a subjective response based on individual perspectives and circumstances can help mitigate its emotional impact.

Ultimately, this section aims to empower readers by providing them with knowledge and insights into the fear of rejection. By recognizing this fear, they can start the journey towards building confidence and resilience. Armed with this understanding, readers will be better equipped to navigate the challenges and uncertainties that come their way, embracing rejection as an opportunity for growth rather than a deterrent to success.

Recognizing Negative Thought Patterns: This part of the chapter focuses on helping readers identify and address negative thought patterns that contribute to their fear of rejection. Negative thought patterns, such as self-doubt, perfectionism, and negative self-talk, can significantly impact one's confidence and ability to face rejection.

Through practical exercises and self-reflection prompts, readers will gain the tools and insights needed to recognize these detrimental thought patterns. By becoming aware of the negative thoughts that arise when faced with potential rejection, readers can begin challenging these beliefs and replacing them with more positive and empowering ones.

Self-reflection prompts will encourage readers to explore their own inner dialogue and pinpoint moments where they engage in self-doubt or negative self-talk. By examining and questioning these thoughts, readers will realize that these limiting beliefs are often unfounded or distorted. They will learn to challenge their negative thoughts by asking themselves if there is evidence to support these beliefs and if there are alternative perspectives that are more empowering.

Furthermore, practical exercises will be provided to help readers cultivate a more positive mindset. For example, readers may be encouraged to create a list of their strengths and accomplishments to remind themselves of their capabilities. Another exercise may involve reframing negative thoughts into more positive and realistic statements.

By recognizing and addressing these negative thought patterns, readers will develop a more resilient mindset and build the confidence necessary to face rejection head-on. They will understand that failure and rejection are not indicative of their worth or abilities but rather stepping stones towards growth and success.

Building Resilience: Resilience is a key factor in overcoming the fear of rejection and developing confidence. It involves the ability to bounce back from setbacks, learn from failures, and view them as opportunities for growth. Building resilience begins with reframing our perception of failures and setbacks. Instead of seeing them as personal shortcomings or reasons to give up, we can view them as valuable lessons that propel us forward.

Cultivating a growth mindset is essential for building resilience. A growth mindset is the belief that our abilities and intelligence can be developed through dedication and hard work. With a growth mindset, we understand that failure is not a reflection of our worth but rather an indication that we are pushing ourselves beyond our comfort zones. By adopting this mindset, we position ourselves to embrace challenges and view them as opportunities to learn and improve.

Developing a strong sense of self-worth is also crucial for building resilience. When we have a healthy self-image and believe in our own value, we are better equipped to handle rejection. We understand that rejection does not define us but is merely a temporary setback on our journey towards success. By recognizing and appreciating our own worth, we can bounce back from rejection more quickly and confidently.

In addition to reframing failures and cultivating a growth mindset, building resilience involves taking care of ourselves mentally and physically. Engaging in activities that promote mental well-being such as practicing mindfulness, journaling, or seeking therapy can help us manage stress and build emotional resilience. Taking care of our physical health through regular exercise, proper nutrition, and adequate sleep also supports overall resilience by ensuring we have the energy and stamina to face challenges head-on.

By consciously working on building resilience, we can overcome the fear of rejection, develop confidence, and pursue our goals with determination. Remember, setbacks and rejections are not signs of inadequacy but stepping stones towards growth and achievement. Embrace them as opportunities to become stronger, more resilient individuals who are capable of overcoming any obstacle that comes our way.

Stepping out of our comfort zones is a critical step in overcoming the fear of rejection and building confidence. It is natural to feel comfortable in familiar surroundings and routines, but true growth and self-discovery lie just beyond our comfort zones. By pushing ourselves to explore new experiences and take risks, we challenge ourselves to grow and expand our potential for success.

To encourage readers to step out of their comfort zones, here are some practical tips and exercises:

1. Start small: Begin by taking small steps outside your comfort zone. Set achievable goals that slightly push your boundaries without overwhelming you. For example, if you're shy, start by striking up a conversation with a stranger or volunteering to give a presentation to a small group.

2. Embrace discomfort: Understand that discomfort is a natural part of stepping out of your comfort zone. Embrace the feeling of being uncomfortable as a sign of growth and progress. Remember that the most rewarding experiences often come from challenging yourself.

3. Challenge negative beliefs: Identify any negative beliefs or self-doubt that may be holding you back from stepping out of your comfort zone. Challenge these beliefs by questioning their validity and replacing them with positive affirmations. Remind yourself that failure is not the end, but rather an opportunity for growth and learning.

4. Surround yourself with support: Seek out supportive friends, mentors, or communities who can encourage and motivate you on your journey outside your comfort zone. Having a strong support system can provide reassurance and guidance during times of uncertainty.

5. Reflect on past successes: Recall previous situations where you successfully stepped out of your comfort zone and achieved positive outcomes. Remind yourself of your capabilities and the strength you have shown in the past. This reflection can boost your confidence and help you overcome future challenges.

6. Celebrate progress: Acknowledge and celebrate every step you take outside your comfort zone, no matter how small. Rewarding yourself for your bravery and progress will reinforce positive behavior and motivate you to continue pushing your boundaries.

Remember, stepping out of your comfort zone is a continuous process. As you become more comfortable with discomfort, gradually increase the level of challenge and push yourself to explore new opportunities. By consistently stepping outside your comfort zone, you'll not only build confidence but also unlock a world of possibilities and personal growth.

Developing Effective Communication Skills: Effective communication is a fundamental skill in building confidence and overcoming the fear of rejection. This section focuses on various communication techniques that can help individuals express themselves confidently and assertively.

1. **Active Listening:** Active listening is an essential aspect of effective communication. It involves fully engaging in a conversation, paying attention to the speaker, and responding appropriately. By actively listening, readers can demonstrate respect and understanding towards others, fostering stronger connections and reducing the fear of rejection.

2. **Assertiveness Training:** Developing assertiveness skills is crucial for overcoming the fear of rejection. This involves expressing one's thoughts, feelings, and needs in a respectful yet direct manner. Readers will learn strategies for assertive communication, such as using "I" statements, setting boundaries, and expressing disagreement constructively. By practicing assertiveness, individuals can increase their self-assurance and reduce anxiety around potential rejection.

3. **Conflict Resolution Skills:** Conflict is a natural part of human interactions, but it can often lead to fear of rejection if not handled properly. This section provides readers with practical techniques for resolving conflicts peacefully and constructively. They will learn how to approach conflicts with empathy, actively listen to different perspectives, find common ground, and negotiate win-win solutions. By mastering conflict resolution skills, individuals can navigate challenging conversations with confidence and minimize the likelihood of rejection.

4. **Communicating Needs and Setting Boundaries:** Being able to effectively communicate one's needs is essential for building healthy relationships and reducing the fear of rejection. In this part, readers will explore strategies for clearly expressing their desires, expectations, and boundaries. They will also learn how to ask for support, seek help when needed, and prioritize self-care without feeling guilty or fearing judgment.

5. **Handling Rejection Gracefully:** Despite our efforts, rejection is an inevitable part of life. This section offers guidance on how to handle rejection gracefully and maintain self-confidence in the face of setbacks. Readers will learn strategies for reframing rejection as an opportunity for growth, practicing self-compassion, and using rejection as feedback to improve their skills and approaches. By embracing rejection as a normal part of the journey towards success, individuals can bounce back stronger and overcome the fear of future rejection.

Through the development of effective communication skills, readers can enhance their ability to express themselves confidently and assertively, ultimately reducing the fear of rejection. By implementing these techniques in their personal and professional lives, individuals can build stronger relationships, navigate conflicts with ease, and approach new opportunities with resilience and self-assurance.

Chapter 8

Dealing with Life's Uncertainties: Coping Strategies

****

Understanding the nature of uncertainty:

Uncertainty is an inevitable part of life, and it manifests itself in various aspects such as career choices, relationships, and personal development. It is essential to explore the concept of uncertainty and understand its presence in these areas. By acknowledging that uncertainty is a natural and common experience, readers can begin to approach it with a more rational perspective.

Additionally, it is crucial to address the psychological impact that uncertainty can have on individuals. Uncertainty often leads to feelings of anxiety and stress, especially when faced with important decisions or unknown outcomes. By highlighting these emotional responses, readers can gain self-awareness and better understand their own reactions to uncertain situations.

While uncertainty can be challenging, it is important to note that it also presents opportunities for growth and personal development. Research supports the idea that uncertainty can act as a catalyst for innovative thinking and creative problem-solving. By embracing uncertainty instead of avoiding it, individuals can open themselves up to new possibilities and experiences that may ultimately lead to success and fulfillment.

By providing research-based insights into the nature of uncertainty, this chapter equips readers with a deeper understanding of its presence in their lives and the potential impact it can have on their well-being. By reframing their mindset and perceiving uncertainty as an opportunity for growth, readers can develop effective coping strategies to navigate uncertain situations with confidence and resilience.

Developing resilience is a crucial skill when it comes to navigating uncertain situations. In this chapter, we delve into the concept of resilience and its significance in building the strength and adaptability needed to face life's uncertainties.

Resilience can be defined as the ability to withstand and recover from adversity or change. It involves cultivating a growth mindset, which is the belief that challenges and setbacks are opportunities for growth and learning. By adopting a growth mindset, individuals can reframe their perspective on uncertainty, seeing it as a chance for personal development rather than an obstacle to overcome.

One strategy for building resilience is practicing self-compassion. This involves treating oneself with kindness and understanding, especially in the face of failure or disappointment. Instead of engaging in self-criticism or negative self-talk, individuals who practice self-compassion offer themselves support and encouragement. By being kind to oneself, individuals can bounce back from setbacks more quickly and effectively.

Another important aspect of developing resilience is honing problem-solving skills. When faced with uncertainty, being able to identify potential solutions and take action is essential. Problem-solving skills can be developed through practice and reflection. By breaking down challenges into manageable steps and seeking creative solutions, individuals can build their capacity to navigate uncertain situations successfully.

Real-life examples and success stories can offer inspiration and guidance when it comes to building resilience. Hearing about others who have displayed resilience in the face of uncertainty can provide valuable insights into the strategies they used and the lessons they learned. These stories can help individuals see that they are not alone in their struggles and that resilience is attainable with effort and determination.

By focusing on developing resilience, individuals can equip themselves with the tools needed to navigate uncertainty in their twenties and beyond. With a growth mindset, self-compassion, problem-solving skills, and inspiration from others, individuals can cultivate the resilience necessary to thrive in the face of life's uncertainties. Remember, developing resilience is a journey, and each step taken brings us closer to becoming resilient individuals capable of overcoming any challenges that come our way.

Building a support system:

In times of uncertainty, having a strong support system can make all the difference. Surrounding yourself with individuals who provide emotional support and guidance can help alleviate stress and make navigating uncertain situations more manageable.

It is essential to identify and nurture relationships that are positive and uplifting. Seek out friends, family members, mentors, or even support groups who genuinely care about your well-being and can offer valuable insights during challenging times. Look for individuals who have demonstrated resilience and success in their own lives and can serve as sources of inspiration and guidance.

When seeking support, effective communication is key. Clearly express your concerns, fears, and needs to trusted individuals. Be open and honest about what you are going through, allowing them to understand your perspective and offer valuable advice or assistance. Remember that vulnerability is not a sign of weakness but rather a strength that allows others to connect with you on a deeper level.

In addition to seeking support from others, it is important to actively listen and be there for those in your support system when they need you. Cultivating mutually beneficial relationships creates a network of trust, understanding, and reciprocity.

Remember, building a support system takes time and effort. It may involve reaching out to new people, attending networking events or social gatherings, or joining groups centered around shared interests or goals. Be patient with the process, as authentic connections cannot be rushed.

By proactively building a support system filled with individuals who genuinely care about your well-being, you create a valuable resource to lean on during uncertain times. Their presence will provide emotional stability, guide you through challenges, and remind you that you are not alone in your journey towards success and fulfillment.

Practicing self-care is a crucial aspect of managing uncertainty and maintaining overall well-being during challenging times. It involves engaging in activities that promote physical, mental, and emotional health, ultimately enhancing resilience and coping abilities. In this section, we will explore the significance of self-care and provide practical tips for implementing self-care routines.

Emphasizing the significance of self-care in managing stress and uncertainty is essential. When faced with uncertainties, it is common to feel overwhelmed and anxious. By prioritizing self-care, individuals can effectively manage stress levels, reduce anxiety, and maintain a sense of balance.

One key aspect of self-care is engaging in regular exercise. Physical activity helps release endorphins, which are known as the "feel-good" neurotransmitters. Whether it's going for a jog, practicing yoga, or participating in a team sport, regular exercise can significantly improve mood and reduce stress.

Mindfulness practices also play a vital role in self-care. Engaging in mindfulness exercises such as meditation or deep breathing techniques can help individuals become more present and aware of their thoughts and emotions. By cultivating mindfulness, individuals can develop a greater sense of calmness and clarity, enabling them to navigate uncertain situations with a clearer mindset.

In addition to exercise and mindfulness, maintaining a healthy diet is crucial for overall well-being. During uncertain times, it is easy to turn to comfort foods or neglect proper nutrition. However, consuming a balanced diet rich in fruits, vegetables, lean proteins, and whole grains provides essential nutrients that fuel both the body and mind. A healthy diet can enhance energy levels, improve focus, and support optimal brain function.

Adequate sleep is another critical component of self-care. Sleep deprivation can negatively impact mood, cognitive function, and overall well-being. Establishing a consistent sleep routine and prioritizing quality sleep can increase resilience and improve the ability to cope with uncertainty effectively.

Developing a self-care routine has numerous benefits for mental and emotional resilience. By regularly engaging in self-care activities, individuals can reduce stress, boost mood, and enhance their overall well-being. Having a self-care routine also promotes self-awareness and self-compassion, enabling individuals to nurture their own needs and better manage uncertainties that arise.

By incorporating these practical self-care tips into your daily life, you will equip yourself with the tools needed to navigate uncertainty effectively and maintain a strong sense of well-being. Remember, practicing self-care is not selfish but rather a necessary investment in your mental, emotional, and physical health during this formative period of your twenties.

Cultivating adaptability plays a crucial role in successfully navigating uncertain situations. In this section, we will discuss the importance of adaptability and provide readers with strategies for effectively adapting to change.

Uncertainty can often bring about fear and resistance, but by reframing our perspectives, we can embrace the opportunities that arise from being adaptable. Instead of seeing uncertainty as a threat, we can view it as a chance for growth and innovation. By shifting our mindset to one of curiosity and openness, we can approach uncertain situations with optimism and confidence.

Embracing flexibility is another key aspect of cultivating adaptability. Rigidity and a resistance to change can hinder our ability to adapt effectively. It's important to remain flexible and open to new possibilities, even if they deviate from our original plans. Being willing to adjust our goals and strategies when necessary allows us to navigate uncertain circumstances with greater ease.

Seeking new opportunities is also essential for developing adaptability. Uncertainty often presents hidden chances for growth, learning, and success. By actively seeking out new opportunities, whether they be in our careers or personal lives, we can expand our horizons and discover new paths forward. Embracing change and taking calculated risks can lead to unexpected and positive outcomes.

To illustrate the power of adaptability, we will share stories of individuals who have successfully embraced uncertainty in their own lives. These real-life examples will highlight the transformative impact that adaptability can have on personal and professional growth. By showcasing the journeys of these individuals, readers can gain inspiration and learn from their experiences.

By incorporating these strategies for cultivating adaptability into their lives, readers will be equipped with the tools needed to effectively manage uncertainty. They will learn how to embrace change, see it as an opportunity for growth, and navigate uncertain situations with resilience and confidence. Cultivating adaptability will empower readers to thrive in an ever-changing world and seize the potential that uncertainty holds.

Chapter 9

The Ups and Downs of Early Adulthood

Understanding the Transition: Early adulthood marks a significant transition phase between adolescence and adulthood. It is a time of tremendous change and growth, both personally and professionally. This section focuses on exploring the various aspects of this transition, including the psychological, emotional, and societal changes that individuals commonly experience during this period.

Psychologically, early adulthood can be characterized by an increased sense of self-awareness and self-reflection. It is a time when individuals begin to question their identity, values, and beliefs in a more profound way. This process of self-discovery often involves reevaluating one's goals, aspirations, and priorities. By understanding the psychological shifts that occur during early adulthood, readers can gain valuable insights into their own thought processes and motivations.

Emotionally, early adulthood can be challenging as individuals navigate the complexities of their emotions and relationships. It is a time when feelings of uncertainty, confusion, and even anxiety may arise. The pressures to make important life decisions and establish oneself can be overwhelming. By acknowledging and understanding the emotional aspects of this transition, readers can develop strategies to effectively manage their feelings and maintain a balanced state of mind.

Societally, early adulthood brings with it a host of new responsibilities and expectations. From entering the workforce to pursuing higher education or starting a family, young adults are faced with numerous choices that have long-term implications. The societal pressures to conform or meet certain milestones can add to the already existing challenges. By recognizing the external factors influencing their lives, readers can navigate through societal expectations while staying true to their authentic selves.

By comprehending the unique challenges that come with the transition into early adulthood, readers will be better equipped to deal with potential obstacles. Understanding the psychological, emotional, and societal changes that occur during this phase will provide clarity and perspective on their own personal journey. With this knowledge, individuals can approach this transitional phase with confidence, embracing the opportunities for growth and success that lie ahead.

The Ups and Downs of Early Adulthood: Dealing with Identity Crisis

During early adulthood, many individuals experience an identity crisis as they transition from adolescence to adulthood. This phase involves a period of self-exploration, embracing uncertainty, and navigating the process of self-discovery. Understanding and addressing this identity crisis is crucial for building a strong sense of self.

To begin the journey of self-exploration, readers are encouraged to embrace the uncertainties that come with early adulthood. It is natural to feel overwhelmed by the choices and responsibilities that lie ahead, but by approaching this phase with an open mind and heart, individuals can lay the foundation for personal growth and development.

Navigating the process of self-discovery involves understanding one's values, beliefs, and personal aspirations. By examining what truly matters to them, readers can gain clarity about their authentic selves and align their decisions accordingly. This introspective journey allows individuals to build a strong sense of identity based on their own unique traits and passions.

One effective strategy for self-discovery is engaging in activities that foster personal growth. This could include pursuing new hobbies, traveling, volunteering, or taking up new challenges. By stepping out of comfort zones and embracing diverse experiences, individuals can uncover hidden talents, interests, and passions that contribute to their identity.

Self-reflection plays a crucial role in understanding oneself better. Encouraging readers to set aside time for introspection, this book provides prompts and exercises to help them explore their thoughts, emotions, and desires. Journaling, meditation, and seeking solitude are effective practices for deepening self-awareness.

It is important to remember that an identity crisis is a normal part of the journey towards self-discovery. It is not uncommon for individuals in their twenties to question their purpose and direction in life. The key is to have patience and be kind to oneself during this process. By embracing uncertainty, exploring different paths, and staying true to their values, readers can navigate this phase with resilience and confidence.

Building a strong sense of self lays the foundation for personal growth, decision-making, and overall well-being. As readers delve into the intricacies of their identity during early adulthood, they will develop the self-assurance and clarity necessary to navigate life's challenges and embrace opportunities for success and fulfillment.

Managing Relationship Transitions:

During early adulthood, relationships go through significant changes, including friendships, romantic partnerships, and family dynamics. This period is marked by exploration and growth, which can lead to shifts in social circles and the need for recalibration in existing relationships. In this section, we will explore strategies for managing relationship transitions effectively, fostering healthy connections, and establishing fulfilling relationships.

1. Embracing Change: As individuals navigate their twenties, it is common for friendships to evolve or even fade away. This can be due to various factors such as relocation, changing interests, or differing life paths. It is essential to understand that change is a natural part of life and to embrace it rather than resisting it. By acknowledging the ebb and flow of relationships, individuals can adapt and forge new connections that align with their current aspirations and values.

2. Communicating Effectively: Communication plays a central role in any relationship. Developing strong communication skills allows individuals to express their needs, concerns, and boundaries clearly. Active listening, empathy, and respect are crucial elements of effective communication. By honing these skills, individuals can foster understanding and strengthen their relationships.

3. Setting Healthy Boundaries: Boundaries are essential in all relationships. They serve as guidelines that promote mutual respect and understanding. Establishing healthy boundaries involves identifying one's personal limits and communicating them respectfully to others. This ensures that individuals have their needs met while respecting the autonomy of others. Learning to set boundaries helps create balanced and harmonious relationships.

4. Nurturing Meaningful Connections: As early adulthood brings new opportunities for personal growth and self-discovery, it is important to invest time and energy into nurturing meaningful connections. Building strong relationships requires effort and commitment from both parties involved. By prioritizing quality over quantity, individuals can cultivate bonds that provide support, encouragement, and shared experiences.

5. Managing Conflicts Constructively: Conflicts are inevitable in any relationship. However, the way they are handled can make a significant difference. It is important to approach conflicts with an open mind, seeking resolution rather than engaging in blame or defensiveness. Practicing active listening, compromise, and empathy can help turn conflicts into opportunities for growth and understanding.

Navigating relationship transitions during early adulthood can be challenging, but it also presents a chance for personal development and the formation of lasting connections. By embracing change, communicating effectively, setting healthy boundaries, nurturing meaningful relationships, and managing conflicts constructively, individuals can build strong support systems that contribute to their overall well-being and happiness.

Coping with Financial Pressures: This part of the chapter "The Ups and Downs of Early Adulthood" focuses specifically on addressing the financial challenges that young adults often face during this phase of life.

One of the primary concerns for many individuals in their twenties is how to manage their finances effectively. This section provides practical advice and strategies for budgeting, saving money, and managing debt. By gaining a solid understanding of these financial concepts, readers can develop healthy financial habits that will set them up for long-term success.

Budgeting is an essential skill for managing personal finances. It involves creating a plan for allocating income towards various expenses, such as housing, transportation, food, utilities, and entertainment. This section guides readers on how to create a realistic budget that aligns with their income and goals. It emphasizes the importance of tracking expenses, identifying areas where cutbacks can be made, and prioritizing savings.

Saving money is crucial for building a strong financial foundation. This section explores different strategies for saving, such as setting aside a percentage of each paycheck or automating transfers into separate savings accounts. It also highlights the advantages of establishing an emergency fund to cover unexpected expenses. By prioritizing saving, young adults can develop a safety net that provides peace of mind and financial stability.

Managing debt is another significant aspect addressed in this section. It offers practical advice on how to handle student loans, credit card debt, and other forms of borrowing. Readers will learn about strategies for paying off debt efficiently, such as the snowball or avalanche method. Additionally, this section emphasizes the importance of maintaining good credit by making timely payments and being mindful of credit utilization.

In addition to discussing traditional sources of income, this section also explores alternative income streams and investment options available to young adults. It introduces concepts such as side hustles, freelancing, and investing in stocks or real estate. By diversifying income sources and exploring investment opportunities, readers can work towards attaining financial stability and creating wealth for the future.

By covering these practical aspects of coping with financial pressures, readers will gain a comprehensive understanding of how to manage their finances effectively. This section ensures that young adults are equipped with the knowledge and tools necessary to make informed financial decisions, ultimately working towards achieving long-term financial stability during this crucial stage of early adulthood.

Overcoming Mental Health Struggles:

This section of the chapter "The Ups and Downs of Early Adulthood" delves into the common mental health issues that young adults may face, such as anxiety, depression, and stress. It emphasizes the importance of prioritizing self-care, seeking appropriate support when needed, and developing healthy coping mechanisms to navigate the complexities of early adulthood.

Understanding that mental health struggles are a common experience for many individuals during this phase of life, this section provides readers with useful strategies for maintaining positive mental well-being. It emphasizes the significance of self-awareness and self-reflection, encouraging readers to monitor their own mental health and seek professional help if necessary.

Furthermore, this section promotes the importance of integrating self-care practices into daily routines. It emphasizes the value of activities like exercise, meditation, journaling, and relaxation techniques in reducing stress and improving overall mental well-being. By incorporating these practices into their lives, readers can build resilience and manage their mental health effectively.

The section also highlights the significance of building a strong support network. It encourages readers to foster meaningful relationships with friends, family members, mentors, or therapists who can provide guidance, understanding, and emotional support. By surrounding themselves with positive influences, individuals can feel less isolated and more supported during challenging times.

Additionally, this section acknowledges the potential impact of societal stigma surrounding mental health issues. It empowers readers to challenge and overcome such stigmas by educating themselves and promoting open conversations about mental health. By normalizing discussions around mental health, individuals can reduce the negative stereotypes associated with it and create a more supportive and inclusive society.

Overall, this section provides readers with practical strategies for managing common mental health struggles during early adulthood. By emphasizing self-care, seeking support, and developing healthy coping mechanisms, young adults can prioritize their mental well-being and navigate the challenges of this phase with resilience and strength.

Celebrating Successes: Recognizing Your Wins

****

The Importance of Celebrating Successes

In "Build Your Character at Twenty: Writing the Life Success Script at the Age of 20," it is essential to emphasize the significance of celebrating successes and recognizing achievements. Many individuals often overlook the importance of taking a moment to acknowledge their accomplishments and give themselves credit for their hard work. However, celebrating successes is vital for several reasons.

First and foremost, celebrating successes boosts motivation. When we celebrate our achievements, no matter how big or small, we provide ourselves with positive reinforcement. This positive reinforcement acts as fuel to keep us going and motivates us to continue working towards our goals and aspirations. The acknowledgment of success helps foster a positive mindset and instills a sense of confidence in our abilities.

Moreover, celebrating successes improves self-confidence. By recognizing our wins, we build trust in ourselves and our capabilities. We gain a greater belief in our potential to achieve future goals and overcome challenges. This increased self-confidence not only impacts our personal lives but also has professional implications. Confident individuals are more likely to take risks, seize opportunities, and assert themselves in various aspects of life.

In addition to motivation and self-confidence, celebrating successes contributes to overall well-being. Taking the time to acknowledge our accomplishments promotes a sense of pride, satisfaction, and fulfillment. It allows us to recognize the progress we have made and appreciate our efforts. By prioritizing celebration, we create a positive and supportive relationship with ourselves, which significantly impacts mental and emotional well-being.

Lastly, it is crucial to understand that celebrating small wins and milestones is just as important as acknowledging significant achievements. While major accomplishments may occur less frequently, celebrating even the smallest victories keeps us engaged and motivated along the journey to success. Celebrating milestones along the way reinforces the idea that progress is being made, even if it may not be immediately evident.

Overall, the act of celebrating successes is transformative. It boosts motivation, enhances self-confidence, and improves overall well-being. By taking the time to recognize our wins, no matter how big or small, we set ourselves up for continued growth and achievement. In the next sections of this chapter, we will explore techniques for setting meaningful goals and milestones, developing a rewards system, reflecting on achievements, and sharing our successes with others. Together, these strategies will empower you to fully embrace the practice of celebrating successes and recognizing your wins in life.

Setting Meaningful Goals and Milestones

Setting meaningful goals and milestones is a crucial step in achieving success and recognizing your wins. When you have a clear vision of what you want to accomplish, it becomes easier to stay motivated and focused on your journey to success. Here, we will explore the process of setting meaningful goals and provide techniques for creating realistic and achievable objectives.

The first step in setting meaningful goals is to identify your passions and values. Take some time to reflect on what truly matters to you and what brings you joy and fulfillment. Consider both short-term and long-term goals, as well as various aspects of your life, such as career, personal relationships, health, and personal development.

Once you have identified your passions and values, you can begin to set specific, measurable, achievable, relevant, and time-bound (SMART) goals. Start by breaking down your larger goal into smaller, actionable steps that will lead you towards its accomplishment. This allows you to maintain focus and track your progress along the way.

It's important to ensure that your goals are realistic and attainable. While it's great to dream big, setting unrealistic goals can often lead to disappointment and discouragement. Assess your resources, capabilities, and timeline to determine if your goals are within reach. If necessary, adjust your goals to make them more achievable while still challenging enough to inspire growth.

Another technique for setting meaningful goals is to consider the impact they will have on your life and others around you. Will your goals align with your values and contribute positively to your overall well-being? Will they create a positive ripple effect in other areas of your life? By considering these factors, you can ensure that your goals are not only fulfilling but also aligned with who you are and what you stand for.

Lastly, remember to regularly review and revise your goals as needed. As you grow and evolve, your priorities may change, and new opportunities may arise. By staying flexible and open-minded, you allow yourself to adapt your goals and milestones accordingly.

By setting meaningful goals and breaking them down into achievable milestones, you create a roadmap for success. This approach keeps you motivated, focused, and accountable as you work towards your desired outcomes. Remember, the journey towards success is just as important as the destination, so celebrate each milestone along the way as a recognition of your progress and achievement.

Developing a Rewards System

When it comes to achieving our goals and celebrating successes, having a rewards system in place can be an effective way to stay motivated and maintain momentum. A personalized rewards system provides an extra incentive to work towards our goals and offers a tangible representation of our achievements. In this section, we will explore the importance of developing a rewards system and discuss different types of rewards that can be utilized.

A rewards system serves as a powerful tool for reinforcing positive behavior and creating a sense of accomplishment. By attaching rewards to the completion of certain tasks or milestones, we are more likely to stay engaged and committed to our goals. Rewards can serve as a form of self-appreciation and acknowledgment for the hard work and effort we have put in.

When developing a rewards system, it is important to consider personal preferences and values. Different individuals are motivated by different things, so it is essential to choose rewards that align with our interests and desires. Some people may be motivated by experiences, such as treating themselves to a concert, spa day, or vacation. Others may find material items more rewarding, such as buying a new gadget or indulging in a favorite hobby.

To determine appropriate rewards, start by identifying what brings you joy and satisfaction. Consider the activities or items that make you feel excited and fulfilled. Reflect on experiences that you have always wanted to try or possessions that would enhance your life in meaningful ways. By selecting rewards that truly resonate with you, you increase the likelihood of staying committed to your goals.

Additionally, it is essential to establish a hierarchy of rewards based on the magnitude of the accomplishments. For smaller milestones or short-term goals, smaller rewards may be more appropriate. These could include enjoying a special treat, having a leisurely day off, or engaging in a favorite hobby. For larger achievements or long-term goals, more significant rewards can be implemented. These might involve splurging on a luxury item, taking a dream vacation, or investing in personal growth experiences.

Remember, the purpose of a rewards system is to motivate and celebrate your accomplishments. It should be enjoyable and meaningful to you personally. Take the time to plan your rewards system thoughtfully, ensuring that it aligns with your values and serves as a genuine source of inspiration. By incorporating a rewards system into your journey towards success, you can enhance your overall experience, boost motivation, and sustain long-term progress.

Reflecting on achievements is an essential step in celebrating successes and recognizing personal growth. Taking the time to reflect allows individuals to acknowledge their accomplishments, learn from their experiences, and gain a deeper understanding of their own progress. In this section, we will explore the importance of reflection, techniques for self-reflection, and tools and exercises to help evaluate progress.

Reflection is a powerful tool that allows individuals to pause and appreciate how far they have come. It provides an opportunity to recognize the hard work, dedication, and resilience that led to achievements. Without reflection, it is easy to overlook the milestones along the way and neglect the valuable lessons learned from each experience.

One technique for self-reflection is journaling. Regularly writing down thoughts, feelings, and observations can help individuals gain clarity and insight into their journey. Journaling prompts, such as "What am I most proud of accomplishing?" or "What challenges did I overcome recently?" can guide the reflection process and encourage deep introspection.

Another effective technique is visualization. Take a moment to close your eyes and envision your past successes. Recall the emotions you felt when achieving those milestones and allow yourself to bask in the sense of accomplishment. Visualization not only reinforces positive feelings but also fuels motivation and confidence for future endeavors.

In addition to these techniques, various tools and exercises can aid in evaluating progress and acknowledging achievements. One such tool is creating a gratitude list. List all the accomplishments, big or small, that you are grateful for. This exercise helps shift focus towards positivity and encourages appreciation for the journey so far.

Another exercise involves charting progress over time. Use a visual representation, such as a graph or chart, to track achievements in different areas of life. This not only provides a visual reminder of progress but also highlights any patterns or trends that can inform future actions.

Remember, reflection is not about dwelling on past success but rather about celebrating personal growth and using it as a stepping stone for future achievements. By incorporating self-reflection techniques and utilizing tools and exercises for evaluation, individuals can gain a clearer perspective on their journey, appreciate their progress, and continue striving towards even greater success.

Sharing and Celebrating with Others:

Sharing our successes with others can have numerous benefits beyond simply basking in the joy of achievement. It not only allows us to deepen our connections with loved ones but also provides an opportunity for growth, support, and inspiration. Here are some strategies for effectively communicating achievements to friends, family, and mentors, as well as ideas for celebrating successes collectively:

1. Choose your audience wisely: When sharing your successes, it's important to consider the people you share them with. Seek out individuals who genuinely care about your well-being and are supportive of your goals. Surrounding yourself with positive and uplifting individuals will enhance your celebration experience.

2. Tailor your message: Depending on the nature of your success, it may be helpful to tailor your message to different audiences. For example, when sharing professional achievements with colleagues or mentors, focus on specific details that showcase your growth or impact within the organization. On the other hand, when celebrating personal achievements with loved ones, you may want to emphasize the emotional significance or lessons learned from the experience.

3. Show gratitude and reciprocity: Expressing gratitude to those who have supported you in your journey is a wonderful way to celebrate your successes. Take the time to acknowledge their contributions and express genuine appreciation for their role in your achievements. Additionally, be mindful of reciprocating support and celebrating the successes of others in return, fostering a culture of celebration within your social circle.

4. Seek feedback and insights: Sharing your successes can create an opportunity for learning and growth. Openly discuss your achievements with trusted mentors or peers who can provide valuable feedback and insights. This feedback can help you refine your skills and strategies for future endeavors, enhancing your chances of continued success.

5. Celebrate collectively: Celebrating successes collectively can amplify feelings of joy and accomplishment. Consider hosting a gathering or creating a gratitude ritual to commemorate milestones with friends and family. This collective celebration not only strengthens relationships but also provides a supportive network for future challenges and endeavors.

Remember that sharing and celebrating successes should not be seen as boasting or seeking validation. Instead, view it as an opportunity to inspire others, foster deeper connections, and create a positive ripple effect in your social circle. By sharing your achievements with others, you contribute to a culture of celebration and support, ultimately enhancing your own well-being and that of those around you.

Part 9:
Adventure and
Life Experience

Chapter 1

Saying Yes to New Experiences: Living Life Fully

****

Benefits of embracing new experiences:

Stepping out of our comfort zones and embracing new experiences is crucial for personal growth and development. By venturing into uncharted territory, we open ourselves up to a world of possibilities and opportunities that can profoundly impact our lives.

Firstly, embracing new experiences helps us broaden our perspectives. When we expose ourselves to different people, cultures, and environments, we gain a deeper understanding and appreciation for the diversity of the world. This exposure allows us to challenge our preconceived notions, break down stereotypes, and develop empathy towards others. By broadening our perspectives, we become more open-minded and adaptable individuals, better equipped to navigate the complexities of an interconnected global society.

Secondly, stepping outside of our comfort zones cultivates resilience. New experiences often come with uncertainty, fear, and challenges. However, by pushing through these discomforts, we develop resilience and the ability to overcome obstacles. Each time we embrace something new, whether it's starting a new job or traveling to a foreign country, we build confidence in our ability to adapt and thrive in unfamiliar situations. This resilience becomes a valuable asset in both personal and professional spheres, enabling us to bounce back from setbacks and persevere in the face of adversity.

Research has also shown that embracing new experiences enhances creativity. When we step outside our routine and engage with novel situations or environments, our brains are stimulated in unique ways. This stimulation fuels our imagination and enables us to think outside the box, generating innovative ideas and solutions. By actively seeking out new experiences, we can tap into our creative potential and cultivate a mindset of curiosity and exploration.

Furthermore, embracing new experiences improves our problem-solving skills. Venturing into unfamiliar territory forces us to adapt quickly and find solutions to unforeseen challenges. As we navigate these unknown territories, we develop critical thinking skills, resourcefulness, and the ability to think on our feet. These problem-solving abilities become invaluable assets in all aspects of life, from personal relationships to professional endeavors.

In summary, embracing new experiences offers a multitude of benefits. It broadens our perspectives, nurtures resilience, enhances creativity, and sharpens our problem-solving skills. By saying yes to new opportunities and stepping outside our comfort zones, we invite personal growth and open ourselves up to a world of possibilities. So, let go of fear and uncertainty, embrace the unknown, and watch as your life transforms in extraordinary ways.

Overcoming fear and uncertainty when faced with new experiences is essential for personal growth and development. In this section, we will explore strategies to manage fear, reframe negative thoughts, and build confidence in navigating unfamiliar situations.

To begin, it's important to acknowledge that fear and uncertainty are normal when stepping outside of our comfort zones. These emotions can serve as indicators of growth and remind us of the potential rewards that lie beyond our current boundaries. By reframing our perspective, we can view fear as an opportunity for personal expansion rather than a deterrent.

One effective strategy for managing fear is to break down the experience into smaller, more manageable steps. By taking gradual, incremental actions towards the new experience, we can gradually acclimate ourselves and build confidence along the way. For example, if the new experience involves public speaking, we can start by practicing in front of a mirror or a small group of supportive friends before progressing to larger audiences.

Another technique for overcoming fear and uncertainty is reframing negative thoughts. Often, our fears are rooted in self-doubt and negative self-talk. By consciously replacing negative thoughts with positive affirmations and empowering beliefs, we can shift our mindset from one of doubt to one of possibility. For instance, instead of thinking, "I'm not good enough," we can reframe it as "I am capable of learning and growing through this experience."

Building confidence and self-belief is crucial in navigating unfamiliar situations. One way to cultivate confidence is through preparation and knowledge acquisition. By researching and learning as much as possible about the new experience beforehand, we can feel more equipped and competent. Additionally, seeking support from mentors or individuals who have successfully navigated similar experiences can provide guidance and encouragement.

Practicing self-care and prioritizing our well-being can also contribute to building confidence. Engaging in activities that make us feel good about ourselves, such as exercise, meditation, or pursuing hobbies, can boost self-esteem and resilience. Taking care of our physical and mental health creates a strong foundation for facing challenges with greater confidence.

In summary, overcoming fear and uncertainty when confronted with new experiences requires deliberate strategies and a shift in mindset. By breaking down experiences into manageable steps, reframing negative thoughts, and building confidence through preparation and self-care, we can embrace new opportunities with courage and open ourselves up to personal growth and fulfillment.

Seeking opportunities for personal growth:

In order to fully embrace new experiences and live life to the fullest, it is essential to actively seek out opportunities for personal growth. This involves identifying and pursuing experiences that align with your personal interests and goals. By stepping outside of your comfort zone and trying new things, you can expand your horizons, develop new skills, and discover hidden passions.

To begin, take some time to reflect on your interests and aspirations. What are the activities or areas of knowledge that genuinely excite you? Are there any hobbies or subjects that you have always wanted to explore but haven't had the chance to yet? Make a list of these potential avenues for personal growth.

Once you have identified your areas of interest, it's time to take action. Start by researching opportunities that allow you to dive deeper into these areas. For example, if you have always been fascinated by photography, consider enrolling in a photography class or joining a local photography club where you can learn from experienced photographers and engage with fellow enthusiasts.

Don't limit yourself to traditional forms of education or structured programs. Seek out unconventional ways to grow personally as well. This could involve attending workshops or conferences related to your interests, participating in community events, volunteering for causes you care about, or even embarking on solo travel adventures.

Stepping outside of your comfort zone is crucial for personal growth. Push yourself to try things that may feel unfamiliar or intimidating. If you're typically introverted, challenge yourself to attend social gatherings or networking events where you can meet new people and expand your network. If you tend to stick with what's familiar, consider traveling to a destination vastly different from your own culture and immersing yourself in a whole new way of life.

To further inspire you on this journey of seeking new experiences for personal growth, here are a few stories of individuals who have embraced new opportunities and reaped the rewards:

1. Sarah, a recent college graduate, had always been passionate about environmental sustainability. Instead of immediately accepting a desk job after graduation, she decided to volunteer for an organization that focused on marine conservation in a remote island community. There, she not only learned about the importance of preserving delicate ecosystems but also honed her leadership skills, developed a deep appreciation for cultural diversity, and made lifelong friends.

2. Mark, a software engineer, felt disconnected from his creative side despite having a successful career in technology. He decided to join an improv theater group to push himself out of his comfort zone and explore a different form of expression. Through improv, he not only discovered a newfound love for performing but also developed stronger communication skills, increased self-confidence, and the ability to think on his feet – qualities that later proved invaluable in his professional life as well.

3. Maria, a young student studying abroad, found herself in a foreign country with no one she knew. In an effort to immerse herself in the local culture and meet new people, she joined a local dance class. Not only did she learn traditional dances and gain insight into the local customs, but she also formed meaningful connections with her fellow dancers and experienced personal growth through embracing a new art form.

By seeking opportunities for personal growth and actively saying yes to new experiences, you open yourself up to a world of possibilities. Each new venture has the potential to expand your horizons, enhance your skills, and enrich your life. So don't hesitate to step outside of your comfort zone and embrace the unknown – the rewards might just be beyond what you could ever imagine.

Navigating challenges and setbacks is an inevitable part of any new experience, and it is crucial to have strategies in place to deal with them effectively. In this section, we will explore specific strategies for overcoming obstacles and setbacks that may arise during new experiences, emphasizing the importance of resilience, patience, and perseverance.

1. Embrace a growth mindset: When faced with challenges, it is important to shift our perspective and view them as opportunities for growth. Instead of seeing setbacks as failures, recognize them as valuable learning experiences. Adopting a growth mindset allows us to see challenges as stepping stones towards personal development and success.

2. Develop problem-solving skills: Challenges often require creative problem-solving. Break down the problem into smaller parts and brainstorm potential solutions. Consider seeking advice or guidance from mentors or experts in the field who have faced similar challenges. By developing strong problem-solving skills, we can overcome obstacles more effectively and learn valuable lessons along the way.

3. Cultivate resilience: Resilience is the ability to bounce back from setbacks and adapt to change. Cultivating resilience involves learning how to manage stress, maintain a positive mindset, and stay motivated in the face of adversity. Practice self-care techniques such as meditation, exercise, and self-reflection to build resilience and inner strength.

4. Seek support from others: Surround yourself with a supportive network of friends, family, mentors, or peers who can provide guidance and encouragement during challenging times. Sharing your struggles with others can offer fresh perspectives, valuable insights, and emotional support that can help you navigate setbacks more effectively.

5. Learn from failures: Setbacks and failures are valuable opportunities for learning and growth. Instead of dwelling on the negative aspects of a setback, reflect on what went wrong, what you could have done differently, and how you can improve in the future. Use failures as stepping stones towards personal growth by adapting your approach and trying again with renewed determination.

Remember that setbacks are not indicative of your worth or potential. They are simply part of the journey towards success and personal growth. By developing strategies to navigate challenges and setbacks effectively, you will build resilience, perseverance, and the ability to overcome obstacles, ultimately leading to greater personal and professional fulfillment.

Cultivating a mindset of gratitude and appreciation is crucial when it comes to fully experiencing and benefiting from new experiences. By practicing gratitude and mindfulness, individuals can enhance their enjoyment of these experiences and gain even more from them.

Gratitude plays a significant role in shaping our perspectives and attitudes towards life. When we approach new experiences with a mindset of gratitude, we are more open to the possibilities they bring, and we appreciate the opportunities that come our way. By acknowledging and expressing gratitude for the chance to have these experiences, we cultivate a positive outlook and mindset, which in turn enhances our overall well-being.

Practicing mindfulness during new experiences allows us to fully immerse ourselves in the present moment. It involves paying attention to our thoughts, feelings, and sensations without judgment. By being fully present and engaging our senses, we can savor every aspect of the experience and make the most of it. Mindfulness helps us avoid distractions and truly appreciate the details, whether it's the taste of a new cuisine, the sounds of a concert, or the beauty of a scenic location. This heightened awareness enriches our overall experience and deepens our connection with the moment.

To enhance the enjoyment of new experiences through gratitude and mindfulness, here are some techniques to consider:

1. Keep a gratitude journal: Take a few minutes each day to write down three things you are grateful for related to your new experiences. It could be something specific about the experience itself or an aspect of personal growth that resulted from it. Reflecting on these moments of gratitude reinforces a positive mindset and encourages you to seek out more opportunities for growth and appreciation.

2. Practice mindful breathing: Before engaging in a new experience, take a few moments to center yourself through mindful breathing. Close your eyes, take slow deep breaths, and focus your attention on the present moment. Allow any worries or distractions to fade away as you fully immerse yourself in the upcoming experience.

3. Engage your senses: During the experience, intentionally engage your senses to enhance your awareness and appreciation. Notice the colors, textures, smells, tastes, and sounds around you. Take time to savor each moment and fully absorb the sensory details. By doing so, you create lasting memories and deepen your connection with the experience.

4. Share your gratitude: Express your gratitude to others who contributed to the new experience or supported you along the way. Thank them for their role in making the experience possible or for any guidance and encouragement they provided. Sharing your gratitude not only strengthens relationships but also allows others to feel appreciated for their impact on your life.

Reflection exercises are also valuable in appreciating the lessons learned and celebrating personal growth through saying yes to new experiences. Consider asking yourself the following questions:

1. What did I learn from this experience?

2. How did it contribute to my personal development and growth?

3. How did I step out of my comfort zone during this experience?

4. What obstacles or challenges did I overcome along the way?

5. How can I apply the lessons learned from this experience to future endeavors?

By regularly practicing gratitude and mindfulness, reflecting on new experiences, and celebrating personal growth, individuals can fully embrace the power of saying yes to new opportunities. This cultivates a positive mindset, deepens their appreciation for life's blessings, and propels them towards continued growth and fulfillment.

Chapter 2

Creative Outlets and Hobbies: More Than Just Pastimes

****

Introduction to the importance of creative outlets and hobbies:

In our fast-paced, demanding world, it's easy to get caught up in the hustle and bustle of everyday life. We often overlook the importance of carving out time for our own personal well-being and self-expression. That's where creative outlets and hobbies come in.

Engaging in creative activities and pursuing hobbies goes beyond mere pastimes. They serve as powerful tools for self-expression, stress relief, and personal growth. In fact, numerous studies have shown that participating in creative endeavors can have a profound impact on our overall well-being.

First and foremost, creative outlets allow us to tap into our emotions and express ourselves in unique ways. Whether it's through painting, writing, photography, music, cooking, or crafting, these activities provide a platform for us to communicate our thoughts and feelings without limitations. They offer an avenue for self-discovery and self-expression, allowing us to explore our innermost thoughts and bring them to life.

Additionally, engaging in creative pursuits can be a form of therapy. It allows us to channel our emotions into something tangible, providing a healthy outlet for stress relief and emotional release. The act of creating something can be immensely cathartic, giving us a sense of accomplishment and fulfillment.

Moreover, creative outlets contribute to personal growth by challenging us to think outside the box and expand our perspectives. They encourage us to push our boundaries, experiment with different mediums, and embrace new ideas. Through this process, we develop problem-solving skills, learn to adapt to new situations, and enhance our ability to think creatively.

Furthermore, creative hobbies have the power to foster connections with others who share similar interests. Participating in hobby groups or joining online communities allows us to connect with like-minded individuals, forming friendships based on shared passions. These connections provide a sense of belonging and support, enriching our lives beyond measure.

As you embark on your journey towards success and fulfillment, don't underestimate the importance of incorporating creative outlets and hobbies into your life. By making time for these activities, you are investing in your own well-being and personal growth. So, unleash your creativity, explore different avenues of self-expression, and witness the transformative power of engaging in creative pursuits.

Exploring different types of creative outlets: This section will delve into various forms of creative expression, such as painting, writing, photography, music, cooking, and crafting. Each activity will be explored in detail, discussing the unique benefits they offer and how they can be incorporated into daily life.

Painting:

Painting allows individuals to express their emotions and thoughts through visual art. It provides a means of creative self-expression and can be incredibly therapeutic. Whether it's using watercolors, acrylics, or oils, painting offers a way to explore different techniques and experiment with colors and textures. Additionally, painting can enhance mindfulness and promote relaxation by immersing oneself in the artistic process.

Writing:

Writing is a powerful tool for self-reflection and personal growth. It can take various forms, including journaling, poetry, short stories, or even blogging. Through writing, individuals can gain clarity, process their thoughts and experiences, and explore their creativity. Writing can also be a form of catharsis, helping individuals release emotions and find solace. Moreover, writing can improve communication skills and cultivate a deeper understanding of oneself and others.

Photography:

Photography is a way to capture moments and tell stories through visual imagery. With smartphones readily available, photography has become more accessible than ever before. It allows individuals to document their lives and the world around them while honing their creativity and perspective. Through photography, one can develop an eye for beauty, learn about composition and lighting, and share their unique viewpoint with others.

Music:

Music is a universal language that transcends boundaries. Playing a musical instrument or singing can provide immense joy while improving cognitive skills and emotional well-being. Music allows individuals to express themselves creatively, connect with others through collaboration or performance, and find solace in difficult times. Learning to play an instrument or sing can foster discipline, patience, and perseverance.

Cooking:

Cooking is not only a practical skill but also a creative outlet. It allows individuals to experiment with flavors, textures, and presentation while nourishing themselves and others. Cooking provides a sense of accomplishment and can be a form of self-care. Exploring different cuisines and techniques can expand one's culinary repertoire and foster creativity in the kitchen.

Crafting:

Crafting encompasses various activities such as knitting, sewing, woodworking, or jewelry making. These hands-on activities allow individuals to create tangible objects while engaging in a therapeutic process. Crafting promotes focus, patience, and problem-solving skills, while also providing opportunities for self-expression and personalized gifts for loved ones.

By exploring these different types of creative outlets, readers will gain insights into the benefits each activity offers and discover new avenues for personal growth and self-expression. Incorporating one or more of these creative outlets into daily life can bring about a sense of fulfillment, stress relief, and personal satisfaction.

Unleashing creativity: This section will provide readers with practical tips and techniques for tapping into their creativity and overcoming creative blocks. It will go beyond the surface level advice of "just be creative" and instead explore specific methods to help readers truly unlock their creative potential.

One effective technique for unleashing creativity is brainstorming. Encourage readers to set aside dedicated time for brainstorming sessions, where they can freely generate ideas without judgment or limitations. Emphasize the importance of capturing every idea that comes to mind, no matter how outlandish or unconventional it may seem. This process will help readers break free from self-imposed restrictions and explore new possibilities.

Another useful tool is journaling. Encourage readers to keep a dedicated creativity journal where they can jot down their thoughts, ideas, and inspirations. Journaling can serve as a valuable outlet for self-expression and reflection, helping readers delve deeper into their thoughts and emotions. Suggest prompts for journaling, such as writing about their dreams, aspirations, or even their favorite childhood memories. This practice can stimulate their imagination and uncover hidden passions or interests.

Setting goals is another effective strategy for unlocking creativity. Encourage readers to set specific and achievable goals related to their creative pursuits. Whether it's completing a painting, writing a short story, or learning a musical instrument, having clear objectives provides a sense of focus and direction. Guide readers in breaking down their goals into smaller, manageable tasks, allowing them to track their progress and experience a sense of accomplishment along the way.

Seeking inspiration from various sources is crucial for igniting creativity. Encourage readers to explore different art forms, visit museums or galleries, read books or articles on a wide range of topics, and even engage in conversations with people from diverse backgrounds. By exposing themselves to new ideas and perspectives, readers can broaden their creative horizons and develop fresh insights.

Finally, encourage readers to experiment with different mediums or art forms. They may discover talents or passions they were not previously aware of. Suggest engaging in activities such as photography, sculpting, cooking, or even learning a new dance style. By embracing experimentation, readers can unlock their creative potential and find the most suitable outlet for their artistic expression.

By exploring these practical tips and techniques for unleashing creativity, readers will gain the confidence and inspiration needed to overcome creative blocks and tap into their fullest creative potential.

Benefits of engaging in hobbies: In this section, we explore the numerous advantages of pursuing hobbies beyond mere enjoyment. Engaging in hobbies can have a profound impact on personal development and offer benefits that extend far beyond leisure time.

Boosting confidence: Pursuing a hobby allows individuals to develop skills and competence in a specific area. As they gain proficiency, their confidence naturally grows, leading to a greater sense of self-assurance. Whether it's mastering a musical instrument, honing artistic abilities, or excelling in a sport, the progress made through hobbies reinforces self-belief and fosters a positive self-image.

Improving problem-solving skills: Hobbies often require creative problem-solving and critical thinking. Whether it's finding the right solution to an artistic challenge, strategizing for a board game, or troubleshooting technical issues related to a hobby, individuals are regularly presented with opportunities to exercise their problem-solving skills. The ability to think creatively and approach challenges from different angles cultivated through hobbies can translate into improved problem-solving abilities in other areas of life as well.

Providing opportunities for social connections: Engaging in hobbies can create opportunities for individuals to connect with like-minded people who share similar interests. Whether it's joining a local book club, participating in community sports leagues, or attending art classes, hobbies provide a platform for individuals to build social connections outside of their immediate circles. These new relationships can lead to lasting friendships, networking opportunities, and valuable support systems.

Enhancing professional development: Hobbies can also play a significant role in professional growth. Many successful entrepreneurs and professionals credit their hobbies as sources of inspiration and innovative thinking in their careers. The skills developed through hobbies, such as discipline, perseverance, creativity, and time management, can be transferable to various professional settings. Additionally, hobbies can open doors to side businesses or freelance opportunities, allowing individuals to monetize their passion and turn it into a fulfilling career.

Real-life examples and success stories: Throughout this section, we will feature real-life examples and success stories of individuals who have leveraged their hobbies to achieve great things. These stories will demonstrate how pursuing a hobby can lead to unexpected opportunities and accomplishments. From hobbyist photographers whose work has been exhibited in galleries to amateur chefs who have launched successful catering businesses, these stories will inspire readers to explore the potential that lies within their own hobbies.

By discussing the benefits of engaging in hobbies in this chapter, readers will gain a deeper understanding of how pursuing their passions can positively impact various aspects of their lives. This section will provide motivation for individuals to embrace hobbies not only for enjoyment but also as powerful tools for personal growth, professional development, and building meaningful connections.

Incorporating creative outlets into a busy lifestyle is a common challenge faced by individuals in their twenties. With numerous responsibilities and time constraints, it can be difficult to find the time and energy to engage in hobbies and creative pursuits. However, it is essential to prioritize and make space for these activities, as they contribute to overall well-being and personal growth.

One practical strategy for integrating creative pursuits into a busy schedule is to utilize effective time management techniques. By carefully planning and scheduling dedicated time for hobbies, individuals can ensure that they prioritize their creative outlets amidst their other commitments. This might involve setting specific times during the week for pursuing hobbies or blocking out small pockets of time each day for short bursts of creativity.

Creating dedicated spaces for creativity can also help in incorporating hobbies into a busy lifestyle. Designating a physical area in one's home or workspace solely for creative pursuits can provide a visual reminder and encourage individuals to engage in their hobbies regularly. Whether it's a corner with art supplies, a writing nook, or a music studio, having a dedicated space helps to create an environment conducive to creativity.

In addition to time management and designated spaces, prioritizing self-care is crucial when incorporating creative outlets into a busy routine. Taking breaks, practicing self-compassion, and setting boundaries are essential components of maintaining well-being while pursuing hobbies. It is important to remember that engaging in creative activities should bring joy and relaxation rather than becoming another source of stress or pressure.

Furthermore, finding local hobby groups or online communities can provide support and foster connections with like-minded individuals. Joining these communities allows individuals to share their interests, exchange ideas, and collaborate on projects. It can also offer opportunities for networking, mentorship, or even turning hobbies into potential career paths.

By implementing these practical strategies, individuals can successfully integrate creative outlets into their busy lifestyles. Remember, making time for hobbies is not frivolous; it is an investment in personal fulfillment, stress relief, and overall well-being. So, carve out that time, create an inspiring space, prioritize self-care, and connect with others who share your passions.

Chapter 3

Volunteerism: The
Joy of Giving Back

****

Introduction to Volunteerism:

Volunteerism plays a vital role in personal growth and community development. It is the act of selflessly offering one's time, skills, and resources to benefit others and make a positive impact on society. In today's fast-paced world, volunteerism serves as a powerful reminder of the importance of compassion, empathy, and social responsibility.

Throughout history, volunteerism has been deeply ingrained in various cultures and societies. From religious teachings that emphasize the value of selfless service to the community to movements that fought for social justice and equality, volunteerism has shaped the fabric of our society. By understanding its historical and cultural significance, we can appreciate its timeless relevance and the transformative power it holds.

Engaging in volunteer work offers numerous benefits beyond the impact it has on others. Studies have shown that volunteering can have a profound positive effect on our well-being, both emotionally and mentally. It provides a sense of purpose, fulfillment, and satisfaction that comes from knowing we are making a difference in the lives of others. Volunteering also enables us to develop new skills, broaden our perspectives, and gain valuable experiences that can enhance our personal and professional growth.

Furthermore, volunteerism opens doors to valuable networking opportunities. Through engagement with various organizations and communities, we have the chance to connect with like-minded individuals, expand our social circles, and build relationships with people who share similar passions and values. These connections can lead to new friendships, mentorship opportunities, and even potential career prospects.

As we delve deeper into the joys of giving back through volunteerism, it is important to recognize that this book aims to provide a comprehensive guide for individuals in their twenties seeking personal growth, professional achievement, and financial prosperity. While some aspects of volunteerism may be discussed in other chapters, this chapter focuses specifically on exploring the significance of volunteerism, helping readers identify their passions and interests for effective volunteering, finding meaningful opportunities, making a positive impact, and understanding the long-term benefits of being involved in philanthropic activities.

With a solid understanding of the importance of volunteerism, readers can embark on a journey towards personal growth and community impact, knowing that their actions have the potential to create a ripple effect of positive change in their lives and the lives of others.

Identifying Personal Passion and Interests:

Begin by engaging in self-reflection exercises that encourage readers to explore their passions, interests, and causes they feel most strongly about. Encourage them to think deeply about what brings them joy, what issues they feel passionate about, and what talents or skills they possess that could be utilized in volunteer work.

- Prompt readers to consider their values and beliefs, as these will play a crucial role in guiding their volunteer choices. Encourage them to think about the causes that align with their personal values and the impact they hope to make in the world.
- Provide examples of various volunteer opportunities that exist, such as working with children, environmental conservation, animal welfare, or social justice. Remind readers that there is a wide range of causes and organizations to choose from, ensuring there is something for everyone.
- Emphasize the importance of finding meaning and purpose in volunteer work. Share stories of individuals who have found deep fulfillment by dedicating their time and talents to a cause they

are passionate about. Encourage readers to think about how volunteering can personally enrich their lives and contribute to their own personal growth and development.

- Remind readers that identifying personal passions and interests is an ongoing process. Encourage them to remain open to new experiences, try out different types of volunteering, and continually reassess their interests over time.

Finding Volunteer Opportunities:

Volunteering is a powerful way to give back to the community and make a positive impact. To get started on your volunteer journey, it's important to know where to find opportunities that align with your interests and values. Here are some effective ways to research and discover local organizations, community programs, and non-profit initiatives that need volunteers:

1. Online Volunteer Databases:

Explore online platforms dedicated to connecting volunteers with organizations in need. Websites like VolunteerMatch, Idealist, and All for Good provide comprehensive databases of volunteer opportunities across various causes and locations. These platforms allow you to search based on your interests, skills, and availability, making it easy to find opportunities that resonate with you.

2. Non-Profit Websites:

Visit the websites of non-profit organizations that align with your passions. Many organizations have dedicated volunteer sections on their websites, where they list current volunteer openings or provide information on how to get involved. Take the time to understand their mission, values, and projects before reaching out or applying.

3. Local Community Centers and Libraries:

Check out your local community centers, libraries, or town halls for bulletin boards or community event calendars that often highlight volunteer opportunities. These physical spaces can be great resources for finding local organizations or events seeking volunteers. Additionally, community centers may offer specific volunteering programs themselves that you can participate in.

4. Social Media:

Utilize social media platforms like Facebook, Twitter, and Instagram to find volunteer opportunities in your area. Many organizations promote their events or fundraising campaigns through social media, so following or liking their pages can keep you updated on upcoming volunteer opportunities. Joining local community groups or forums can also provide valuable insights into volunteer needs in your area.

5. Networking:

Tap into your personal and professional networks to discover volunteer opportunities. Talk to friends, family members, colleagues, or mentors who are involved in community service or have connections with non-profit organizations. They may be able to introduce you to volunteering opportunities or recommend organizations that align with your interests.

Remember, when searching for volunteer opportunities, it's important to consider not only the cause or organization but also the specific tasks involved and the time commitment required. Take into account your skills, availability, and personal preferences to find opportunities that will be fulfilling and manageable for you. By leveraging these various resources and strategies, you can discover volunteer opportunities that make a meaningful difference both in your life and in the community.

Making a Difference through Volunteerism:

Preparing for Volunteer Activities:

To make the most out of your volunteer experience, it is essential to come prepared. Before starting a volunteer role, take the time to understand the organization's mission, goals, and expectations. This will help you align your own values and objectives with those of the organization, ensuring a meaningful and impactful experience.

Research the specific activities or tasks you will be involved in as a volunteer. This knowledge will enable you to arrive prepared with any necessary skills or knowledge. If there are any training sessions or orientations offered by the organization, be sure to attend them. These sessions often provide valuable insights into the organization's operations and the impact you can make.

Maximizing Impact as a Volunteer:

While volunteering, focus on maximizing your impact by using your unique skills, talents, and resources. Consider what sets you apart and how you can contribute in a way that makes a real difference. For example, if you have marketing expertise, offer to create promotional materials or assist with fundraising campaigns. If you enjoy working with children, consider volunteering at an after-school program or mentoring organization.

Additionally, be proactive in seeking feedback from the organization and fellow volunteers. This will allow you to continuously improve and adapt your approach to have an even greater impact. By actively engaging with the organization and its beneficiaries, you can uncover new opportunities for making a difference.

Commitment, Reliability, and Professionalism:

When giving back to the community through volunteer work, it is crucial to maintain a high level of commitment, reliability, and professionalism. Treat your volunteer commitments as seriously as you would a job. Show up on time and follow through on your responsibilities.

Always be respectful and courteous to fellow volunteers, staff members, and the individuals you serve. Demonstrate professionalism by adhering to the organization's code of conduct and dress code, if applicable. Remember that you represent not only yourself but also the organization, so let your dedication and professionalism shine through.

By being well-prepared, maximizing your impact, and exemplifying commitment, reliability, and professionalism, you can truly make a difference as a volunteer. Your efforts will not only positively impact the lives of others but also contribute to your own personal growth and sense of fulfillment.

The long-term impact of volunteerism extends far beyond the immediate benefits gained from giving back to the community. Through reflection on personal growth and transformation, individuals can appreciate the profound effects that volunteer experiences have on shaping their character and values.

Volunteerism serves as a catalyst for personal development, allowing individuals to discover new strengths, talents, and passions. By engaging in meaningful volunteer work, readers have the opportunity to explore different areas of interest and gain valuable skills that can be applied to various aspects of their lives. Whether it's developing leadership abilities, improving communication skills, or enhancing problem-solving capabilities, the lessons learned through volunteering contribute to a well-rounded and accomplished individual.

Furthermore, volunteerism creates a ripple effect that positively impacts not only individuals but also communities and society as a whole. The acts of kindness and service provided by volunteers inspire others to take action, creating a culture of empathy and compassion. By sharing their experiences and encouraging others to get involved, readers can multiply their impact and contribute to the greater good.

Beyond the immediate fulfillment derived from volunteer work, it is important for readers to recognize the long-term benefits of continued philanthropic efforts. By incorporating volunteering into their lives beyond their twenties, individuals can cultivate a sense of purpose and maintain a strong connection with their communities. This ongoing commitment to service not only fuels personal growth but also strengthens social bonds, fosters understanding among diverse groups, and promotes positive change at both the local and global levels.

In conclusion, reflecting on personal growth and transformation through volunteer experiences allows individuals to fully appreciate the long-term impact of their philanthropic efforts. By examining the ripple effect of volunteer work on individuals, communities, and society as a whole, readers are inspired to continue their involvement in giving back beyond their twenties.

Chapter 4

Adventure Sports and Physical Activities: Challenging Yourself

****

Introduction to Adventure Sports and Physical Activities

Adventure Sports and Physical Activities offer a unique and exhilarating way to challenge oneself physically and mentally, fostering personal growth and development. Engaging in these activities can provide a range of benefits that go beyond just physical fitness.

By participating in adventure sports and physical activities, individuals can cultivate resilience, enhance problem-solving skills, and develop a greater sense of self-confidence. These endeavors push individuals out of their comfort zones, encouraging them to face fears, confront obstacles, and overcome limitations.

There is a wide range of adventure sports and physical activities available for individuals to explore. From rock climbing and hiking to kayaking and skydiving, the options are diverse and cater to different interests and preferences. Each activity presents its own set of challenges, allowing individuals to test their limits and discover new capabilities.

The importance of challenging oneself physically and mentally cannot be overstated. It is through these challenges that personal growth occurs. By stepping outside of one's comfort zone, individuals can push past self-imposed limitations and unlock unrealized potential. Challenging oneself fosters a growth mindset, encouraging continuous learning, adaptability, and perseverance.

It is essential to approach adventure sports and physical activities with the right mindset. Embrace each opportunity as a chance to learn and grow. Stay open to new experiences, embrace the unknown, and view challenges as opportunities for personal development.

Adventure sports and physical activities offer a powerful avenue for self-discovery, character building, and personal growth. By incorporating these endeavors into one's life, individuals can embark on a journey of empowerment and unlock their full potential. Through these activities, individuals can build resilience, nurture a positive mindset, and lay the foundation for a successful and fulfilling life.

Choosing the Right Adventure Sport or Physical Activity:

When it comes to engaging in adventure sports and physical activities, it is essential to choose an activity that aligns with your individual interests, abilities, and goals. Consideration of factors such as fitness level, preferred environments (land, water, air), and available resources can help you make an informed decision. Additionally, evaluating the potential risks and safety measures associated with each activity is crucial for ensuring a safe and enjoyable experience.

Start by reflecting on your interests and passions. What types of activities excite you? Are you drawn to water-based sports like surfing or kayaking, or do you prefer land-based activities such as rock climbing or hiking? Maybe you have a desire to soar through the air and are interested in activities like skydiving or paragliding? By considering your preferences, you can narrow down your options and find an activity that truly resonates with you.

Next, assess your abilities and current fitness level. Some adventure sports and physical activities require a certain level of strength, agility, or endurance. It's important to be realistic about your capabilities and choose an activity that suits your current fitness level. If you're just starting out, consider beginner-friendly options that allow for gradual progression and skill development.

Take into account the environment in which the activity takes place. Do you feel more comfortable on land, in water, or in the air? Some people thrive in the calming presence of the ocean or enjoy the tranquility of hiking through forests and mountains. Others may find exhilaration in high-altitude activities or the rush of adrenaline from extreme water sports. Understanding your preferred environment can help you select an adventure sport or physical activity that resonates with your natural inclinations.

Additionally, consider the availability of resources required for the chosen activity. Are there local facilities or clubs that offer training or equipment rental? Is there easy access to suitable locations for the activity? Assessing the practical aspects can make it easier to incorporate the chosen adventure sport or physical activity into your routine.

Lastly, it is vital to evaluate the potential risks and safety measures associated with each activity. Some adventure sports carry inherent risks, such as rock climbing or whitewater rafting. Ensure that you thoroughly research and understand the safety protocols, training requirements, and equipment needed for the activity. Taking necessary precautions will help minimize the risks involved and ensure a safe experience.

By carefully considering these factors - your interests, abilities, preferred environment, available resources, and potential risks - you can choose an adventure sport or physical activity that suits you perfectly. Remember to listen to your instincts and select an activity that ignites passion within you. The right choice will provide opportunities for personal growth, challenges that push you beyond your limits, and unforgettable experiences that shape your character at this critical stage of life.

Building Skills and Confidence:

Developing the necessary skills and techniques required for adventure sports and physical activities is essential for both safety and enjoyment. In this section, we will explore strategies to help readers build these skills and gain confidence in their abilities.

1. Start Slowly and Progress Gradually:

- It's important to start with activities that match your current fitness level and skill set. Begin with beginner-friendly sports or activities that allow you to learn and progress at your own pace.
- Gradually increase the difficulty or intensity of the activities as you become more comfortable and proficient. This gradual progression will prevent overwhelming yourself and reduce the risk of injuries.

2. Learn from Experts:

- Seek out professionals or experienced individuals who can provide guidance and instruction in the particular adventure sport or physical activity you are interested in.
- Enroll in classes, workshops, or training programs to learn the proper techniques, safety protocols, and best practices.
- Take advantage of opportunities to receive feedback and constructive criticism to improve your skills.

3. Set Achievable Goals:

- Setting clear and achievable goals is crucial for building skills and maintaining motivation.
- Break down larger goals into smaller milestones that can be accomplished over time. Celebrate each milestone as it is achieved, which will boost confidence and encourage continuous improvement.
- Regularly reassess and adjust your goals to ensure they remain challenging but attainable.

4. Practice Consistently:

- Consistent practice is key to developing any skill. Dedicate regular time to practice the techniques and exercises associated with your chosen adventure sport or physical activity.
- Engage in deliberate practice, focusing on specific areas that need improvement. Work on refining technique, increasing speed or endurance, or tackling more advanced maneuvers.
- Find ways to incorporate related exercises or drills into your daily routine to reinforce muscle memory and enhance overall performance.

5. Embrace Fear and Step Out of Your Comfort Zone:

- Overcoming fear is a fundamental aspect of building skills and confidence in adventure sports and physical activities.
- Recognize that fear is a natural response when pushing your limits, but it should not hold you back from trying new things.

- Challenge yourself by gradually exposing yourself to slightly more difficult or unfamiliar situations. This will help expand your comfort zone and build resilience.

By following these strategies, readers can develop the necessary skills, techniques, and confidence required for their chosen adventure sports or physical activities. Remember to start slowly, seek guidance from experts, set achievable goals, practice consistently, and embrace fear as an opportunity for growth.

Safety Precautions and Risk Management:

Adventure sports and physical activities offer exhilarating experiences and opportunities for personal growth. However, it is essential to prioritize safety to ensure a positive and enjoyable experience. In this section, we will delve into the detailed explanation of safety precautions to be followed before, during, and after engaging in adventure sports and physical activities.

Before embarking on any adventure sport or physical activity, it is crucial to conduct thorough research and gather information about the specific activity. Understanding the potential risks and hazards associated with the activity will allow you to make informed decisions and take necessary precautions.

Proper equipment usage is paramount to ensuring safety during adventure sports. Each activity requires specific gear and equipment designed to protect participants from potential injuries. It is essential to invest in high-quality equipment, regularly inspect it for any signs of wear or damage, and follow manufacturer's guidelines for maintenance and usage.

Training is another key aspect of risk management in adventure sports. Before attempting any activity, seek professional guidance and training to learn the proper techniques, skills, and safety protocols. Participating in certified training programs or under the supervision of experienced instructors will significantly reduce the risk of accidents or injuries.

Emergency preparedness is crucial when engaging in adventurous pursuits. Familiarize yourself with emergency procedures specific to the activity you choose. Ensure that you know how to respond effectively in case of an emergency or unexpected event. Carry a first aid kit with you at all times and be aware of nearby medical facilities or contact numbers in case of emergencies.

Additionally, always assess the weather conditions before participating in outdoor activities. Unfavorable weather can pose significant risks, including increased chances of accidents or exposure to extreme temperatures. Stay updated on weather forecasts and exercise caution by rescheduling or canceling activities if conditions are unfavorable or unsafe.

Awareness of potential hazards is vital for minimizing risks in adventure sports. Conduct a comprehensive risk assessment before engaging in any activity. Identify potential dangers, such as rough terrain, deep water, heights, or extreme weather, and take steps to mitigate risks. Understanding your personal limitations and abilities will allow you to make informed decisions and avoid unnecessary risks.

Remember that safety should always be the top priority during adventure sports and physical activities. By following proper safety precautions, using appropriate equipment, receiving adequate training, and being aware of potential hazards, you can ensure a safe and enjoyable experience.

In summary, this section highlighted the importance of safety precautions and risk management in adventure sports and physical activities. We discussed the need for thorough research, proper equipment usage, training, emergency preparedness, awareness of potential hazards, and assessing weather conditions. By implementing these measures into your adventure pursuits, you can minimize risks and create a safe environment for personal growth and enjoyment.

Embracing the Adventure Mindset:

Engaging in adventure sports and physical activities not only challenges us physically but also has a profound impact on our mental well-being and personal growth. By embracing the adventure mindset, we can develop crucial qualities such as resilience, adaptability, and problem-solving skills that are essential for navigating through life's unexpected situations.

1. Developing Resilience:

- Adventure sports often push us to our limits, both mentally and physically. During these challenging moments, we have an opportunity to cultivate resilience – the ability to bounce back from setbacks and persevere in the face of adversity.

- Encountering obstacles and overcoming them while participating in adventure sports helps build mental toughness and the capacity to handle stress.
- By learning to adapt to changing circumstances, we become better equipped to deal with the uncertainties and challenges that life throws at us.

2. Fostering Adaptability:

- Adventure sports provide us with a unique environment where we must constantly adapt to new situations, whether it be weather conditions, terrain variations, or unexpected obstacles.
- Being willing to adapt and adjust our plans in real-time fosters adaptable thinking, enabling us to find creative solutions when faced with uncertainty.
- The more we expose ourselves to different adventure sports and physical activities, the more adaptable we become in unfamiliar environments, broadening our perspective and enhancing our ability to navigate through various life situations.

3. Cultivating Problem-Solving Skills:

- Adventure sports frequently present us with challenges that require us to think critically and solve problems on the spot.
- From navigating complex terrains to strategizing against unforeseen circumstances, these activities demand us to assess risks, make quick decisions, and execute effective solutions.
- The problem-solving skills developed through adventure sports can be transferred to other areas of our lives, equipping us with the ability to address challenges in our personal relationships, careers, and other endeavors.

4. Enhancing Mental Well-being:

- Engaging in adventure sports and physical activities has been proven to have a positive impact on mental health.
- The exhilaration of pushing our boundaries, combined with the release of endorphins during physical exertion, promotes a sense of well-being and reduces stress levels.
- Adventure sports also offer an opportunity to disconnect from the pressures of daily life, fostering mindfulness and promoting a greater appreciation for the present moment.

By embracing the adventure mindset, we can harness the mental benefits that adventure sports and physical activities provide. Through cultivating resilience, adaptability, and problem-solving skills, we empower ourselves to thrive in the face of challenges and uncertainties. Moreover, by prioritizing our mental well-being through these experiences, we cultivate a foundation for personal growth and long-term success.

Assessing Risks and Setting Boundaries:

When planning adventurous activities, it is crucial to prioritize safety and take the necessary precautions to protect yourself. Assessing risks and setting boundaries will help ensure that you have an enjoyable experience without compromising your well-being.

One of the first steps in assessing risks is conducting thorough research about the adventure you are planning. This includes understanding the potential hazards involved, such as extreme weather conditions, physical exertion, or unfamiliar surroundings. By being aware of these risks, you can make informed decisions and take appropriate measures to mitigate them.

Consider evaluating your own comfort levels before embarking on any adventure. Understand your limitations and be honest with yourself about what you are truly capable of. Pushing beyond your limits may result in injuries or accidents that could have been prevented with proper self-assessment.

Another aspect of risk assessment is gathering information from reliable sources. Seek advice from experts, experienced individuals, or professionals who have knowledge in the specific adventure you are planning. They can provide valuable insights, tips, and recommendations to help you navigate potential risks more effectively.

Setting boundaries is equally important when it comes to ensuring your safety during adventurous activities. Establishing limits helps define what you are comfortable with and allows you to communicate those boundaries to others involved in the adventure. It could include specific conditions or restrictions that must be respected by all participants.

Remember to be realistic when setting boundaries. While it's important to step out of your comfort zone and challenge yourself, pushing too far beyond what you are comfortable with may lead to unnecessary risks. Find a balance between pushing your limits and staying within a reasonable range of safety.

Ultimately, assessing risks and setting boundaries is about being proactive in protecting yourself while still allowing room for exploration and growth. By conducting research, evaluating potential hazards, and considering personal comfort levels, you can embark on adventurous activities with confidence, knowing that you have taken the necessary precautions to ensure your safety.

Building a Safety Net: In this section, we will delve into the essential precautions and safety measures that readers should take to ensure their well-being during adventurous activities. While spontaneity and embracing new experiences are important, it is crucial to prioritize safety to avoid unnecessary risks.

One of the first steps in building a safety net is packing essential safety gear. Depending on the nature of the adventure, this may include items such as a first aid kit, water purification tablets, maps or GPS devices, extra clothing layers, flashlights, and emergency signaling devices. By being prepared with these supplies, readers can mitigate potential risks and respond effectively to unforeseen situations.

In addition to packing the necessary gear, informing others about travel plans is a crucial step in ensuring safety. Sharing details such as the intended destination, anticipated timeline, and contact information with trusted individuals can provide an additional layer of security. This way, someone will be aware of the reader's whereabouts and can initiate appropriate actions in case of emergencies or unexpected delays.

Understanding emergency protocols in different environments is also essential for safeguarding personal safety during adventures. Whether it's hiking in the mountains, camping in remote areas, or engaging in water sports, each environment has its unique set of risks and potential emergencies. Readers should familiarize themselves with relevant safety guidelines, local regulations, and emergency procedures specific to their chosen activity and location.

Furthermore, researching and assessing potential risks associated with the planned adventure can help readers make informed decisions to minimize hazards. This may involve evaluating weather conditions, understanding wildlife encounters, considering terrain challenges, and assessing the current condition of any equipment or vehicles involved. By being aware of potential risks, readers can take appropriate precautions and adjust their plans accordingly.

Overall, building a safety net is crucial when embarking on adventurous activities. Packing essential safety gear, informing others about travel plans, understanding emergency protocols, researching potential risks, and taking proactive steps to mitigate hazards all contribute to a safer and more enjoyable adventure. By prioritizing safety, readers can maximize their experiences while minimizing potential risks and ensure that their adventures are memorable for all the right reasons.

Chapter 5

Planning Your Adventures: Balancing Safety and Spontaneity

****

Planning Your Adventures: Balancing Safety and Spontaneity: Embracing Spontaneity

In this section, we will explore the importance of embracing spontaneity while still prioritizing safety. While planning and preparing for adventures is crucial, there are certain moments when unexpected opportunities arise, and it is essential to seize them. However, it is equally important to approach these experiences with mindfulness and consideration for potential risks.

1. Seizing Unexpected Opportunities:

Embracing spontaneity allows us to step out of our comfort zones and embrace new experiences. When unexpected opportunities present themselves, it is vital to assess the potential benefits and risks before making a decision. By being open to unplanned adventures, we allow ourselves to grow, discover new passions, and create unforgettable memories.

2. Assessing Potential Risks:

While spontaneity can be exciting, it is crucial not to throw caution to the wind. Before engaging in unplanned activities, take a moment to consider the potential risks involved. Evaluate the level of physical risk, the reliability of the situation or individuals involved, and any potential consequences that may arise. By being mindful of these factors, you can make informed decisions that prioritize your safety.

3. Utilizing Intuition and Gut Feelings:

Sometimes, our instincts can guide us in making spontaneous decisions. If something feels off or unsafe, trust your intuition and proceed with caution. Listen to your gut feelings and honor your own boundaries. Remember that it's okay to decline an opportunity if it doesn't align with your intuition or if it compromises your safety.

4. Seeking Local Advice and Insights:

When embracing spontaneity in unfamiliar territories, tap into local knowledge and seek advice from trusted sources. Locals can provide valuable insights on hidden gems, off-the-beaten-path destinations, and safety concerns specific to the area. Engaging with the local community not only enhances your experience but also ensures that you are well-informed about potential risks and precautions.

5. Preparing for the Unexpected:

While spontaneity can be exhilarating, it is important to be prepared for unforeseen circumstances. Prioritize essential safety measures such as carrying emergency contact information, a first aid kit, and appropriate safety gear specific to the adventure you are embarking on. These preparations will allow you to embrace spontaneity while ensuring your well-being.

6. Reflecting and Learning:

After engaging in spontaneous adventures, take the time to reflect on your experiences. Consider what worked well and what could have been done differently to enhance safety. Reflecting on these experiences not only helps you learn from any mistakes but also enables you to make more informed decisions in the future.

Embracing spontaneity can lead to incredible opportunities for growth and self-discovery. By incorporating these tips into your adventures, you can strike a balance between embracing the unexpected and prioritizing your safety. Remember to trust your instincts, seek local advice, and reflect on each experience to ensure that your spontaneous adventures are both thrilling and secure.

Seeking expert advice and tapping into local knowledge is crucial when planning adventurous activities. By consulting professionals or experienced individuals, readers can gain valuable insights, guidance, and recommendations specific to their chosen adventure.

When embarking on an adventure, it is essential to seek the expertise of those who have firsthand experience in the particular activity or destination. Whether it's rock climbing, backpacking, or scuba diving, consulting with professionals or seasoned adventurers can provide invaluable information regarding safety protocols, necessary equipment, and potential risks.

Local knowledge is another invaluable resource that can enhance the planning process. Locals possess a wealth of information about their surroundings, including hidden gems, lesser-known trails, and cultural nuances that can greatly enrich the adventure. By tapping into this knowledge, readers can uncover unique experiences and avoid common pitfalls.

To seek expert advice and tap into local knowledge effectively, readers can utilize various sources:

1. Guidebooks and Online Resources: Guidebooks and reputable online resources are excellent starting points for gathering general information about an adventure. These resources often provide insights from experts in the field and offer tips on the best routes, equipment recommendations, and safety guidelines.

2. Adventure Clubs and Organizations: Joining adventure clubs or organizations dedicated to a specific activity can provide access to a network of experienced individuals who are passionate about the same pursuits. These groups often arrange group outings or have forums where members can share their expertise and offer advice to fellow adventurers.

3. Local Expert Guides: Engaging the services of local expert guides can further enhance the adventure experience. These professionals have extensive knowledge of the area, including insider tips, historical context, and safety precautions specific to the destination. They can also tailor the adventure to individual preferences and skill levels.

4. Online Communities and Forums: Participating in online communities and forums dedicated to adventure travel allows readers to connect with fellow enthusiasts who have firsthand knowledge of specific destinations or activities. These platforms offer opportunities to ask questions, seek recommendations, and learn from others' experiences.

When seeking expert advice and tapping into local knowledge, readers should remember to approach the process with an open mind and be willing to adapt their plans based on the insights received. It is essential to prioritize safety and ensure that the information obtained aligns with personal comfort levels and risk tolerance.

By incorporating expert advice and local knowledge into their adventure planning, readers can make more informed decisions, maximize enjoyment, and minimize potential risks. These valuable insights from experienced individuals will enhance the overall experience and broaden perspectives while ensuring a safe and fulfilling adventure.

Learning from Experience:

As young adults embark on various adventures, it is crucial for them to reflect on these experiences and extract valuable lessons. Learning from past adventures not only enhances future planning and decision-making but also cultivates personal growth and resilience. In this final part of the chapter, readers will discover strategies for effectively reflecting on their experiences and adapting their plans for more successful and fulfilling adventures in the future.

1. Reflecting on Experiences: Taking the time to reflect on past adventures allows individuals to gain insights into their strengths, weaknesses, and preferences. Encourage readers to ask themselves questions such as:

- What were the highlights and challenges of the adventure?
- How did I handle unexpected situations?
- Did I push myself outside of my comfort zone?
- What did I learn about myself during this experience?

By actively engaging in self-reflection, readers can uncover valuable lessons that can inform their future decisions.

2. Identifying Lessons Learned: Once readers have reflected on their adventures, they can begin to identify specific lessons they have learned. Encourage them to consider both positive outcomes and areas for improvement. Some potential lessons may include:

- The importance of thorough research before embarking on an adventure.
- The value of maintaining good physical fitness for certain activities.
- The significance of effective communication and teamwork during group adventures.
- The need to be adaptable and flexible in unpredictable situations.

By identifying these lessons, readers can build upon their strengths and address areas that require growth or development.

3. Adapting Plans Accordingly: Armed with newfound knowledge, readers can adapt their plans for future adventures. Encourage them to incorporate the lessons learned into their decision-making process. This may involve:

1. Adjusting the level of difficulty or risk involved in an adventure based on previous experiences.
2. Researching and implementing new safety measures or precautions.
3. Seeking out opportunities that align with their newfound understanding of their preferences and strengths.

Adapting plans based on past experiences allows individuals to make more informed choices and increases their chances of success and fulfillment in future adventures.

By emphasizing the importance of learning from experience, readers are encouraged to view setbacks as valuable learning opportunities and to approach future adventures with an open mind and a willingness to adapt. Through reflection and adaptation, young adults can continue to build their character and pave the way for even more rewarding and enriching experiences in the years to come.

Epilogue: Embracing a Lifetime of Growth and Fulfillment

****

As we come to the end of our journey together in "Build Your Character at Twenty: Writing the Life Success Script at the Age of 20" it is important to acknowledge that self-assessment is not a destination but a lifelong practice. The process we have explored throughout this book is just the beginning of a continuous cycle of growth, reflection, and adaptation.

You have embarked on a remarkable path of self-discovery, gaining insights into your core values, beliefs, passions, strengths, and areas for improvement. Armed with this knowledge, you have created an action plan that aligns with your authentic self and sets the stage for personal and professional growth. But remember, this plan is not set in stone. It is a living document that can and should be revisited and revised as you continue to evolve and navigate the twists and turns of life.

Life is a series of chapters, and each chapter presents new opportunities for growth and transformation. The skills and tools you have acquired in self-assessment will serve as constant companions, guiding you through the challenges and uncertainties that lie ahead. As you encounter new experiences, relationships, and milestones, take the time to reflect and reassess.

One of the keys to lifelong success is the willingness to embrace change and adapt to new circumstances. Your values, passions, and goals may shift as you gain new perspectives and face different challenges. By staying open-minded and receptive to growth, you can seize the opportunities that arise and continue to shape your life in alignment with your authentic self.

As you navigate the complexities of adulthood, remember the importance of self-care and self-compassion. Along your journey, you may encounter setbacks, failures, and moments of self-doubt. These are natural parts of the human experience. Embrace them as opportunities for learning and growth. Be kind to yourself, celebrate your successes, and learn from your mistakes.

Surround yourself with a supportive network of individuals who inspire and challenge you. Seek out mentors who can guide and encourage you along the way. Remember that you are not alone on this journey. By connecting with like-minded individuals, sharing experiences, and building meaningful relationships, you can find strength and support to overcome obstacles and reach new heights.

Never underestimate the power of continuous learning. The world is constantly evolving, and acquiring new knowledge and skills is essential for personal and professional development. Stay curious, seek out opportunities for growth, and embrace a mindset of lifelong learning. Whether it's through formal education, reading, attending workshops, or engaging in experiential learning, the pursuit of knowledge will enrich your life and open doors to new possibilities.

RephraseAs you navigate the complexities of life, remember the importance of giving back. Use your unique talents, skills, and resources to make a positive impact on the world around you. Whether through volunteer work, mentorship, or advocating for causes you believe in, your actions have the power to create meaningful change. Embrace the responsibility of being a global citizen and strive to leave a lasting legacy.

Finally, never lose sight of your own growth and fulfillment. Success is a deeply personal concept, and it is essential to define it on your own terms. Stay true to your values, passions, and purpose, even when faced with societal expectations or external pressures. Your journey is unique, and your definition of success may evolve over time. Embrace the beauty of your individuality and create a life that brings you joy, fulfillment, and a sense of meaning.

As we conclude this book, I want to express my deepest gratitude for accompanying me on this transformative journey. It has been an honor to be your guide and witness your growth. Remember, the power to shape your life lies within you. Embrace self-assessment as a lifelong practice, and may you continue to write a success story that is uniquely yours.

The adventure continues. Embrace it with courage, curiosity, and an unwavering belief in your own potential. The world awaits your extraordinary contributions.

"According to Douglas Adams, the answer to life, the universe and everything may be 42, but we all know the real question is when did it all start, when did it all begin? And, the answer to that is 20 when life hits you like a big bang, so don't just be 20, get out there and DO 20!"

Appenidices

Sample Meal Plan 1

1 WEEK MEAL PLAN

	Breakfast	Lunch	Dinner
MONDAY	Veggie Omelette	Quinoa salad	Baked salmon with roasted veggies
TUESDAY	Overnight oats with fruits	Chickpea salad wrap	Grilled chicken with sweet potato
WEDNESDAY	Spinach and mushroom frittata	Lentil soup with whole wheat bread	Stir-fried tofu with brown rice
THURSDAY	Whole grain toast with avocado	Quinoa and black bean bowl	Baked cod with quinoa and steamed broccoli
FRIDAY	Green smoothie	Greek salad with grilled chicken	Zucchini noodles with marinara sauce
SATURDAY	Vegetable scramble	Beef Lasagne	Grilled steak with roasted sweet potatoes
SUNDAY	Overnight oats with fruits	Chickpea salad wrap	Grilled chicken with sweet potato

Sample Meal Plan 2

7-DAY MEAL PLAN

1600-1800 calories/day

SUNDAY

Breakfast: berry blend smoothie

Lunch: egg salad sandwich

Dinner: chicken and veggie soup salad

MONDAY

Breakfast: banana walnut pudding

Lunch: lettuce wraps and vegan salad

Dinner: beer-braised pot roast

TUESDAY

Breakfast: berry blend smoothie

Lunch: egg salad sandwich

Dinner: chicken and veggie soup salad

WEDNESDAY

Breakfast: berry blend smoothie

Lunch: egg salad sandwich

Dinner: chicken and veggie soup salad

THURSDAY

Breakfast: berry blend smoothie

Lunch: egg salad sandwich

Dinner: chicken and veggie soup salad

FRIDAY

Breakfast: berry blend smoothie

Lunch: egg salad sandwich

Dinner: chicken and veggie soup salad

SATURDAY

Breakfast: berry blend smoothie

Lunch: egg salad sandwich

Dinner: chicken and veggie soup salad

Meal Planning Sheet

MEAL PLANNER WEEK OF _____

	BREAKFAST	LUNCH	DINNER	SNACKS
SUN				
MON				
TUE				
WED				
THU				
FRI				
SAT				

Goal Setting Sheet

Goal SETTING

START DATE: __/__/____   END DATE: __/__/____

MY GOAL IS ...

MY WHY	TO REMEMBER

ACTION STEPS

- [ ] _____
- [ ] _____
- [ ] _____
- [ ] _____
- [ ] _____
- [ ] _____
- [ ] _____

THINGS TO USE

- [ ] _____
- [ ] _____
- [ ] _____
- [ ] _____
- [ ] _____
- [ ] _____
- [ ] _____

DRAW / SKETCH

GRATEFUL FOR

"

"

SWOT Sheet

BUSINESS WORKSHEET

SWOT ANALYSIS

A SWOT analysis helps you understand your business's strengths, weaknesses, opportunities, and threats. Fill in the following sections:

STRENGTHS	WEAKNESSES

OPPORTUNITIES	THREATS

BUSINESS SWOT ANALYSIS WORKSHEET | OLIVIA WILSON, BUSINESS COACH

Further Reading

Dweck, Carol S. Mindset: The New Psychology of Success. Random House, 2006.

Covey, Stephen R. The 7 Habits of Highly Effective People: Powerful Lessons in Personal Change. Simon and Schuster, 2013.

Pink, Daniel H. Drive: The Surprising Truth About What Motivates Us. Penguin, 2009.

Carmichael, Darcie. You Are a Badass: How to Stop Doubting Your Greatness and Start Living an Awesome Life. Workman Publishing, 2013.

Acuff, Jon. What I Wish I Knew When I Was 20: A Crash Course on Making Your Place in the World. Harper Business, 2008.

Robbins, Anthony. Unlimited Power: The New Science of Personal Achievement. Simon and Schuster, 2007.

Godin, Seth. The Dip: A Little Book That Teaches You When to Quit (and When to Stick). Penguin, 2008.

Levine, Sheen. Always Hungry? Conquer Cravings, Retrain Your Fat Cells, and Lose Weight Permanently. Hay House, 2016.

Ramsey, Dave. The Total Money Makeover: A Proven Plan for Financial Fitness. Thomas Nelson, 2013.

Stanley, Thomas J. The Millionaire Mind. Andrews McMeel Publishing, 2001.

Rath, Tom. Eat Move Sleep: How Small Choices Lead to Big Changes. Missionday, 2013.

Manning, Brené. Braving the Wilderness: The Quest for True Belonging and the Courage to Stand Alone. Random House, 2018.

Hanson, Rick. Hardwiring Happiness: The New Brain Science of Contentment, Calm, and Confidence. Harmony, 2014.